THE HOLY SPIRIT AND THE CHURCH

THE HOLY SPIRIT AND THE CHURCH

by
Rev. Hyung Yong Park, Th.M., S.T.D.
Professor Emeritus of Hapdong
Theological Seminary

HAPDONG THEOLOGICAL SEMINARY PRESS
Suwon, Korea

Copyright©2011 by Hyung Yong Park
Published by Hapdong Theological Seminary Press
address | 610 DongSuwon-Ro, Youngtong-Gu, Suwon,
Kyeonggi-Do, Korea 443-791
Telephone | +82-31-217-0629
Fax | +82-31-212-6204
homepage |www.hapdong.ac.kr
e-mail | press@hapdong.ac.kr
All rights reserved

Printed in Korea

Library of Congress Cataloging-in-Publication Data

Park, Hyung Yong
The Holy Spirit and the Church / by Hyung Yong Park
294p
Includes bibliographical references and indexes
ISBN 978-89-86191-00-4
1. Bible-N.T. 2. Theology-Holy Spirit. 3. N. T. Church. 4. Pentecost.
5. Redemptive History

A catalogue records for this book is available from the National Library of Korea
e-CIP Homepage: http://www.nl.go.kr/ecip
(CIP control number. CIP2011003300)

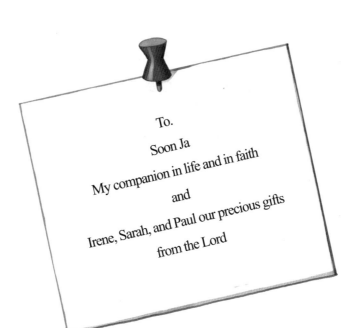

To.

Soon Ja

My companion in life and in faith

and

Irene, Sarah, and Paul our precious gifts

from the Lord

Preface

Jesus explains to Nicodemus how the Holy Spirit works mysteriously. He says, "The wind blows wherever it pleases. You hear its sound, but you cannot tell where it comes from or where it is going. So it is with everyone born of the Spirit" (John 3:8). Because of this mysterious works of the Spirit, there are divergent opinions on the subject, which indicates that one tends to become subjective in its studies. Therefore, one should be guided by a few principles in approaching the works of the Holy Spirit.

First, one must believe that the Holy Spirit is God Himself who inspired the chosen servants to write the 66 books of the Bible. Therefore, one ought to study the works of the Spirit on the basis of the Scripture. We tend to approach the works of the Holy Spirit subjectively because we experience the Spirit's dynamic activities in our daily lives. As we consider our experiences as the basis for the study of the works of the Spirit, our results do not agree. Thus, we must expound the biblical texts in order to understand the Spirit's works, and this book is written with the conviction that the Bible explains the full picture of the works of the Holy Spirit.

Second, one ought to approach the works of the Spirit with the understanding that God sends the Spirit for the building of the Church and has publicly given the 66 books of the Bible as the criteria of faith and life for His Church. Private religious experience cannot act as the criteria of the life of the Church. One ought to understand that the Holy Spirit works along with the Word, the inspired Scriptures. The Holy Spirit works to build and strengthen the Church with the Word He has inspired. This book is written in the belief that there is a close relationship between the works of the Spirit and the building of the Church.

Third, one ought to be humble in approaching the works of the Spirit and in conforming to the life of his Lord Jesus Christ. It is true that one must be humble as he studies any subject of the Bible. However, it is more important that we should be humble as we study the works of the Spirit because individual Spiritual experiences can be the occasion for self-centeredness. So, even though someone has a different understanding of the works of the Spirit, our attitude should be like a brother to brother in the kingdom of God. We should have a tolerant mind towards other Christians who have different opinions on the works of the Spirit.

I am deeply grateful to the editors of *Journal of Korean Evangelical Society of New Testament Studies* (Vol. 8, No. 3, pp. 497-520), *Hapdong Theological Journal* (Vol. 28, No. 2, pp. 390-407), and *Biblical Theological Journal* (Vol. 2, pp. 37-62; Vol. 3, pp. 86-118) for the permission to use the materials here which appeared in their Journals.

I also want to express my gratitude to my children, Irene, Sarah and Paul who helped me proofread parts of the text and to Dr. Dong-Geun Park who made the indexes for this book.

It is the hope of the author that this book would help Bible-believing Christians understand the works of the Spirit in an appropriate and profound manner and allow them to live closer to the teachings of the Bible. It is also the hope of the author that this book in a small way helps pastors and evangelists of local churches and theological students who are preparing for pastoral ministries in the third world, to stand firmly on the Word of God in understanding the works of the Holy Spirit. The author prays that this book would strengthen the body of Jesus Christ all over the world.

August, 2011
Hyung Yong Park

Contents

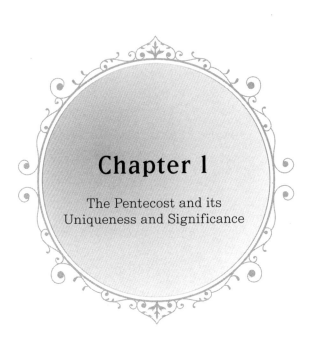

Chapter 1

The Pentecost and its
Uniqueness and Significance

The Holy Spirit works to unite all Christians (Eph. 4:2-6). Yet ironically, the churches are sometimes divided because of their different opinions about the Holy Spirit. Though everyone uses the same Bible, each person interprets it in their own way, giving them a different perspective. Readers who disagree with the contents in this book may criticize that I, the author, like the others, interpreted these Bible verses with my own presuppositions.

I am aware of this hermeneutical tendency. But as I believe that the Bible is necessary to properly study the works of the Holy Spirit, I will confine myself to its text to explain this topic. Some scholars argue that one must also personally experience the Spirit to fully understand the Spirit's activity. They either believe that God the Spirit should not be bound within the limitations of the Bible or that the biblical description of the works of the Holy Spirit is insufficient.

On the contrary, the Scriptures provide, not only the rules for our faith and our daily lives, but also supply an overly adequate explanation of the Spirit's work. In fact, the Spirit is the real author of the Scriptures, so there can be no better source than the Scriptures in studying the work of the Spirit. Moreover, when God gave the Scriptures to the church, He intentionally gave us the 66 books of the Bible as an objective revelation, which is the norm for our faith and life. Hence, we must rely on the Scriptures when discussing the work of the Spirit.

In this chapter, I will try to explain how to understand the phrase "the Baptism of the Holy Spirit" and to prove the uniqueness of the Pentecostal event in Acts 2.

1. Biblical usage of the Term "Baptism of the Holy Spirit"

The term "Baptism of the Holy Spirit" can confuse people

because it is understood in several different ways. Therefore, it is necessary to explain this term in the context of the Scriptures. The word "baptism" appears often in the Bible (80 times in the verb form, 22 times as a noun), but it does not appear too frequently in connection to the Holy Spirit. The terms "Holy Spirit" and "baptism" appear together only in Matthew 3:11, Mark 1:8, Luke 3:16, John 1:33, Acts 1:5; 11:16, and I Corinthians 12:13.

From among the verses, those from the four Gospels show a comparison between John the Baptist's ministry and Jesus' ministry. Hence, in Luke 3:16, John the Baptist says, "I indeed baptize you with water; but One mightier than I is coming, whose sandal strap I am not worthy to loose. He will baptize you with the Holy Spirit and fire" (NKJV). Matthew 3:11, Mark 1:8, and John 1:33 also record verses with a similar content.[1] The verses in Acts initiate a chain of events in which the contents of Acts 11:16 refers to Acts 1:5, which, in turn, refers to Luke 3:16. Thus, a special emphasis must be given to Luke 3:16, Acts 1:5, and Acts 11:16 when studying the baptisms in lieu with the Holy Spirit.

We look at the three verses, Acts 1:5, 11:16 and Luke 3:16. When Jesus first began his public ministry, John the Baptist in Luke 3:16 prophesized of how Jesus' ministry would progress. The central aspect of Jesus' ministry will be "the baptism of the Holy Spirit and

---

1) Among the four Gospels, only Matthew and Luke mentioned "the baptism with both Spirit and fire." Mark and John referred to the baptism of the Spirit without any reference to the baptism with fire. Why did Mark and John exclude the baptism with fire? In Mark 1:1, Mark writes, "the beginning of the gospel about Jesus Christ," emphasizing the idea of an element of joy, "the gospel" and "Good News." Baptism with fire, on the other hand, is related to Judgment Day, a time of sorrow and punishment. Hence, Mark would not have mentioned fire." In John's case, a special characteristic of John's Gospel was its use of "prophetic foreshortening" which is illustrated in John 4:23; 5:25; 8:56; 13:32, to name a few. John adequately explains a broad subject in a short summary. cf. William Hendriksen, *Exposition of the Gospel According to John,* vol. 2 (*NTC,* Grand Rapids: Baker, 1975), pp. 279-80.

with fire." Acts 1:5 then, anticipating the Pentecost, records the words of Jesus in reference to the events of the Pentecost. Before Jesus ascended into Heaven, He reflected on the words of John the Baptist (Luke 3:16). In Acts 11:16, on the other hand, Peter describes to the Jews the events of Cornelius' family. And in this narrative, Peter repeats the words of Jesus in Acts 1:5. It is evident that Peter, in Acts 11:16-17, retrospects to the event of the Pentecost.

Now the attention should be addressed on Luke 3:16, Acts 1:5, and I Corinthians 12:13. Luke 3:16 records the words of John the Baptist in the early part of Jesus' ministry, Acts 1:5 records Jesus' words after his resurrection, and I Corinthians 12:13 explains how one becomes a member of Christ's body by the baptism of the Holy Spirit. Among the four Gospels, the Gospel of Luke is used in this argument because the Book of Acts was written in sequence to the Gospel of Luke. Luke had purposely written these two books as two sequential volumes.[2]

Our interest lies in Luke 3:16 and Acts 1:5, which closely associates with Acts 2 to explain the events of the Pentecost.[3] At the beginning of Jesus' ministry, John the Baptist announces that Jesus will baptize with the Holy Spirit and with fire and says "His

---

2) In his Gospel, Luke focuses on Jesus' person and ministry as he records the events of His public life up until the time of ascension. Then in the Book of Acts, he writes about the Christ who sits on the right hand of God and who sends the Holy Spirit to work through the Church and continue the ministry of God's Kingdom (see Acts 8:12; 19:8; 20:25; 28:23, 31). In Acts 1:1-11, Luke clearly indicates that the Gospel of Luke and the Book of Acts are indeed two sequential parts of a whole. See Park, Hyung Yong, *An Exposition of the Acts of the Apostles* (Korean) (Suwon: Hapdong Theological Seminary Press, 2003), p. 18; F. F. Bruce, *The Acts of Apostles: The Greek Text with Introduction and Commentary* (Grand Rapids: Eerdmans, 1975), p. 65.

3) Max Turner concurs with the idea of inter-relatedness of these verses by saying that "Luke himself came to see the Baptist's promise of (Luke) 3.16-17 fulfilled in an unanticipated way, mainly beyond Pentecost (Acts 1.5; 11.16)." Cf. Max Turner, *Power from on High: The Spirit in Israel's Restoration and Witness in Luke-Acts* (Sheffield: Sheffield Academic Press, 1996), p. 187.

winnowing fork is in his hand to clear his threshing floor and to gather the wheat into his barn, but he will burn up the chaff with unquenchable fire" (Luke 3:17, NIV) to explain the meaning of such a baptism. "Baptizing with the Holy Spirit and fire" is the eschatological work of Jesus after His death and resurrection. For the eschatological harvest, the Lord Jesus will complete his redemptive ministry by collecting the good grain (those who accept Christ) in Heaven's storage and by burning the chaff (those who reject Christ) in the everlasting fire of hell (see Luke 12:49-53; Mark 13:30).

As John the Baptist predicted, Jesus died on the cross and rose from the dead on the third day, fulfilling redemption according to God's plan (Rom. 4:25).[4] After His resurrection, Jesus remained on earth for 40 more days and said, "You will be baptized with the Holy Spirit" (Acts 1:5). No matter how we read this verse, from the context of the entire Book of Acts, it refers to the events of the Pentecost in Acts 2. Hence, there is no problem in accepting the events of the Pentecost in Acts 2 as the events of "the baptism of the Holy Spirit." The Bible is the best evidence that calls the Pentecost an event of "the baptism of the Holy Spirit."

The remaining verse we need to deal with regarding "the Baptism of the Holy Spirit" is I Corinthians 12:13. "For we were all baptized by one Spirit into one body- whether Jews or Greeks, slave or free- and we were all given the one Spirit to drink" (I Cor. 12:13, NIV). The phrase "baptism of the Holy Spirit" is used in both Acts 1:5 and I Corinthians 12:13, but they do not mean the same thing. Looking at the immediate context of the Bible, it is certain that "the

---

4) The word βαπτισθήσεσθε is future passive. This passive means that the baptism of the Holy Spirit shall not be the result of the recipients' activity. The subject of the baptism is the one who promised. Cf. Frederick Dale Bruner, *A Theology of the Holy Spirit* (Grand Rapids: Eerdmans, 1976), p. 158.

baptism of the Holy Spirit" mentioned in I Corinthians 12:13 does not refer to the events of the Pentecost or a specific historical event in Acts 2:1-4. Rather, I Corinthians 12:13 refers to a personal salvation experience of each Christian individual.

I Corinthians 12:12-27 compares the Christian Church to a human body. Verse 13 explains that Christians must receive the Holy Spirit's baptism to become a part of the body of Christ. "For in one Spirit we were all baptized into one body - Jews or Greeks, slaves or free - and all were made to drink of one Spirit" (I Cor. 12:13, ESV). Paul states that, like the human body whose different parts work together to function as a whole, each individual of the Church has different responsibilities and talents that make up the body of Christ. Though each person is of a different race and gender, we all can become a member of the body of Christ through the work of the one and only Spirit. The Church consists of different individuals with a variety of characteristics, but she is one body in Christ through the work of the Spirit. The step in becoming a body of Christ is to experience "the baptism of the Holy Spirit." [5] One cannot do so without experiencing "the baptism of the Holy Spirit." Paul is saying in I Corinthians 12:13 that by the baptism of the Holy Spirit, we are grafted into Christ as a branch is grafted into the vine (see John 15:1-9; Rom. 11:17-24). [6]

The term "baptism of the Holy Spirit" used in Acts 1:5 and I Corinthians 12:13 should be understood differently. They must be considered in light of the context to prevent any confusion on the subject.

---

5) F. W. Grosheide, *Commentary on the First Epistle to the Corinthians* (*NICNT*, Grand Rapids, Eerdmans, 1968), p. 293.

6) Robert K. Churchill, *Glorious is the Baptism of the Spirit* (Nutley: Presbyterian and Reformed Publishing Co., 1976), pp. 9-11.

In our studies, Acts 1:5 directs the focus on Acts 2, the Pentecostal event that should be examined in reference to Jesus' death, resurrection, and ascension. Hence, Acts 1:5 should be seen through the perspective of God's redemptive history for humankind. On the other hand, I Corinthians 12:13 explains the salvation experience of an individual Christian. From our studies thus far, we have learned that, though Luke 3:16, Acts 1:5 (Acts 2:1-4), and I Corinthians 12:13 all mention a baptism of the Holy Spirit, the former two verses refer to the Pentecostal event and the latter verse refers to an individual Christian's personal salvation experience.[7] We should not be confused by the use of "the Baptism of the Holy Spirit" in each context of the Bible.

2. The Pentecost: "The Baptism of the Holy Spirit" (Acts 2:1-4)

---

7) This writer believes that the "baptism of the Holy Spirit" in an individual Christian occurs when he is born again in Christ. In I Cor. 12: 13, Paul uses the phrase, "baptism of the Holy Spirit," rather than "regeneration" for two reasons. First, the redemptive act of Christ's death and resurrection is applied to each individual Christian through the activity of the Holy Spirit. Without the Spirit, no one can confess that Jesus is their Savior (I Cor. 12:3). The Holy Spirit gives faith to a Christian and allows one to confess that Jesus is the Savior. The presence of the Holy Spirit designates the Christian as a righteous person and a child of God, and from then on, the Spirit resides within the person (I Cor. 3:16; 6:19). Secondly, the word "baptism" is more appropriately used when a Christian joins a body of Christ (church). Circumcision in the Old Testament represents the act of accepting a Gentile as a member of God's people (Israel), and it corresponds to the baptism in the New Testament, by which the New Testament Church accept new believers into their congregation. So rather than "regeneration" and "justification," Paul uses the word "baptism" more appropriately to portray the idea that a Christian joins a Church. See Hyung Yong Park, "Baptism of the Holy Spirit and Salvation of a Christian" *Journal of Reformed Theology*, vol. 9, No. 1(1991, 7), pp. 38-40; Michael Green, *I Believe in the Holy Spirit* (Grand Rapids: Eerdmans, 1977), pp. 130-131; Anthony A. Hoekema, *Holy Spirit Baptism* (Grand Rapids: Eerdmans, 1972), p. 21; Gordon D. Fee, *The First Epistle to the Corinthians* (*NICNT*, Grand Rapids: Eerdmans, 1987), p. 605: "Most likely, therefore, Paul is referring to their common experience of conversion, and he does so in terms of its most crucial ingredient, the receiving of the Spirit."

(1) The Fulfillment of the Old Testament Prophecy

As the Old Testament prophets prophesied (Joel 2:28-32, MT 3:1-5) and as Jesus predicted (John 14:16, 26; 16:7-14), the baptism of the Holy Spirit occurs at the Pentecost after Jesus' crucifixion and resurrection. The Pentecost is celebrated 50 days after the Jewish Passover. Jewish people from everywhere congregate in Jerusalem to celebrate the event. While the Jewish Passover is meant to celebrate the freedom gained from their physical shackles in the land of slavery, the Pentecost observes the gaining of the Promised Land. Hence, the festivities of the Pentecost overflow with joy and thankfulness to the Lord.

There were two characteristics observed in the events of the baptism of the Holy Spirit during the Pentecost. The people could hear what was happening at the Pentecost (Acts 2:2), and they could also see the events (Acts 2:3).[8] As a result, all the disciples who gathered there were filled with the Spirit and began to preach the Good News in many different tongues.[9] In view of the redemptive history, the curse at the Tower of Babel (Gen. 11:1-9) was broken in order to spread the gospel. The people who were gathered to celebrate the Pentecost were surprised at the sudden event, and some even concluded that the disciples were drunk with fresh wine (Acts 2:7-13).

In response to those onlookers who thought the disciples were drunk, Peter uses the text Joel 2:28-32 (MT 3:1-5) to say that this

---

8) The word ἦχος(echos) for "sound" is used to illustrate the cries of the sea (see Luke 21:25), and the word, ὁράω, related to sight, is used to show that the events of the Pentecost could be observed by the naked eye.

9) Kistemaker (Simon J. Kistemaker, *Exposition of the Acts of the Apostles, NTC*, Grand Rapids: Baker, 1990, pp. 77-78) interprets that the word *tongue* is equivalent to the concept of a *spoken language*. Richard N. Longenecker (*The Acts of the Apostles: The Expositor's Bible Commentary*, vol. 9, ed. Frank E. Gaebelein, Grand Rapids: Zondervan, 1981, p. 271) also says that " 'the tongues' in [Acts] 2:4 are best understood as 'languages.'"

event had already been prophesied by Joel (Acts 2:15, 16). Through Joel, God promised to pour His Spirit on all His people on the Last Day. The prophecy of Joel clearly indicates that the Pentecost is an eschatological event and the beginning of the Last Day. Peter says "in the last days" (Acts 2:17) referring to the Pentecost. Peter uses the Book of Joel to explain the events of the Pentecost and inserts a phrase "they will prophesy (propheteusoosin: προφητεύσουσιν)" as a transition between Acts 2:17-18 and Acts 2:19-20.

Luke 3:16 states that Jesus will administer His baptism of the Holy Spirit as well as of fire, while Acts 1:5 refers to the Pentecost and portrays only "the baptism of the Spirit." The reason for this difference can be found in Acts 2:17-18 and Acts 2:19-20.[10]

<Acts 2:17-18>
1) Your children will prophesy.
2) Your youth will see visions.
3) Your elderly will dream dreams.
4) Both your male and female servants will receive the Holy Spirit.

"They will prophesy."

<Acts 2:19-20>
1) The heavens will show wonders, and signs will be given on earth.
2) The sun will be turned to darkness, and the moon will change into blood.

As we study the contents above, Acts 2:17-18 clearly describes the events of the Pentecost. On the contrary, Acts 2:19-20 does

---

10) The U.B.S. version which quotes the Old Testament and the Nestle-Aland Greek Testament (27th edition) show this point clearly.

not; rather, it goes beyond the events of the Pentecost and refers to the events of the end of the world.[11] Other places in the Bible also depict the Judgment Day in a similar tone: "By the same word the present heavens and earth are reserved for fire, being kept for the Day of Judgment and destruction of ungodly men" (II Peter 3:7, NIV) and "the day of the Lord will come like a thief. The heavens will disappear with a roar; the elements will be destroyed by fire, and the earth and everything in it will be laid bare" (II Peter 3:10, NIV). Revelation 6:12 illustrates the day of God's wrath as follows: The sun will become dark like a horse, the moon will become blood red, and other dramatic events will occur to signify the Last Day.

It is of great significance that the depiction of the Judgment Day appears in the description of the Pentecost. At the beginning of Jesus' ministry, John the Baptist illustrates that Jesus' ministry is characterized by the baptism of the Holy Spirit and fire, when he said, "He will baptize you with the Holy Spirit and with fire. His winnowing fork is in his hand to clear his threshing floor and to gather the wheat into his barn, but he will burn up the chaff with unquenchable fire" (Luke 3:16, 17, NIV). While the baptism of the Holy Spirit is a baptism of blessing, the baptism of fire is a baptism of judgment. This does not mean they are two separate baptisms; rather, they are two different aspects of a single baptism. Consequently, Acts 2:17, 18 illustrates a baptism of blessing given to the believers (the Church) through the Holy Spirit during the Pentecost (Acts 1:5), and Acts 2:19, 20 portrays one of judgment that will fall on the

---

11) Hagner (Donald A. Hagner, "The Old Testament in the New Testament," *Interpreting the Word of God*, ed. S.J. Schultz and M.A. Inch, Chicago: Moody Press, 1976, p. 98) in interpreting Peter's use of the Book of Joel, says, "Eschatology has been inaugurated yet not completed; the blessings of the Kingdom are presently enjoyed, while the accompanying judgment is delayed. Thus, theologically the two parts of the quotation stand together; chronologically they do not."

unbelievers on Judgment Day.[12]

Using the book of Joel to explain the Pentecost, Peter gives a good example of how the Old Testament prophecies should be applied. It shows how they can be used within the perspective of the New Testament. Peter's interpretation of the Book of Joel simultaneously compares two historical events from two completely different time periods. The first section is associated with the events of the Pentecost, and the second section is associated with the last events of the Judgment Day. Peter gives a synchronistic account of the two events as though he was looking through a pair of binoculars. These two events are separated by a long time interval, but the continuity is not destroyed nor is the meaning of the contents ruined. The events of the Pentecost and the Last Judgment possess the "already but not yet" character of time, which clearly displays the two aspects of the one and only Coming of Jesus. Jesus' teachings about the Kingdom and Paul's epistles all point toward these two facets of the **One Coming**. Hence, there lies a dual focus on the "present" and the "future" and on the "already" and the "not yet."

By the inspiration of the Holy Spirit, Peter adds the phrase, "they will prophesy" (kai propheteusoosin: καὶ προφητεύσουσιν) between Acts 2:17, 18 where he explains the Pentecost and Acts 2:19, 20 where he explains the events of the Judgment Day. The phrase, "they will prophesy" is not mentioned in the Book of Joel. Yet, Peter intentionally includes this phrase between Acts 2:17, 18 and Acts 2:19, 20 to show that verses 17 and 18 have a different emphasis from verses 19 and 20. Looking at the whole of the Old Testament prophecy, Peter recognizes a special structure in the text and decides to add something extra to the end of verse 18. Through the Pentecost,

---

12) See, Hyung Yong Park, *An Exposition of the Acts of the Apostles,* pp. 66-69.

Peter was able to see another aspect of Jesus' baptism, which was the element of judgment (Luke 12:49-53).

However, until the Day of Judgment, there is to be a period of God's abundant grace. During that period, "everyone who calls on the name of the Lord will be saved" (Acts 2:21). Those who accept that Christ died and rose from the dead for them will be saved from the Last Judgment. In turn, we can see that the events of the Pentecost are not meant for the individual to experience salvation but to accomplish a large part of God's redemptive plan. Hence, the Pentecost plays a unique role in acting out the Old Testament prophecy.

(2) The Witness of John the Baptist

When Jesus first started his public ministry, John the Baptist prophesied that "He will baptize you with the Holy Spirit and with fire. His winnowing fork is in his hand to clear his threshing floor and to gather the wheat into his barn, but he will burn up the chaff with unquenchable fire" (Luke 3:16, 17). These words refer to Jesus' ministry as the baptism of the Holy Spirit and fire. John the Baptist said these words in order to resolve the doubts that possessed the public. When the Israelites witnessed the work of John the Baptist, they believed him to be the expected Christ (Luke 3:15). They believed that he would establish the expected eschatological rule; in other words, they thought John the Baptist would build the promised Kingdom. These beliefs were rooted in the Old Testament prophecies about the coming Messiah, and John's reply was a one-sentence description of Jesus' position and his relationship to Him on the subject of the promised Kingdom. Comparing John's baptism to Jesus' baptism was neither to attract people's attention nor to dramatize John's work. Rather, it taught that the central focus of both

John and Jesus' works was baptism.

John the Baptist clearly indicates that the special focus of Jesus' Kingdom is baptism and prepares for it by ministering through the baptism of repentance. There is a definite difference between John's ministry and Jesus' ministry.[13] John told his followers and the people that he was not the 'Messiah-King' whom they were looking for. He was simply leading the way with water baptism in preparation for the real Messiah (Luke 3:4-6). John explained that the expected 'Messiah-King' was an omnipotent being who would come later in time and who would baptize with the Holy Spirit and with fire. By this, John the Baptist meant that his baptisms were an external symbol of forgiveness, while Jesus Christ would offer baptisms that would bring true internal purification and regeneration.

John the Baptist pointed out that the centrality of Jesus' ministry of the Kingdom is "the baptism with the Holy Spirit and with fire." John gave external and symbolic baptisms by water, but Jesus would give true internal baptisms with the Holy Spirit and with fire.[14] "Baptism with the Holy Spirit and with fire" does not mean that Jesus gives two kinds of baptisms. In the Greek biblical text, the elements

---

13) The Bible makes a clear distinction between John the Baptist's ministry and Jesus' ministry. Matt. 4:12-17 records, "When Jesus heard that John had been put in prison, he returned to Galilee. Leaving Nazareth, he went and lived in Capernaum, which was by the lake in the area of Zebulun and Naphtali — From that time on Jesus began to preach, 'Repent, for the kingdom of heaven is near.'" while Mark 1:14-15 says, "After John was put in prison, Jesus went into Galilee, proclaiming the good news of God. 'The time has come,' he said. 'The kingdom of God is near. Repent and believe the good news!'" Then Luke 3:20-22 first records the imprisonment of John the Baptist (vs. 20) and then Jesus' baptism by John the Baptist which signals the beginning of his public ministry (vs. 21-22).

We cannot pinpoint the specific time when John the Baptist's ministry ended and Jesus' ministry began, but the authors of the Gospels clearly relate the events in a proper chronological order.

14) Norval Geldenhuys, *Commentary on the Gospel of Luke* (*NICNT*, Grand Rapids: Eerdmans, 1968), p. 140. In comparing the baptisms of John the Baptist and Jesus, John's baptisms only symbolized the baptism of the Holy Spirit, while Jesus' baptisms actually

of the Holy Spirit and fire are expressed as one, using one preposition (en: ἐν). If Luke had believed that there were two different baptisms, he would have used two different prepositions. Hence, Jesus' baptism can be seen as one baptism with two unique aspects.[15] Jesus' baptism with the Spirit and with fire is one baptism that presents both a blessing and judgment, respectively.

But how can Jesus give both a baptism of blessing and of judgment at the same time? In order to answer this question, we must remember the reason why Jesus came down to earth. He came to save us from our sins. Because "the wages of sin is death" (Rom. 6:23), and "just as man is destined to die once, and after that to face judgment," (Heb. 9:27), human beings must die and experience judgment because of their sins. Jesus "has appeared once for all at the end of the ages to do away with sin by the sacrifice of himself " (Heb. 9:26, NIV).

Jesus died on the cross to nullify the necessity of punishing the sinners and to save them. Paul testifies that "God made him who had no sin to be sin for us, so that in him we might become the righteousness of God" (II Cor. 5:21, NIV). In reality, Jesus' death on the cross is the baptism of judgment that originally belonged to

---

brought the complete cleansing by the Holy Spirit. See, I. Howard Marshall, *Commentary on Luke* (*NIGTC*, Grand Rapids: Eerdmans, 1978), pp. 147f.

15) Lenski (R.C.H. Lenski, *The Interpretation of St. Luke's Gospel,* Minneapolis: Augsburg Publishing House, 1961, p. 201) believed that the Spirit and fire are the "work of grace," so he interprets the fire as a symbol of cleansing or purification. cf. R.C.H. Lenski, *The Interpretation of the Acts of the Apostles* (Minneapolis: Augsburg Publishing House, 1961), p. 59. On the other hand, Summers (Ray Summers, *Commentary on Luke,* Waco: Word Books, 1972, p. 48) believed that the Holy Spirit represented salvation and that the fire represented judgment. Summers explains that Christ's coming was a blessing to some and a judgment to others. Then Nolland (John Nolland, *Luke 1-9:20: Word Biblical Commentary,* vol. 35a. Dallas: Word Books, 1989, p. 153) presents "the view that sees in both Spirit and fire the means of eschatological purgation experienced by the penitent as purification in the refiner's fire and by godless as destruction by wind and fire."

us. Instead, he accepted the judgment and he received the baptism of judgment in place of us. Luke 12:50 says, "But I have a baptism to undergo, and how distressed I am until it is completed!" This meant that Jesus' death on the cross was the baptism He had come to receive on earth. Then Mark 10:38 says, "Can you drink the cup I drink or be baptized with the baptism I am baptized with," and John 18:11 says, "Shall I not drink the cup the Father has given me?" These two verses ascertain that His death on the cross is the baptism of judgment He will receive because of our sins. And because He did so, if anyone accepts Jesus as his Savior and is united with Him, he will be cleansed from his sins. As a result, our sins have been washed away.

After Jesus received this baptism of judgment and then resurrected from the dead, He directs our attention to the Pentecost when he says "For John baptized with water, but in a few days you will be baptized with the Holy Spirit" (Acts 1:5). We must keep in mind that, in the beginning of Jesus' public ministry, John the Baptist referred to Jesus' ministry as "the baptism with the Holy Spirit and with fire" (Luke 3:16), but after Jesus experienced the baptism of judgment on the cross, the resurrected Christ only mentioned "the baptism with the Holy Spirit" (Acts 1:5), no longer referring to the element of fire but only to the Pentecost.

After Jesus' crucifixion and resurrection, "The baptism of the Spirit and fire" changed to "the baptism of the Spirit." What brought about this transformation? Without further consideration, the Bible states that Jesus came as our substitute to receive the baptism of judgment, so those who are united with Christ as a part of His body are exempt from it. Therefore, the baptism of the Holy Spirit that occurred during the Pentecost represents a blessing in which God seals His people as His own. The fact that a single author recorded such a flow of history using the Gospel of Luke and the book of Acts

(Luke 3:16; 12:50; Acts 1:5; 2:1-4) confirms our claims up to this point.

John the Baptist's words about Jesus' ministry, Jesus' death on the cross, and the Holy Spirit's baptism during the Pentecost are directly related to one another. This, in turn, shows that Jesus accepted the baptism of judgment on the cross to solve the problem of sin and to give His people the benefit of receiving the baptism of blessing by the Holy Spirit. The redemptive events that Jesus fulfilled during the Pentecost were the inevitable result of His own death and resurrection.[16] Hence, the baptism of the Holy Spirit at Pentecost was a unique and once-for-all event in history.

(3) The Testimony of Jesus

Jesus' life heads toward the cross and resurrection. The reason Jesus incarnated in the form of a human was to walk the path of the cross. While portraying His public ministry, the Gospels say that no one and nothing could interfere with this plan. Peter, who had previously spoken the famous confession, "You are the Christ, the Son of the living God" (Matt. 16:16, NIV) in Caesarea, Philippi, tried to hinder Jesus' death on the cross. Jesus then scolded Peter by saying, "Get behind me, Satan! You are a stumbling block to me; you do not have in mind the things of God, but the things of men" (Matt. 16:23, NIV). Though Jesus knew His path of the cross was a bitter fruit to reap, He wanted His life which was in God's hands, to follow God's plan.

In foreseeing His redemptive mission on the cross, Jesus makes a definite statement about the baptism of the Holy Spirit during the Pentecost:

---

16) D. A. Carson, *Showing the Spirit: A Theological Exposition of I Corinthians 12-14* (Grand Rapids: Baker, 1987), pp. 139-143.

"But I tell you the truth: It is for your good that I am going away. Unless I go away, the Counselor will not come to you; but if I go, I will send him to you. When he comes, he will convict the world of guilt in regard to sin and righteousness and judgment" (John 16:7-8).[17]

"But when he, the Spirit of truth, comes, he will guide you into all truth. He will not speak on his own; he will speak only what he hears, and he will tell you what is yet to come. He will bring glory to me by taking from what is mine and making it known to you" (John 16:13-14).

"When the Counselor comes, whom I will send to you from the Father, the Spirit of truth who goes out from the Father, he will testify about me" (John 15:26).

"And I will ask the Father, and he will give you another Counselor to be with you forever" (John

---

17) Hendriksen (W. Hendriksen, *The Gospel of John, NTC*. Vol. II. Grand Rapids: Baker, 1953, p. 323) appropriately interprets Christ's departure in relation to the events of the cross. "The basic reason why Christ's departure means triumph and not tragedy, the reason why it is a help and not a hindrance for these men (and for the Church in general) is this, that otherwise *the Helper* (see on 14:16), namely, the Holy Spirit, will not come to them. Jesus does not explain why the Spirit cannot come unless the Son departs from the earth and returns to his home above. Suggestions which probably point in the right direction are these: the Son's *going away* is a departure via *the cross*. By his going away he merits redemption for his people. Now the Holy Spirit is the One whose special task it is to apply the saving merits of Christ to the hearts and lives of believers (Rom. 8: Gal. 4:4-6). But the Spirit cannot apply these merits when there are no merits to apply. Hence, unless Jesus *goes away*, the Spirit cannot come."

14:16).

"But the Counselor, the Holy Spirit, whom the Father will send in my name, will teach you all things and will remind you of everything I have said to you" (John 14:26).

"I will not leave you as orphans; I will come to you" (John 14:18).

In summary, if Jesus did not die on the cross, no other Comforter (parakletos: παράκλητος)[18] would have been sent to take His place, and that would not have been beneficial for the disciples. So, Jesus needed to walk the path of the cross, and after His resurrection, another Comforter, the Holy Spirit, would descend upon the disciples to be with them forever. It is important to note here that Jesus referred to the Holy Spirit as "another Comforter" which means that His disciples already had one, the one who is departing. The present advocacy of Jesus for His disciples is discharged in the courts of heaven.[19] And His death on the cross does not mean the end of his work on earth but rather a new beginning that will, by the sending of the Spirit, bring His work to full manifestation.[20] Through them, the Spirit would give witness about Jesus, sin, righteousness, and judgment. Through the Spirit, Jesus would permanently remain with

18) The word *paracletos* is found once in I John 2:1 where Jesus is described as "our paraclete" and four times in the last discourse of Jesus (John 14:16, 26; 15:26; 16:7). It does not otherwise occur in the New Testament or in the entire Old Testament. *Paracletos* means "one who is called alongside." In secular Greek, *paracletos* mainly means "legal assistant" as an advocate or a witness.

19) D. A. Carson, *The Gospel According to John* (Grand Rapids: Eerdmans, 1991), p. 500.

20) Herman Ridderbos, *The Gospel of John: A Theological Commentary* (Grand Rapids: Eerdmans, 1997), p. 530.

the disciples (see, John 14:18).

In sequence to His death, resurrection, and ascension, Jesus was looking towards the Baptism of the Holy Spirit at the Pentecost. Therefore, He ties the events of His death, resurrection, ascension, and Pentecost together. If Jesus' death and resurrection are considered as unique and once-for-all events, and if the Pentecost is considered inseparable from Jesus' death and resurrection, then the Pentecost must also be considered unique and once-for-all. Likewise, the baptism of the Holy Spirit at the Pentecost is closely connected to the redemptive events in history and is definitely a unique event in all of history.[21]

God planned the baptism of the Holy Spirit to occur after Christ's death and resurrection, which shows that this event was, not simply a model for the individual Christian, but that God was using it as an important epoch-making event in the history of His redemption. Thus, the Pentecost is associated with the events of Jesus' death, resurrection, and ascension in the past, and it is also related to the spreading of the gospel by the New Testament Church until Jesus' Second Coming in the future.

The focus of this study, in view of the redemptive history, presents the Holy Spirit's descent at Pentecost (Acts 2:1-4) as a fulfillment of the Old Testament prophecies, a fulfillment of John the Baptist's prophecies, and a fulfillment of Jesus' promise. The events recorded within the Bible must be interpreted within the context of the Bible. The baptism of the Holy Spirit at the Pentecost should be

---

21) Richard B. Gaffin, Jr., *Perspectives on Pentecost* (Grand Rapids: Baker, 1979), pp. 25-28.; Sinclair B. Ferguson, *The Holy Spirit: Contours of Christian Theology* (Downers Grove: IVP, 1996), pp. 86-87. "It is no more repeatable as an event than is the crucifixion or the resurrection or the ascension of our Lord. It is an event in redemptive history (*historia salutis*), and should not be squeezed into the grid of the application of redemption (*ordo salutis*)."

considered in terms of Luke's purpose in writing the Gospel of Luke and the book of Acts as its sequential volume.[22] Thus, the uniqueness of the Pentecost can be recognized and its significance can be brought to light.

---

22) J. I. Packer (*Keep in Step with the Spirit,* Old Tappan: Fleming H. Revell Company, 1984, p. 205) states that if Luke had realized that the future readers of the Pentecostal event would misunderstand its significance, he would have been surprised and concerned at the same time. Packer continues to say that Luke's account of the Pentecost, Samaria, Cornelius' family, and Ephesus gives an object lesson to teach the character and mission of the Church.

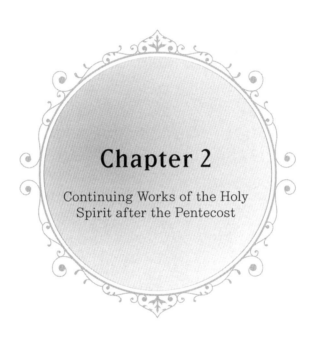

Chapter 2

Continuing Works of the Holy
Spirit after the Pentecost

The Acts records the outpouring of the Holy Spirit in the Pentecost as well as the other special works of the Spirit on several occasions. Questions arise as to what relationship the Pentecost has with these other occasions. How do we interpret the miraculous work of the Holy Spirit in Samaria (Acts 8:4-25)? What about the advent of the Holy Spirit in the household of Cornelius (Acts 10:44-48)? How do we interpret the advent of the Holy Spirit in Ephesus (Acts 19:1-7)? These are a few questions that come to mind while studying the works of the Holy Spirit after the Pentecost (Acts 2:1-4), and we will answer each question in separate sections.

1. The Outpouring of the Holy Spirit in Samaria (Acts 8:4-25)

The martyrdom of Stephen caused believers in Jerusalem to disperse to other places, with the exception of the Apostles (Acts 8:1). Stephen's death initiated the spreading of the gospel outside of Jerusalem. As Luke had said, "but you will receive power when the Holy Spirit comes on you; and you will be my witnesses in Jerusalem, and in all Judea and Samaria, and to the ends of the earth" (Acts 1:8, NIV), the gospel was shared in Samaria.

Among those who had dispersed by persecution was Philip (Acts 8:4-5). He had gone to the city of Samaria, spreading the gospel, performing miracles and converting many people to Christ. From Philip, the people in Samaria heard about Jesus Christ and the Kingdom of Heaven, believed, and became baptized to commit themselves to Christ (Acts 8:12).

Some scholars do not believe that the Samaritans, who became believers through Philip's preaching, had genuine faith.[23] The text

---

23) James Dunn, *Baptism in the Holy Spirit* (London: SCM, 1970), pp. 55-72. Dunn concludes that Luke wants to make only two points: "the Samaritans received the Spirit

does not say that there was a problem in either Philip's understanding of the gospel or in the Samaritan people's faith. Rather, Philip baptized those Samaritans who became Christians (Acts 8:12).[24] However, the book of Acts records that Peter and John were sent by the Jerusalem Church and "they prayed for them that they might receive the Holy Spirit" (Acts 8:15) and "Peter and John placed their hands on them, and they received the Holy Spirit" (Acts 8:17, NIV). The two apostles prayed for the Holy Spirit to come on the Samaritan believers and laid hands on them because "the Holy Spirit had not yet come upon any of them; they had simply been baptized into the name of the Lord Jesus" (Acts 8:16, NIV).

(1) Agreement with Luke's Purpose in Writing the Acts

We must study the work of the Holy Spirit in Samaria in Luke's perspective and by considering the special circumstances of the history of Samaria. Luke wanted to inform the readers of the fact that the gospel of redemption accomplished by Christ's death and resurrection was being spread "in Jerusalem, and in all Judea and Samaria, and to the ends of the earth" (Acts 1:8). By the outpouring of the Holy Spirit at Pentecost (Acts 2:1-4), the Church was established, which, in turn, began to spread the gospel in Jerusalem. The gospel proclamation in Jerusalem is the first stage of the accomplishment of the Lord's commands about missions in Acts 1:8.

---

only through the apostles' ministry, and the exposure of Simon." (pp. 67-68). Dunn holds an opinion that the Samaritans were prompted "by the herd-instinct of a popular mass-movement" (p. 65) and they did not become Christians when they were baptized by Philip.

24) C. K. Barrett, *The Acts of the Apostles,* vol. 1 (*I.C.C.*), (Edinburgh: T&T Clark, 1994), pp. 412: "It is unlikely that he means that the baptized Samaritans were not Christians; they were Christians, but they did not manifest the charismatic phenomena of inspiration." Max Turner (*Power from on High: The Spirit in Israel's Restoration and Witness in Luke-Acts,* Sheffield: Sheffield Academic Press, 1996, pp. 360-367) supports an opinion that the Samaritans genuinely believed the Christian message and were baptized.

It is natural for Luke to describe the special manifestation of the Holy Spirit in the next stage of the gospel proclamation in all of Judea and Samaria.

The gospel of salvation in Jesus Christ goes beyond social or racial boundaries. Yet, we must remember the friction and the hate that existed for a long time between the Samaritans and the Jews.[25] In order to unify the two discordant groups of people under the one gospel, the same Holy Spirit, which was manifested among the Jews, had to be manifested among the Samaritans in the same way.[26] When these barriers are lifted, the gospel could continue to overcome all the conflicts that exist in history, and through Christ, the believers in Samaria could become one with the believers in the Jerusalem Church. Moreover, the Jerusalem Church could then throw away

---

25) The quarrel between the Jews and the Samaritans goes far back in history. Assyria conquered the Northern Kingdom's capital Samaria (B.C. 722). Assyria dispersed many Samaritans within the Assyrian kingdom and allowed the Assyrian people to reside within Samaria (II Kings 17:32ff.). The Assyrian people brought their gods (II Kings 17:29-31) and worshipped them, while worshipping Jehovah at the same time (II Kings 17:25, 28, 32, 33, 41). In time, the residents of Samaria had come to worship only the Lord Jehovah as well, which brought a unique character into their religion. For example, from among all the Old Testament books, they only accepted the five books of Moses.

Then when the Jews returned from their Babylonian exile, the Samaritans wanted to help the Jews construct the temple, but the Jews refused the offer (Zechariah 4:2-3). As a result, the tension between the Jews and the Samaritans increased. The Samaritans then refused to worship God in Jerusalem, choosing to worship in their own temple which was built on top of Mount Gerizim in 400 B.C. (see John 4:20). However, this temple was burned down by the Jews in 128 B.C. (by John Hyrcanus). This further deepened the strain between the two. In Jesus' time, the conversation between Jesus and the Samaritan woman (John 4:1-26) portrays the presence of this social tension quite well. The preaching of the gospel in Samaria, recorded in the book of Acts, needs to be compared in relation to this historical circumstance.

26) Bruner explained well on this matter. See, Frederick Dale Bruner, *A Theology of the Holy Spirit* (Grand Rapids: Eerdmans, 1976), p. 176.: "The Samaritans were not left to become an isolated sect with no bonds of union with the apostolic church in Jerusalem." — "The drama of the Samaritan affair in Acts 8 included among its purposes the vivid and visual dismantling of the wall of enmity between Jew and Samaritan and the preservation of the precious unity of the church of God through the unique divine 'interception' and then prompt presentation of the Spirit in the presence of the apostles."

their Jewish pride and greet the Samaritan Christians as their brothers and sisters in Christ.

(2) The Importance of the Apostles and their Teachings

Luke summarized two requirements for an Apostle in Acts 1 when the Apostles chose Matthias as an apostle to replace Judas Iscariot.

First of all, the apostle must have followed Jesus and must have accompanied Jesus along with the disciples during the public ministry of Jesus on earth. Luke said, "it is necessary to choose one of the men who have been with us the whole time the Lord Jesus went in and out among us, beginning from John's baptism to the time when Jesus was taken up from us" (Acts 1:21-22, NIV). The successor for Judas Iscariot's place had to be a person who had followed Jesus during His public ministry.

Secondly, the apostle had to have witnessed Jesus' resurrection first-hand. So, Judas' successor should have been present with the disciples when Jesus appeared to them after His resurrection.[27] In emphasizing these two requirements, Luke states that Judas' successor should not only be a leader in the Church and a person who attains the level of faith of an apostle but must be a witness to the gospel's tradition. An apostle preserves the messages from Jesus and delivers them to others without distortion. Thus, Luke places a special emphasis on the role of the apostle who would replace Judas.[28]

---

27) Park, Hyung Yong, *An Exposition of the Acts of the Apostles* (Korean) (Suwon: Hapdong Theological Seminary Press, 2003), pp. 44-49; S. Kistemaker, *Exposition of the Acts of the Apostles* (*NTC*, Grand Rapids: Baker, 1990), pp. 66; C.K. Barrett, *The Acts of the Apostles* (*I.C.C.*) vol. 1, pp. 102: "The main theme of the apostolic testimony is, according to Luke, the resurrection of the one who was baptized, conducted the ministry described in the gospel, and subsequently was killed."
28) Richard N. Longenecker, *The Acts of the Apostles: The Expositor's Bible Commentary,*

It should be noted that Luke states that the qualifications of an apostle included giving testimonies on Jesus' work and teachings during His public ministry as well as on Jesus' death, resurrection, and ascension. In talking about the writing of scriptural revelation, giving testimonies on Jesus' death, resurrection, and ascension is an extremely important qualification. God gave the last revelation through His Son, Jesus Christ (Heb. 1:1-2). Jesus' person and work are not transitory features; rather, they have the everlasting significance as the final revelation. But the New Testament had not been recorded during Jesus' life on earth. It began to be written about 30 years after the end of Jesus' ministry on earth. With these conditions, only the one who had witnessed and could give a direct testimony on Jesus' person, ministry, and resurrection could properly record the last scriptural revelation. From the time of Jesus' life on earth until the time when the New Testament was recorded, the apostles preserved, passed on, and preached the gospel.

Therefore, the apostles' position bore great importance in the early Church, and it provides a better understanding of the fact that when the Jerusalem Church "heard that Samaria had accepted the word of God, they sent Peter and John to them" (Acts 8:14, NIV). The Apostles Peter and John were sent by the Jerusalem Church to Samaria to supervise over the spreading of the genuine gospel. The book of Acts provides a significant account of the role of the twelve apostles. Their direct role was not recorded in the event of the outpouring of the Holy Spirit at Pentecost (Acts 2:1-4) and in the conversion of Paul (Acts 9:3-18). But it is significant to note that the apostles, as custodians and deliverers of the message from Jesus, were present at the events in Samaria, in Ephesus, and in Cornelius' family.

Vol. 9, ed. Frank E. Gaebelein (Grand Rapids: Zondervan, 1981), p. 265.

Their presence was a confirmation that the New Testament Church was expanding with the same gospel message to the Gentiles.

Luke emphasizes the importance of the part that the apostles and the Jerusalem Church played in the spreading of the gospel. When the gospel had spread to Samaria, the apostles in Jerusalem sent Peter and John. When they were praying for and laying hands on the Samaritans, the Samaritans received the Holy Spirit. The fact that the Samaritans received the Holy Spirit through Peter and John's ministry (Acts 8:15, 17, 18) illustrates that the authority of the apostles rested in the core of the Church's expansion.[29]

The Samaritans needed to comprehend the authority and power of the apostles, while the Jews needed to realize that the Samaritan Christians were also a part of the body of Christ. In addition, the Samaritan Christians had to grasp the fact that their understanding of godly truth came by the mediation of the Jewish Apostles.[30] By His Providence, God allowed the Holy Spirit's extraordinary work to appear to the Samaritans through the laying of hands of Peter and John. As a result, the gospel was spread to other places (Samaria), and at the same time, God proved the unity of the Church.

(3) The Miraculous Work of the Holy Spirit in Samaria

The Holy Spirit finally came to the Samaritans after Peter and John prayed and laid hands on the people. Yet, Luke records that the Samaritans received the Holy Spirit after being baptized "into the name of the Lord" (Acts 8:16). They were first baptized by Philip (Acts 8:12) and then received the Holy Spirit after a visit by the apostles (Acts 8:14-17). This means that the Samaritans received the Spirit after they accepted Christ as their Savior.[31]

---

29) Park, Hyung Yong, *An Exposition of the Acts of the Apostles,* pp. 116-117.
30) John F. MacArthur, Jr., *Charismatic Chaos* (Grand Rapids: Zondervan, 1992), p. 180.
31) For these reasons, the Pentecostal scholars and others with similar views about the

The Samaritans first believed and then received the Holy Spirit at some later point.[32] How do we understand this time difference? In the early Church, people could receive the water baptism in His name only after recognizing Jesus' death and resurrection and repenting their sins because baptism symbolized that they were being cleansed from their sins (Acts 2:36-38; 3:15-19; 5:30-1).[33] The early Church emphasized Jesus' death and resurrection in their message but especially the resurrection (Acts 2:31-32; 3:15-21; 4:10, 33; 5:30-31; 7:52-56). Hence, it is safe to say that the Samaritans received their water baptisms after accepting Jesus' death and resurrection as saving events and after repenting their sins.[34]

In such cases, because the point at which one believes in Jesus and the point at which one receives the Holy Spirit are different, scholars who assert a Pentecostal view use the events from Samaria

---

baptism of the Holy Spirit wish to promote the scheme of pre-conversion and post-Holy Spirit baptism. Thus, they link the event of Samaria with the events of the Pentecost. cf.

D.M. Lloyd-Jones, *Joy Unspeakable* (Sungryung Sehreh, Korean), trans. Chung, Won Tai (Seoul: Christian Literature Crusade, 1986), pp. 135-6, 252; Ann, Young Bok, *A Right Understanding of the Work of the Holy Spirit* (Korean) (Seoul: Christian Literature Crusade, 1987), p. 38; Chung, Won Tai, *Fervent Calvinism* (Korean) (Seoul: Christian Literature Crusade, 1984), p. 53; Myung, Sung Hoon, *With the Holy Spirit* (Korean) (Seoul: Credo, 1993), pp. 75-84; Howard M. Ervin, *Conversion-Initiation and the Baptism in the Holy Spirit: An Engaging Critique of James D.G. Dunn's Baptism in the Holy Spirit* (Peabody, MA: Hendrickson Publishers, Inc., 1984), pp. 25-32.

32) Campbell Morgan asserts that the Samaritans received the Word of God simply by making an intellectual assent (Morgan, *The Acts of the Apostles*. Fleming H. Revell, 1924, p. 157). James Dunn, like Morgan, makes a stand that the Samaritans were led by "the herd-instinct of a popular mass-movement (ὁμοθυμαδόν-v.6)" (James D. G. Dunn, *Baptism in the Holy Spirit*, p. 65). Both Morgan and Dunn state that the Samaritans did not immediately become believers of Christ when they received baptisms in His name.

33) We must note that the Greek expression in Acts 2:38 is "μετανοήσατε, καὶ βαπτισθήτω ἕκαστος ὑμῶν ἐπὶ τῷ ὀνόματι Ἰησοῦ Χριστοῦ εἰς ἄφεσιν τῶν ἁμαρτιῶν ὑμῶν"

34) Nowadays, pastors provide water baptisms only after making sure that the individual truly believes in Jesus' death and resurrection and that the person realizes that one is a sinner.

and other places (Acts chapter 2) to support the pre-conversion and post-baptism scheme. But Luke did not write his Gospel and the book of Acts to create a redemptive pattern for an individual. Rather, Luke wrote the Gospel of Luke to portray Jesus' birth and public ministry until the time of His ascension. And in the book of Acts, he records the process in which Christ's Church, after Jesus' ascension, worked to spread the gospel from Jerusalem to the ends of the earth (Luke 1:1-4; Acts 1:1-2). Hence, we must reflect upon the progression of the redemptive history to properly understand the work of the Holy Spirit in Samaria.

Then how can we understand the miraculous work of the Holy Spirit in Samaria after they believed in Jesus? In order to understand this event, we must be aware of a broader context. The Samaritans received the Holy Spirit (ἐλάμβανον πνεῦμα ἅγιον) after the two apostles laid their hands on them. When Simon witnessed this event, he tried to buy the apostles' power with his money. What does this mean? Simon believed that the power would benefit him because he had seen the external manifestation of the Holy Spirit and so tried to buy it with money. Looking at it in this perspective, God especially allowed the advent of the Holy Spirit in Samaria to bring about a strong external manifestation of the Spirit. This then would open the door for the gospel in a land where its long historical tradition had made it stubborn. The Samaritans had already believed in Jesus and when they had received baptisms from Philip, they also had received the Holy Spirit (see, I Cor. 12:3; Rom. 10:9-10, 17). Thus, Peter and John's visit brought about a powerful external manifestation of the Holy Spirit.[35] Moreover, the outpouring of the Holy Spirit in Samaria provided an opportunity for the gospel to spread from Jerusalem

---

35) Park, Hyung Yong, *An Exposition of the Acts of Apostles*, pp. 116-117; cf. Kistemaker, *op. cit.*, p. 300: "God confirmed this new phase by sending the Holy Spirit as a visible

through all of Judea to the land of Samaria and also played a part in uniting the Samaritan Church to the Jerusalem Church.

2. The Work of the Holy Spirit Within Cornelius' Family (Acts 10:44-48; 11:1-18)

Through the event of Cornelius' family, God was preparing for a mission to the Gentiles. The whole of Acts 10 and Acts 11:1-18 records the event of Gentile Cornelius' conversion. His conversion illustrated how the gospel of Christ would be spread to the Gentiles. The event of Cornelius' family should be seen in light of the entire book of Acts and should be seen in connection to the results of the Jerusalem council in Acts 15.

In response to the Judaizers who tried to impose circumcision on the Gentile believers (Acts 15:1), Peter used the event of Cornelius' family as an example to say "God, who knows the heart, showed that he accepted them by giving the Holy Spirit to them, just as he did to us. He made no distinction between us and them, for he purified their hearts by faith" (Acts 15:8-9, NIV) and testified that "we believe it is through the grace of our Lord Jesus that we are saved, just as they are" (Acts 15:11, NIV). Whether someone is a Jew or a Gentile, Peter affirmed that one would receive salvation under God's grace only through faith in Jesus Christ. God was using the event of Cornelius' family to open the door for missions in the Gentile lands.

---

sign of his divine presence." Wayne Grudem (*Systematic Theology: An Introduction to Biblical Doctrine*. Grand Rapids: Zondervan, 1994, p. 774) explains that the event of Acts 8 illustrates a 'Samaritan Pentecost,' which shows a special outpouring of the Holy Spirit among the Samaritans. Grudem agrees to the fact that the Pentecost in Acts 2 is a turning point between "the Old Covenant Experience of the Holy Spirit" and "the New Covenant Experience of the Holy Spirit" (p. 772). However, because he has already used the term 'Pentecost' to describe Acts 2, his description of Acts 8 as another 'Samaritan Pentecost' is lacking in consistency with his use of the terminology.

(1) The Details of the Event

God arranges a special meeting for Cornelius and Peter. God appears to the Roman Centurion Cornelius in a vision and orders him to invite Peter to his home.[36] God then specifically tells Cornelius that Peter is staying at Simon the tanner's house in Joppa (Acts 10:5-6). Such a method implies that God had a special purpose. At the same time, God was breaking Peter's thoughts of discrimination against the Gentiles.

Peter went up to the roof to pray, and in the midst of his hunger, in a trance, he saw the heavens open and a large sheet descending. Within the sheet were four-legged animals of each kind along with those that crawled on land and those that flew in the sky. At that moment, Peter heard a voice say "Get up, Peter. Kill and eat" (Acts 10:13). Peter insisted that he would not eat any unclean food, but the voice said, "Do not call anything impure that God has made clean" (Acts 10:15, NIV).[37] This curious act in the dream repeated three times, and at that moment, the messenger from Cornelius arrived at Peter's place and asked him to come to the house of the Gentile Cornelius to preach the gospel. Peter then realized through the vision that God does not differentiate between the Gentiles and the Jews. Because Peter had received God's revelation through a vision only a few moments before, he did not hesitate to go to Cornelius' household and preached Christ that one received salvation only through faith (Acts 10:43). When Peter had preached, he had not made a special

---

36) Cornelius was a man who worshipped God, prayed diligently, and helped many people. In looking at the book of Acts, Cornelius could not have been a believer at the time when he saw God's vision. This is because the verses "He will bring you a message through which you and all your household will be saved. 'As I began to speak, the Holy Spirit came on them as he had come on us at the beginning'" (Acts 11:14-15, NIV), imply that Cornelius was saved when Peter was preaching. cf. Donald Macleod, *The Spirit of Promise* (Ross-shire, Scotland: Christian Focus Publications, 1986), p. 17.

37) "What God has made clean, do not call common." (Acts 10:15, ESV).

prayer, and the apostle had not specially asked God nor laid hands on the people gathered there; yet, the Holy Spirit came upon the household. Peter recognized that this was God's plan and without any hesitation, baptized the new believers (Acts 10:44-48).[38]

(2) The Special Work of the Holy Spirit in Cornelius' Household

The miraculous work of the Holy Spirit took place in Cornelius' household while Peter was preaching.[39] Peter's sermon focused on the Christology, portraying Jesus' life in great detail (Acts 10:34-43). The fact that Peter preached in detail about the life and works of Jesus of Nazareth proves, first of all, that the message of the early Church could not do without the historical Jesus[40] and secondly, that the work of the Holy Spirit is closely related to the historical Jesus.

Peter testifies that God poured the Holy Spirit and His power upon Jesus the Nazarene (Luke 3:21-22; see Acts 10:38) and that Jesus' ministry on earth was continued by the power of the Holy Spirit (see Luke 4:1; Matt. 12:28). Jesus was endowed with the power of the Holy Spirit to heal the demon-possessed, and the sick, to spread the gospel to the poor, and to feed the hungry, in order to expand God's Kingdom (Acts 10:38; see Isaiah 61:1-2; Luke 4:18-21). Peter preached, not only about Jesus' earthly ministry, but also went on to

---

38) Park, Hyung Yong, *An Exposition of the Acts of the Apostles,* pp. 119-125.

39) Notice the relationship between the present participle λαλοῦντος and the main verb ἐπέπεσεν in the aorist form from Ἔτι λαλοῦντος τοῦ πέτρου τὰ ῥήματα ταῦτα ἐπέπεσεν τὸ πνεῦμα τὸ ἅγιον ἐπὶ πάντας τοὺς ἀκούντας τὸν λόγον (Acts 10:44). Peter's preaching and the advent of the Holy Spirit occurred simultaneously.

40) Graham N. Stanton (*Jesus of Nazareth in the New Testament Preaching,* Cambridge University Press, 1974) disagrees with R. Bultmann who claims that the early Church was only interested in the resurrected Christ and not the historical Jesus. Stanton continues to say that the early Church was deeply interested in Jesus' past (p. 186), that Jesus' life and special characteristics were an important part of the messages given within the early Church (p. 30), and that the early Church's faith based on the resurrection did not underestimate Jesus' life and ministry (p. 191).

testify about Jesus' death, resurrection, and exaltation. For example, he had witnessed Jesus' death at the hands of the Jews by hanging on a tree (Acts 10:39), which, in fact, is a fulfillment of the Old Testament Scriptures in Jesus. Those who are cursed by God would hang on the cross. And hence, Jesus hung on the cross in place of us to receive God's punishment for our sins (Cf. Deuteronomy 21:22-23; Galatians 3:10-13; I Peter 2:24). Peter further explains that God the Father raised Jesus from the dead in three days and seated him in the seat of triumph and honor. At the same time, God appointed His Son as "judge of the living and the dead" (Acts 10:40-42). Those who believe in Jesus Christ would then receive forgiveness of sins (Acts 10:43).

Luke testifies that the Holy Spirit descended upon all the people who were listening to Peter's sermon. Here are a couple points in summary on the incident in Cornelius' household.

First of all, there is a definite correlation between the activities of the historical Jesus empowered by the Holy Spirit and the work of the Holy Spirit upon Cornelius' household.[41] Jesus said that when the Holy Spirit comes, He "will teach you all things and will remind you of everything I have said to you" (John 14:26), "He will testify about me" (John 15:26), "He will not speak on his own; he will speak only what he hears" (John 16:13), and "He will bring glory to me by taking from what is mine and making it known to you" (John 16:14-15, NIV). Luke states that the advent of the Holy Spirit upon Cornelius' household signifies the fulfillment of Jesus' plan in spreading the gospel from Jerusalem to the ends of the earth.

Secondly, the outpouring of the Holy Spirit in the household

---

41) The fact that Luke portrays Jesus' public ministry in his Gospel and the fact that Luke used this as evidence in the book of Acts to describe the expansion of the gospel from Jerusalem to the ends of the earth, consequently, show that the ministry of the historical

of Cornelius also shows a strong externally visible manifestation of the Spirit. The Lord gives two special revelations, one to Cornelius and the other to Peter, to make way for Peter to go to Cornelius' home. He shows Peter that the Gentiles had the same right as a Jew to become members of the Church as God's people (Acts 10:1-33; 11:17). The advent of the Holy Spirit upon Cornelius' household was not the usual baptismal experience but rather a powerful visible incident. It portrayed an external significance that was beyond a simple laying on of hands on the people (Acts 8:17). In Samaria, the Holy Spirit had come only after the apostles had laid hands on the people. However, this incident in Cornelius' household was the peak event in the history of missions, so there could be no other way than by the direct intervention of the Spirit with a clear external sign of speaking in tongues (Acts 10:46).[42]

Thirdly, Luke strongly testifies that the distinction between Jews and Gentiles was eliminated through the advent of the Holy Spirit upon Cornelius' household. Luke states that the circumcised believers "were astonished that the gift of the Holy Spirit had been poured out even on the Gentiles" (Acts 10:45) and that Peter said "Can anyone keep these people from being baptized with water?" (Acts 10:47, NIV), baptizing them in the name of Jesus Christ (Acts 10:48). Luke testifies that God crumbled the wall between the circumcised Jews and the uncircumcised Gentiles by sending the same Spirit to the Gentiles as to the Jews (see Eph. 2:11-18). Now both the Jews and the Gentiles are equal as children of God. This advent of the Holy Spirit upon Cornelius' household eliminated the discrimination

---

Jesus and the events of the outpouring of the Holy Spirit recorded in Acts have a direct relationship in the expansion of the gospel or the Church. See the relationships between Luke 24:46 and vs. 47; Luke 24:47 and vs. 48; Luke 24:47 and Acts 1:8; and the fact that Acts 1:1-3 makes a distinction between the contents of Luke and Acts.

42) G. W. H. Lampe, *The Seal of the Spirit* (London: S.P.C.K., 1976), p. 75.

between the Jews and the Gentiles, and by elevating the Gentiles' status as equals, formed only a unified people of God in Christ's Church under the guidance of the Holy Spirit.[43]

Fourthly, the incident at Cornelius' house emphasizes the importance of the Jerusalem Church and the role of the apostles. The Jerusalem Church sent Peter and John to Samaria when they heard that the gospel was spread there, and the Lord God used these apostles to bring about the visible manifestation of the Spirit (Acts 8:14-17). Likewise, God used Apostle Peter in the house of Cornelius to cause an outpouring of the Spirit upon the people. Peter explains that, after His resurrection, Jesus was seen "by witnesses whom God had already chosen—by us who ate and drank with him after he rose from the dead" (Acts 10:41), which stresses the importance of the apostles. The apostles had a responsibility for the custodianship of the gospel, the deliverance of the gospel, and the defending of the gospel.[44] As a matter of fact, the one who initiated the advent of the Spirit upon Cornelius' household was the Lord Himself. The Lord used Apostle Peter to illustrate that the gospel given to the Jerusalem Church was the one and the same gospel as the one given to the Gentile Cornelius. The gospel was given to a Gentile for the first time. When a progressive expansion of the gospel occurred, those apostles who

---

43) Richard N. Longenecker, *The Acts of the Apostles* (*The Expositor's Bible Commentary,* vol. 9), pp. 394-395: "Undoubtedly the sign of tongues was given primarily for the sake of the Jewish believers right there in Cornelius's house. But it was also given for Jerusalem believers, who would later hear of what happened, so that all would see the conversion of these Gentiles as being entirely of God and none would revert to their old prejudices and relegate these new converts to the role of second-class Christians."

44) John R. W. Stott, *The Spirit, the Church, and the World: The Message of Acts* (Downers Grove: I.V.P., 1990), p. 193; cf. Ralph P. Martin, *New Testament Foundation,* Vol. II (Grand Rapids: Eerdmans, 1978), p. 283: "Rather, it is in connection with the exercise of authority in the churches – in particular, the custodianship of the traditions, whether oral or written – that we must see their originality."

accompanied Jesus during His public ministry and witnessed His resurrection played an important role in the plan.

3. The Miraculous Work of the Holy Spirit in Ephesus (Acts 19:1-7)

The advent of the Holy Spirit in Ephesus is an event that must be considered when talking about the continuing ministry of the Holy Spirit after the Pentecost. This incident again must be seen in relation to Luke's purpose in writing Acts and must be seen in light of a broader context. Luke wished to pursue the path in which Christ's gospel was being spread from Jerusalem to all of Judea to Samaria to the ends of the earth (Acts 1:8). With the advent of the Holy Spirit during the Pentecost came the establishment of the Jerusalem Church according to God's plan (Acts 2:37-47).

Luke recorded the first chapter of Acts in preparation for the outpouring of the Holy Spirit at Pentecost.[45] Then he wrote about how the gospel spread from Jerusalem to Samaria through the twelve apostles in chapters 2-8. Chapters 9-12 then show how God prepared

---

45) Acts 1 provides a smooth transition between the Gospel of Luke and the book of Acts, and is recorded in preparation for the advent of the Holy Spirit at Pentecost in Acts 2. Acts 1 also talks about how Matthias became the twelfth apostle in place of Judas Iscariot who, before the New Testament Church was established, betrayed Jesus. The Lord God planned to use the apostles and the prophets as foundations upon which to build Christ's Church (Eph. 2:20). Therefore, the apostles had to be twelve in number before the New Testament Church would be established. The number twelve signify the completeness of the New Testament Church. Of course, the sole foundation of the Church is Jesus Christ (I Cor. 3:10, 11). Yet, the Church is formed from the people who believe after listening to the apostles and the prophets' preaching of the Word. So, the apostles and the prophets can be considered the secondary foundation of the Church (see, Park, Hyung Yong, *An Exposition of the Epistle to the Ephesians* (Korean). Suwon: Hapdong Theological Seminary Press, 1998, pp. 141-3). Some argue that Matthias was the wrong choice for the twelfth apostleship. They believe that the apostles should have waited until Paul was selected as the replacement for Judas. cf. Campbell G. Morgan, *op. cit.,* pp. 19-20; R. Stier, *The Words of the Apostles* (Eng. Trans., Edinburgh, 1896), pp. 12ff. However, this is not a convincing argument.

for missions to the Gentiles,[46] and chapters 13-28 record how the gospel was spread to the ends of the earth through the Apostle Paul.

In this way, the advent of the Holy Spirit in Samaria united the Samarian Church to the Jerusalem Church. The same event within the household of Cornelius laid the path for the gospel to reach the Gentiles, and in Ephesus, the event was used by Paul to actually expand the gospel to the Gentiles. The role of Peter, a representative among the twelve apostles, stood out in the event of the advent of the Holy Spirit in Samaria and in the household of Cornelius. Then in Ephesus, the same event accentuated the role of Paul the Apostle for the Gentiles. This fact, first of all, demonstrates the equal status of Apostle Paul to the twelve apostles. Secondly, it shows God's plan in using Paul and the twelve apostles, to spread the gospel from Jerusalem to the ends of the earth, and thirdly, it illustrates Luke's purpose in having followed the progress of God's plan. In fact, we must study the advent of the Holy Spirit in Ephesus while keeping in mind Luke's purpose for writing the event.

(1) The Details of the Event

When Paul was visiting Ephesus, the twelve disciples there[47] (Acts 19:1, 7) received the baptism of John the Baptist (Acts 19:3)

---

46) In Acts 9, Luke records the conversion of Paul, the apostle of the Gentiles (Acts 9:1-30), and in chapter 10, he tells about a particular event that occurred within the household of the Gentile Cornelius, whose conversion came about through a special intervention of God (Acts 10:1-48; 11:1-18). Then Acts 11 talks about the establishment of the Antioch Church, which became the stronghold for Gentile missions (Acts 11:19-26). Chapter 12 records the story of Herod Agrippa the First who imprisoned Peter and killed James with a sword (Acts 12:1-19). In chapter 12, Luke reiterates the ministry of the twelve apostles. In chapter 15, he talks about the activities of the apostles for the last time at the Jerusalem council in relation to the Gentile missions. Henceforth, he does not mention the activities of the apostles. This implies that, in chapters 9-12, Luke wanted to portray how the Gentile missions was being prepared and led by the Apostle Paul from chapter 13.

47) There is much debate on whether or not the "disciples" in the text believed in Jesus.

but neither received nor heard about the Holy Spirit (Acts 19:2). Paul realized the circumstance and patiently explained to the disciples at Ephesus about John the Baptist. He told them that they must believe in Jesus Christ who was to come after John the Baptist (Acts 19:4). John's baptisms signified the cleansing of sins, and the disciples in Ephesus had given their loyalty solely to John the Baptist. After hearing Paul's words (ἀκούσαντες), the disciples in Ephesus received the water baptism in the name of the Lord Jesus and when Paul placed his hands on them, the Holy Spirit came on them. The fact that they were speaking in tongues and prophesying was the external evidence of the outpouring of the Holy Spirit in Ephesus (Acts 19:5-6).

(2) The Work of the Holy Spirit in Ephesus

With Paul's laying of hands on them came the Holy Spirit, and

---

believed in Jesus in order to assert the pre-conversion and post-baptism schema. They further claim that these disciples who believed in Jesus later received the Holy Spirit when Paul laid hands on them. (see Myung, Sung Hoon, *With the Holy Spirit* (Korean). Seoul: Credo, 1993, p. 77; Howard M. Ervin, *Conversion-Initiation and the Baptism in the Holy Spirit*, pp. 55-59). However, the disciples in Ephesus were not converted for several reasons. First of all, the text explains them as "some disciples" (τινας μαθητάς) (Acts 19:1). In the book of Acts, "μαθηταί" generally refers to Christians. Yet, Acts 19:1 is the only example in the book of Acts where the definite article is absent in the usage of the term "μαθηταί." Luke wanted to use the term "τινας μαθητάς" instead of "τοὺς μαθητάς" to distinguish between the disciples in Ephesus and other Christians. Secondly, they had not received the Holy Spirit nor heard about His existence (Acts 19:2). Thirdly, they had been baptized by John the Baptist only (Acts 19:3). Fourthly, Paul considered them as subjects for conversion as he told them about Jesus (Acts 19:4). Fifthly, they received a second baptism, this time, in the name of Jesus Christ (Acts 19:5). For these reasons, they were not considered converts previously. They were converted once they were baptized in the name of Jesus Christ. cf. Simon J. Kistemaker, *Exposition of the Acts of the Apostles* (*New Testament Commentary*, Grand Rapids: Baker, 1990), p. 678: "Although they were learning about Jesus, the men remained closely associated with John the Baptist. They missed the joyful assurance of the Spirit in their lives, had no living relationship with Christ, and were told that John's baptism was inadequate. They were in a phase that was introductory to the Christian faith. And because they were in this phase, Luke and Paul guardedly used the terms disciples (learners) and believe (consent)."

immediately, the disciples in Ephesus began to speak in tongues and prophesy (Acts 19:6). The advent of the Holy Spirit in Ephesus was significant for a few reasons.

First of all, the advent of the Holy Spirit occurred through the laying of hands by Paul. As God used Peter in Samaria and in Cornelius' household, He used Paul at Ephesus. God chose Paul as His instrument (Acts 9:15) and used Him an equal to the twelve apostles. The advent of the Holy Spirit in Samaria and in Cornelius' household occurred with the mediation of the twelve apostles. The fact that the event in Ephesus occurred in connection to Paul's ministry, not only corresponded to God's purpose in selecting Paul, but also to His plan to use the twelve apostles and Paul to spread the gospel.

Secondly, the missions to Ephesus played an important role in the spreading of the gospel. Paul stayed in Ephesus for 3 years, building a church and spreading the gospel in Asia Minor (Acts 20:31). The disciples in Ephesus received the Holy Spirit in the early part of Paul's visit to Ephesus. This event determined the path in which Paul would follow in his ministry for the next 3 years[48] and had a great significance in the spreading of the gospel in Asia Minor with Ephesus as the center.[49] As a matter of course, it is natural that a special manifestation of the Holy Spirit occurred in Ephesus.

Thirdly, the disciples in Ephesus spoke in tongues and prophesied when they received the Holy Spirit. This shows that this phenomenon was externally visible as it indicated the presence of the Holy Spirit. In Samaria, Simon the magician saw the disciples

---

48) Jerome Murphy-O'Connor (*Paul: A Critical Life*. Oxford: Oxford University Press, 1997, p. 29.) states that "Luke gives two figures for the duration of Paul's stay in Ephesus, two years and three months (Acts 19:8-10), and three years (Acts 20:31)." And he suggests that "three years" is a round figure.

49) F. F. Bruce (*The Book of the Acts. NICNT*. Grand Rapids: Eerdmans, 1970, p. 387)

receiving the Holy Spirit and said, "Give me also this ability" (Acts 8:19), wanting to buy the power with money. This shows that the results of the advent of the Holy Spirit could be seen externally. The event in the household of Cornelius allowed the people who received the Holy Spirit to speak in tongues, glorifying God as a result. This event was also an externally observable result of the advent of the Holy Spirit. And consequently, the same event in Ephesus brought the same result.

When Luke describes the advent of the Holy Spirit in Samaria, in Cornelius' household, and in Ephesus, he never used the phrase "baptism of the Holy Spirit." He simply described the three events by saying that "Peter and John placed their hands on them, and they received the Holy Spirit" (Acts 8:17), "the gift of the Holy Spirit had been poured out" (Acts 10:45), "the Holy Spirit came on them" (Acts 11:15), "the Holy Spirit came on them" (Acts 19:6). Luke was trying to distinguish between "the baptism of the Holy Spirit" during the Pentecost and the advents of the Holy Spirit that occurred afterwards in other places.

Each event resulted in the advent of the Holy Spirit, and such a consistent result confirms that Christ's Church is united as one body without any ethnic or social distinction. Whether they be Jew, Samaritan, or Gentile, they formed one Church under the guidance of the Holy Spirit.

---

says that Ephesus is "a new centre of the Gentile mission – the next in importance after Syrian Antioch." G. W. H. Lampe, *The Seal of the Spirit*, p. 76: "Next to Antioch, in fact insuccession to Antioch, Ephesus is the centre of the Gentile mission, the headquarters where St. Paul makes his longest stay, and the centre from which missionary activity radiates into Asia Minor and St. Paul's emissaries visit his churches at Corinth and elsewhere. The planting of the Faith in this centre is clearly an event of immense importance, and it is natural that the first converts should become a nucleus and focus of this new Church, the strategic centre of the Pauline preaching."

A Closing Word

Up to this point, we have discussed the controversial events of the advent of the Holy Spirit in Samaria, in Cornelius' household, and in Ephesus. We are able to observe in these events as to how the Holy Spirit continues to manifest Himself after the Pentecost (Acts 2:1-4). These events witnessed to the special external manifestations according to the purpose of Luke. Through these events, Luke gives witness to how the Holy Spirit of God was uniquely manifested at each crucial step in the spreading of the gospel. In addition, this teaches us that, without the Holy Spirit, the spreading of the gospel is impossible. And Luke conveys the unification of the New Testament Church and the purity of the said gospel by emphasizing the special manifestations of the Holy Spirit which occurred in Jerusalem, in Samaria, in the household of Cornelius, and in Ephesus. The apostles were to be vehicles to spread the gospel from Jerusalem to the ends of the world.

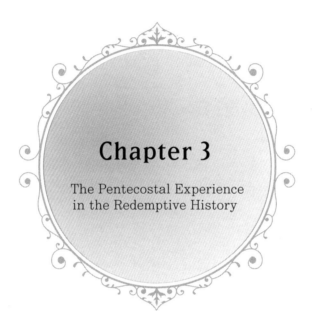

Chapter 3

The Pentecostal Experience
in the Redemptive History

The Pentecost is proven to be unique when it is observed from the perspective of redemptive history. It also plays a pivotal role in the advancement of God's redemptive history. Because the Pentecost is related to Jesus' first coming, His earthly ministry, death, resurrection, ascension, and establishment of the early Church, it is not considered an independent event. In reading the Gospel of Luke and the Book of Acts together, one can clearly see the life and ministry of Jesus Christ moving toward the outpouring of the Holy Spirit at the Pentecost and the establishment of the early Christian Church. As much as God the Father planned the death and the resurrection of Jesus Christ, He also planned for the Coming of the Holy Spirit (the Pentecost) to occur at a specific time.

In addition to the uniqueness of the Pentecost, there is the problem of how to understand the continuous work of the Holy Spirit after the Pentecost, listed in Acts. After the Pentecost, the work of the Holy Spirit continued in Samaria, within Cornelius' family and in Ephesus in a similar manner as the actual Pentecost (Acts 8:14-17; 10:44-48; 19:1-7). Thus, we can naturally assume that, even at present, the Holy Spirit works in the same way as recorded in Acts.

Certainly, the work of the Holy Spirit continues. Who can limit God's activity? But God the Spirit is not a God of confusion; rather, He is a God of order. It is in accordance with His order that God first brought redemption to earth through His Son and then had the gospel of redemption propagated by His church all over the world. Luke succinctly states the two aspects of God's redemptive plan: "Thus it is written, that the Christ should suffer and on the third day rise from the dead, and that repentance and forgiveness of sins should be proclaimed in his name to all nations, beginning at Jerusalem. You are witnesses of these things" (Luke 24:46-48, ESV). What was planned by God even from the Old Testament time is that the death and resurrection of Jesus Christ and the universal proclamation of the Gospel of Jesus Christ. So, the death and resurrection of Jesus Christ must be accomplished first, then, the New Testament Church should be established to proclaim the Gospel of redemption. All this occurred in God's ordained order.

The Bible does not dictate that a certain gift of the Holy Spirit will stop at a particular time and that another gift will continuously be given. However, God has given the gifts of the Spirit to His Church in accordance of His redemptive order. We must remember that the events of the Pentecost, Samaria, Cornelius' family, and the outpouring of the Holy Spirit in Ephesus occurred in the Apostles' lifetime and even before most of the New Testament books were written. Although it is not easy to compare and understand the work of the Holy Spirit in Acts and the current work of the Holy Spirit in the church, a few suggestions can be made in approaching the topic.

1. Once-for-Allness of the Apostleship

Jesus selected the twelve apostles and trained them during his public ministry. He prepared the apostles in order to establish the Church after His death and resurrection. When Jesus first met Peter by Andrew's introduction, Jesus changed Peter's name. "You are Simon son of John. You will be called Cephas" (John 1:42). Then in Caesarea, Philippi when Jesus was soon to face His death on the cross, Simon Peter confesses these famous words, "You are the Christ, the Son of the living God" (Matt. 16:16, NIV). To which, Jesus responds, "Blessed are you, Simon son of Jonah, for this was not revealed to you by man, but by my Father in heaven. And I tell you that you are Peter, and on this rock I will build my church, and the gates of Hades will not overcome it" (Matt. 16:17-18, NIV).

There is a profound meaning embedded in Jesus' act of changing Peter's name. When He first met Peter, He says, "You will be called Cephas" (John 1:42)[50] in the future tense. Then in Caesarea, philippi when Jesus hears Peter's famous confession, He changes the tense from the future to the present and says, "You are Peter" (Matt. 16:18).[51] There is also a great significance when Jesus declares, "You are Peter, and on this rock I will build my church" [52](in the future tense) to say that He is leaving the establishment of the Church until later.

Jesus could not establish the Christian Church at the time when He heard Peter's confession in Caesarea, Philippi because His death and resurrection had not happened yet. If Jesus had established a church during his public ministry, the church would have remained without a proper message of salvation to share. It was God's redemptive plan to establish the New Testament Church after the death and resurrection of Jesus Christ, which would give the Church the message of redemption in Jesus Christ. The New Testament Church was established in lieu with the outpouring of the Holy Spirit at the Pentecost.[53] The New Testament Church was a new community of faith established with the responsibility of giving

---

50) σὺ κληθήσῃ κηφᾶς. "You shall be called Cephas"(ESV). Κληθήσῃ is the future passive tense of καλέω.

51) σὺ εῖ πέτρα.

52) καὶ ἐπὶ ταύτῃ τῇ πέτρᾳ οἰκοδομήσω μου τὴν ἐκκλησίαν.

53) Some scholars assert that the New Testament Church was established during Jesus' public ministry. Ahn Young Bok ([A Right Understanding of the Work of the Holy Spirit (Korean)] Seoul: Christian Literature Crusade, 1987, pp. 41-47) states that the Pentecost did not occur in order to establish the Church but to endow power to an already-established Church and therefore, asserts that the New Testament Church was established before the Pentecost. This assertion is consistent with the pre-conversion and post-Spirit-baptism scheme. However, this assertion is resulted from an improper understanding of the relationships of Jesus on the cross, His resurrection to achieve salvation, the outpouring of the Holy Spirit at the Pentecost, the establishment of the First New Testament Church, and the spreading of the gospel through the Church.

witness to Jesus' death and resurrection (Matt. 28:18-20; Luke 24:46-48; Acts 1:8). The responsibility of giving witness to Jesus' death and resurrection means to spread the message of salvation (Rom. 10:9-10). Then those who would receive and believe the message would join the church and allow it to expand. In this sense, the New Testament Church is confessional and organic, and therefore, she must have the content of confession to proclaim. Jesus Christ accomplished the content of confession for the Church in His death and resurrection. Therefore, the New Testament Church should be established after the death and resurrection of Jesus Christ and on or after the Pentecost.

Before the Pentecost and after Jesus' death, resurrection, and ascension, the apostles choose Matthias in Judas Iscariot's place as the twelfth apostle[54] because Judas had betrayed Jesus and failed in the responsibility of an apostle during Jesus' public ministry. However, the Bible indicates that after the apostle James was martyred, no one was chosen to take his place (Acts 12:2). Why did the remaining eleven apostles choose Matthias to fill Judas Iscariot's spot before the Pentecost but did not choose a successor for the apostle James? (Acts 12:2). Jesus Christ chose the apostles to build the church and trained them to be a second foundation of His church (Eph. 2:20). When the New Testament church was being firmly planted in reality, the apostles left the historical scene one by one. Because they had fulfilled their mission and their responsibilities, God did not need them any longer. The resurrected and ascended Lord Jesus wanted the New Testament church to be established under the leadership of the apostles, and once the church was established, He wanted

---

54) The number twelve signifies completeness or wholeness. The number twelve is used in the New Testament in reference to Jesus' twelve disciples (Matt. 1:1; John 6:70), the twelve tribes of Israel (Matt. 19:28), and the temple in Jerusalem (Rev. 21:9-14).

to continue the building of His Heavenly Kingdom through the church.[55]

The Bible does not clearly give a reason, but we can presume that, once the New Testament Church was firmly established by the work of the apostles, they did not need to find successors for the original twelve apostles. This is supported by the historical fact that, when all the apostles had died, God did not designate any successors for these apostles.

Why did God refrain from designating the apostles' successors? There was no need for successors once they had accomplished their mission. God used the apostles, Paul, and all others who were intimate with the apostles to record His revelation in the books of the New Testament. As a result, the New Testament is an authoritative rule for all those churches that accept and confess Jesus Christ as their Lord. The Lord God inspired the apostles and the New Testament authors in a special way in order that the books of the New Testament may preserve the authority within the churches even after their death.[56] The New Testament (27 books) contains the final revelation, Jesus' life and activity as the fulfillment of the Old Testament. This written revelation is to be the rule and guide for life and faith of the churches and believers.

The Lord God delegated a special mission to the apostles who were living in a special period in history and had given them special powers to achieve this mission. Amongst the gifts of the Holy Spirit

---

55) Jesus begins constructing His Heavenly Kingdom when He receives the baptism from John the Baptist and the power of the Holy Spirit. The resurrected and ascended Christ continues the building of the Heavenly Kingdom by empowering the Church with the Holy Spirit during Pentecost (see Luke 3:21-22; Acts 1:6-8; 2:14-47).

56) John Peck, *What the Bible Teaches About the Holy Spirit* (Wheaton: Tyndale House Publishers, 1979), p. 55: "To put it in a nutshell, he gave the apostles a special authority for the early church, and then brought the New Testament scriptures into being to exercise the same authority in the church after their death."

is the "apostleship" (Eph. 4:11); the duration of this gift, however, ends when the apostle dies. Hence, much difference exists between the gift of the Spirit given to the individual apostles and the gift of the Spirit given to the churches after the apostles' deaths.

2. The Closure of the New Testament Canon

We must consider the work of the Holy Spirit and the continuing gifts of the Holy Spirit in relation to the closure of the New Testament canon. Occasionally, some argue that, since the Holy Spirit of 2000 years ago and the Holy Spirit of today are one and the same, we must not prevent the gifts of the Holy Spirit, as recorded in the Bible, from happening today. They believe that all the gifts of the Spirit revealed in the Bible are still continuing today. Yet, their argument is self-conflicting and is not very convincing. In following their logic, since the 27 books of the New Testament were inspired by the Spirit 2000 years ago, additional books for the New Testament can be written today through the inspiration of the same Spirit. Yet, though they assert the same work of the Holy Spirit, they stand against the possibility of having the 28th, 29th, 30th, and other books of the New Testament from being written. Despite this confusion, however, we must understand that God gave 66 books of the Bible to the New Testament Church as a standard of faith and daily life. The Bible being a standard means that the number of its books cannot increase because once the standard changes, it cannot act as a standard any longer.

God gave us 27 books of the New Testament as a standard. Having 27 books in the New Testament is not a "coincidence." We must understand that the 27 books of the New Testament were fixed into the canon through God's control of history and His Spirit's special guidance.[57] The formative process of the canon is not independent of God's influence; God endowed the canon with a supernatural authority in order for it to work as an official canon.[58] Believing that God revealed all the inspired writings throughout history but ignored the process of creating a canon is a belief in abstract concept of history.[59] This belief comes from misunderstanding of God's purpose for providing these materials to the church.[60]

The written revelation of God is concentrated around redemptive events that occurred in history. They have a close connection to the events of Noah, calling of Abraham, events of the exodus of

---

57) N. B. Stonehouse, "The Authority of the New Testament," *The Infallible Word* (Philadelphia: Presbyterian and Reformed Publ. Co., 1946), p. 139.

58) Apostolicity, antiquity, universality (public acceptance), inspiration, and others are used as the criteria in determining the canon. Although apostolicity is very important in determining a canon, apostolicity as a criterion of canon is greatly weakened because not all the authors of the 27 books of the New Testament are apostles (i.e. Mark, Luke, James, Judas, and etc.). The criterion of antiquity is also inadequate because epistles that were written earlier than the ones in the current New Testament were omitted from the New Testament Canon (see I Cor. 5:9). Even in terms of universality, the early church read the Didache and the Shepherd more than II Peter, I, II, and III Johns, and Judas of the current New Testament. Regarding inspiration, the New Testament books were inspired when they were being written, not when they were being selected as part of the canon. And when the canon was determined in the next generation, not all the inspired writings were selected to be part of the canon (see I Cor. 5:9; Col. 4:16). This shows that inspiration is important in determining a canon but is not the perfect standard by which the canon is determined. Likewise, apostolicity, antiquity, universality, and inspiration are all important, but they cannot be the perfect standard by which the canon is determined. The important fact is that God who controls history used all the criteria and the evidences to create a composite of 27 books in the New Testament Canon. See Park, Hyung Yong, *The New Testament Canon* (Korean), (Suwon: Hapdong Theological Seminary Press, 2002), pp. 91-101.

59) In abstract concept of history, I. Kant uses the contrast between the noumenal world and the phenomenal world. The noumenal world is a realm of faith and freedom, and the phenomenal world refers to a world of human relationships. Religious confirmations and miracles occur in the noumenal world, and historical events happen within the boundaries of the phenomenal world. Therefore, the abstract historical view eliminates God's role as the controller of history. This ideology asserts that the 27 books of the New Testament Canon were determined without the influence of God. However, the Christian concept of history upholds the belief that God determines everything that occurs in this world.

60) Park, Hyung Yong, *The New Testament Canon* (Korean), pp. 101-105.

the Israelites, Israelite kingdom and dynasty, exile and return of the Israelites, and others. They are also related to the events of Christ's birth, crucifixion, and resurrection.

Prior to the incarnation of Jesus Christ, the reconstruction of the temple was an important event in redemptive accomplishment. Malachi, Zachariah, and Haggai wrote about this reconstruction, a period in which God's revelations and prophecies were abundantly given. After the temple was finished, there was a quiet, intermittent period of about 400 years, which ended when Jesus began redemptive activities, fulfilling the Old Testament prophecies. The New Testament revelations are centered on Jesus' birth, His public ministry, crucifixion, and resurrection. Consequently, the New Testament asserts that only one more event – the Second Coming -- needs to occur to complete the process of redemption. The Christians mentioned in the New Testament are people who "wait for his Son from heaven" (I Thess. 1:10). Therefore, after the prophecies regarding Christ's coming and its related events were given, history of revelation enters a period of dormancy.

Special revelation was written as a process in history, and both the Old and New Testaments were recorded in the course of history. However, this special revelation culminates in the person and the activity of Jesus Christ (Heb. 1:1-2). Here, we must underscore the fact that we should consider the special revelation, the historical process, the eschatological event, and Christ together as parts of a whole. If we consider the special revelation as word and act relationship, as an epochal character of Christ's event, and as a covenantal character of revelation, special revelation appears to have stopped after the apostles' witness of the person and work of Jesus Christ and the exaltation of Jesus Christ. Ever since the foundation of the New Testament Church, God finalizes the history of revelation which stretches to Jesus' Second Coming (I Cor. 1:7; II Thess. 1:10). The time during which the apostles maintained spiritual leadership had passed. Now, under the guidance of the church, Christ's complete work is gradually being applied. The closure of the special revelation is related to the once-for-allness of Christ's work.[61] If the once-for-all character of Christ's work is abandoned, it contradicts the argument for the closure of the special revelation, and if we do not recognize the closure of the special revelation, the once-for-all nature of Christ's work will falter.

Saying that the apostles and the prophets are the foundations for the church supports the closure of the New Testament canon (Eph. 2:20). Paul mentions both the apostles and the prophets which indicate that he did not restrict the privilege to the twelve main apostles.[62] Yet, the apostles are the messengers of God's word who received God's authority through inspiration. Jesus selected and called each apostle into the ministry to teach under the authority of His name. The apostles also witnessed Christ's resurrection directly. The title 'apostle' carries the meaning of having witnessed Jesus' teaching, work, and resurrection first-hand and having the ability to pass this on to others. For, the apostles were messengers of God's revelation which was revealed through Jesus Christ. Hence, when they selected Matthias to replace Judas Iscariot in Acts 1:15-26, he had met the two qualifications for the apostleship: 1) He needed to have been with Jesus during His public ministry. 2) He must have witnessed the resurrection (Acts 1:21-22).

These qualifications were extremely crucial because these

---

61) Park, Hyung Yong, *The New Testament Canon,* pp. 108-113.
62) The word 'apostle' (ἀπόστολος), in a stricter sense, refers only to the twelve apostles and the apostle Paul, but in a broader sense, it can also include all the people related to the twelve apostles and the apostle Paul (Phil. 2:25; II Cor. 8:23; John 13:16).

apostles were responsible for teaching Jesus' words and activity from the time when Jesus ascended into Heaven until the time when the New Testament revelation was recorded. Consequently, the apostles' teachings were recorded in the New Testament. The prophets were also inspired to teach through a close relationship with the apostles. The New Testament records their teachings as well. In Ephesians 2:20, Paul refers to both the apostles and the prophets as the foundation for the Church because of their role as teachers. In turn, through their teachings, Jesus' words became the foundation for the Church (see Rom. 15:20). Salmond correctly says, "Here, therefore, it seems best on the whole to understand the Gospel of Christ as preached by the Apostles to be the 'foundation' on which their converts were built up into the spiritual house."[63] Realistically, the teaching of "the apostles and the prophets" is the New Testament; therefore, the Church was established on the basis of the New Testament. The New Testament, in turn, is God's revelation. Like the foundations of a life-size building which cannot be easily altered, the New Testament foundations of the Church also cannot be destroyed or altered. This foundation is complete and final.

Then what is the relationship between the closure of the special revelation and the Holy Spirit's continuous work? God brings closure to the New Testament revelation but also mentions that, within the revelation, there is one more redemptive event yet to come. This event is Jesus' return to earth. What was God's purpose in using the apostles and others to reveal the Second Coming and His eternal Kingdom in the New Testament? And after Jesus' exaltation, why did He use the apostles as the foundations for the New Testament Church, and why did He give them the responsibility of spreading the gospel

---

63) S.D.F. Salmond, *The Epistle to the Ephesians: Expositor's Greek Testament,* vol. III (Grand Rapids: Eerdmans, 1980), p. 299.

until Jesus' return?

Until Jesus returns, the Church does not need any other revelation besides the official and objective revelation recorded in the Old and New Testaments. God prophesied Jesus' return in the New Testament revelation, implying that He will not give any other revelation that can be added to the 66 books of the Bible.[64] God did not give a private revelation; rather, He gave only the special written revelations to the Church, which means that the Bible is sufficient for our faith and life. In the New Testament, God included all the commandments and revelations necessary for the life of the Church. Until the time of Jesus' return, the Lord wanted the Church to rely on the written revelations of the New Testament rather than on the private revelations given to individual people.

Scholars, who say that the revelation still continues, maintain a double-standard. On the one hand, they believe that the 66 books of the Bible hold a canonical and redemptive perspective; on the other hand, they believe that there is a private revelation for an individual or group. There is a distinction between the written revelation for the Church and the private revelation for the individual person(s). However, the Bible does not accept such a standard. God did not give us a revelation that has no relationship with redemption. He gave us a revelation that explains redemptive words and acts at the same time. Salvation influences a believer's entire life, not just one area in life. No space exists in a Christian's life for a private revelation that is unrelated to salvation.

God used the gift of prophecy when He laid the foundations for the Church and gave it to those who worked on behalf of Christ before the New Testament was recorded (Acts 21:4-14, The

---

64) Richard B. Gaffin, Jr. *Perspectives on Pentecost* (Grand Rapids: Baker, 1979), pp. 98-99.

prophecies of the daughters of Philip). But He no longer needs to supply that gift for the life of the Church. The Church continues its existence relying on the exposition of the inspired Word of God and not relying on these prophecies. "The closing of the canon has superseded their necessity and value, inasmuch as the Church possesses in the Scriptures all that they were intended to accredit and commend. Beyond the written word which was completed before the apostles passed away, the Spirit has no further revelations or immediate communications of the divine will to impart. The extraordinary gifts, limited as they were to the primitive Church, wholly passed away, because they were no longer necessary."[65]

However, while Christians live with their earthly bodies, the necessary gifts of the Holy Spirit, such as the gifts of healing, leadership, helping each other (I Cor. 12:28-30), teaching, admonishment, charity, compassion (Rom. 12:6-8), evangelism, pastoring, and teaching (Eph. 4:11), and others, must continue.[66]

Likewise, God distinguishes between the gifts of the Spirit used before the completion of the New Testament and the gifts that continue today. The former was given to the apostles and the authors of the Bible and some of the gifts given to them no longer existed now, such as the apostles. The latter ones are the gifts that are profitable for the building of the New Testament Church. It is not

---

65) George Smeaton, *The Doctrine of the Holy Spirit* (Carlisle: The Banner of Truth Trust, 1974), pp. 151-152.

66) The scriptural text that refers to the gifts of the Holy Spirit in detail are Romans 12:6-8, I Cor. 12:8-10, 12:28-30, Eph. 4:11, etc. In making a list of these gifts (ignoring all the repeated ones), there are about 20 gifts of the Holy Spirit. Among them, the apostleship and prophecy are no longer in existence, but the gifts of evangelism, pastoring and teaching, leadership, service, teaching, encouraging, and others still continue within the church today. Just because a certain gift of the Spirit is mentioned in the New Testament revelation does not mean that it must consistently be in existence today. Such an argument goes against the nature of the New Testament revelation.

right to assume that all the gifts mentioned in the Bible should always exist within the Church.

3. The Significance of the Pastoral Epistles in Understanding the Ministry of the Church with Regards to the Work of the Holy Spirit

The study of the Holy Spirit's continuous ministry and gifts within the Pastoral Epistles reveal how the Church maintained itself after Paul's lifetime. Paul instructed Timothy on how to properly minister and maintain the Church after his death. Though Paul planted a Church in Ephesus, Timothy was responsible for its ministry without Paul's presence. Likewise, Titus also took care of the Cretan church when Paul was away (Titus 1:5). The pastoral epistles show a continuation of the Church's activities without the presence of the apostles' guidance; hence, we can compare the work of the Holy Spirit in the life of the Church during the apostles' lifetime to the work of the same Spirit in the life of the Church without the apostles' presence.

(1) The pastoral epistles describe a Church that emphasized the Word. For example, they mention that "the law is good" (I Tim. 1:8), "for whatever else is contrary to the sound doctrine" (I Tim. 1:10), "in keeping with the prophecies" (I Tim. 1:18),[67] "by the word of God and prayer" (I Tim. 4:5), "in the truths of the faith and of the good teaching" (I Tim. 4:6), "through a prophetic message" (I Tim. 4:14), "a

---

67) This prophecy (ἐπὶ προφητείας) refers to the one given to Timothy through Paul. The expression "through a prophetic message" (διὰ προφητείας) is used again in I Tim. 4:14. The prophecy mentioned in the text does not foreshadow future events, but rather, it refers to the message delivered to Timothy at some point in time in the past. cf. J.N.D. Kelly, *A Commentary on The Pastoral Epistles* (Grand Rapids: Baker, 1981), p. 57.

workman who correctly handles the word of truth" (II Tim. 2:15), "all scripture is God-breathed" (II Tim. 3:16), "preach the Word" (II Tim. 4:2), "holding firmly to the trustworthy message" (Titus 1:9), "here is a trustworthy saying" (I Tim. 1:15; 3:1; 4:9, II Tim. 2:11, Titus 3:8), and "teach what is in accord with sound doctrine" (Titus 2:1). Why do the pastoral epistles emphasize the Word of God? It is because God wants the Christian Church to live by and rely on His written objective Word instead of the Holy Spirit's direct work which was manifested through the apostles.

(2) The leaders of the Church portrayed in the pastoral epistles are not required to prophesy, speak in tongues, or perform miracles; rather, they must discipline themselves daily to be models for their families, the Church, and the unbelievers (I Tim. 3:1-13; Titus 1:5-9). The qualifications of a Church leader "must be above reproach, the husband of but one wife, temperate, self-controlled, respectable, hospitable, able to teach, not given to drunkenness, not violent but gentle, not quarrelsome, not a lover of money" (I Tim. 3:2, NIV). The scriptural text suggests seven important qualifications of a Church leader. They must: ①be respected by their co-workers, ② have a healthy marriage life, ③have a sound lifestyle, ④have a sound mind, ⑤generally be respectable and virtuous, ⑥be hospitable to their guests and ⑦teach well.[68] These seven qualifications, as well as, the seven precautions that are mentioned thereafter (I Tim. 3:3-4), all relate to the daily lifestyles of a Church leader.

(3) Paul provides rules of guidance for the daily lifestyles according to the sound doctrine of the Church. Older men must be temperate,

---

68) William Hendriksen, *I~II Timothy and Titus* (*N.T.C.*) (Grand Rapids: Baker, 1974), pp. 120-124.

pious, and discrete and must live out faith, love, and patience. Older women must live a reverent life, refrain from slandering others, and restrain themselves from getting drunk. Younger women must love their husbands and children, take care of the household, and be pure and pious (Titus 2:1-10). These instructions for a humble life imply that the lifestyle of the Church does not rely on a special gift of the Holy Spirit but on the Word of God.

(4) Some words and phrases are mentioned quite frequently in the pastoral epistles, such as "a pure heart and a good conscience and a sincere faith" (I Tim. 1:5, 19), "godliness and holiness" (I Tim. 1:9; 2:2; 4:8; II Tim. 3:5, 12; Titus 2:12), "prayers, intercession and thanksgiving" (I Tim. 2:1, 8; 4:5), "considerate and true humility" (I Tim. 3:3; Titus 3:2), "in faith, love and holiness with propriety" (I Tim. 2:15), "set an example for the believers in speech, in life, in love, in faith and in purity" (I Tim. 4:12; 5:12; 6:5, 11), "with faith and love in Christ Jesus" (II Tim. 1:13), "unlimited patience" (I Tim. 1:16), and "endure hardship and sufferings" (II Tim. 2:3, 9; 3:11). These words seem to suggest the kind of lifestyle Paul wants to see in the life of the Church without his presence.

(5) Why did Paul mention the most important lesson about the inspiration of the Bible in the book of II Timothy, which he wrote prior to his martyrdom (II Tim. 3:14-17)?[69] Paul states that the Bible would teach "which are able to make you wise for salvation through faith in Christ Jesus" (II Tim. 3:15). He writes that all scriptures are

---

69) Some do not acknowledge the term "God-breathed" (θεόπνευστος) to imply the inspiration of the Holy Spirit. Schweizer states that Paul is not authenticating the theory of inspiration with this term. See E. Schweizer, "Θεόπνευστος," *Theological Dictionary of the New Testament*, vol. 6 (Grand Rapids: Eerdmans, 1971), pp. 454, n. 7. He cites I Cor. 7:10, 40 as the scriptural references.

inspired by the Holy Spirit (II Tim. 3:16). Then he continues to say that the Scripture is "useful for teaching, rebuking, correcting and training in righteousness" (II Tim. 3:16, NIV) for all believers. This implies that the Church must continue to rely on the written objective Word of God and serve Him accordingly.

(6) In Titus, Paul mentions "the works of the Holy Spirit" in the context of personal salvation (Titus 3:5, 6). "He saved us, not because of righteous things we had done, but because of his mercy. He saved us through the washing of rebirth and renewal by the Holy Spirit, whom he poured out on us generously through Jesus Christ our Savior, so that, having been justified by his grace, we might become heirs having the hope of eternal life" (Titus 3:5-7, NIV). The Holy Spirit's ministry mentioned in the scriptural text does not refer to a visual, external evidence of miracles but to a spiritual rebirth within a believer unseen by others.[70] Paul does not emphasize an external and dynamic ministry; instead, he stresses the internal and orderly ministry. God the Spirit continuously transforms a person to firmly establish Christ's Church.

In the Pastoral Epistles, we can see the regular works of the Church instead of the extraordinary works of the Holy Spirit. The activities of the Church do not portray the same miraculous works of the Holy Spirit that were shown in the apostles' life time. How can we explain the transformation? Such a transformation indicates that the Church moves according to the will of God who superintends all history. Hence, asking for the Spirit's gift as given to the apostles lies contrary to God's historical providence.

Through this research, the outpouring of the Holy Spirit at

---

70) Hendriksen, *I~II Timothy and Titus,* p. 391.

Pentecost should not be seen as a personal salvation experience but as an event of redemptive history.[71] Without the Word of God, it is not possible for one to maintain a proper perspective on the work of the Holy Spirit. Human beings tend to be more subjective, giving more weight on the personal experience of the Spirit than on the objective revelation of God. Hence, it is utmost important that we must rely on the written Word of God given to us and to the Church. God only gave 66 books as His Word to the Church. We have tried to understand the Holy Spirit's work in accordance with the progression of God's redemptive history, such as the death, resurrection, and ascension of Christ, the Pentecost, the establishment of the Christian Church, and the Second Coming. The process of fulfilling God's redemptive history includes the making of the New Testament. Hence, we must accept the New Testament teachings that say that some gifts of the Spirit do not exist anymore, while other gifts still continue today. As we accept this, we can properly serve the Lord our God, the Lord of all history.

The Pastoral Epistles show us the faithful picture of the early church. The church did not depend on the special gifts of the Holy Spirit or on miracles for her growth. The word of God supplies the nutrition for the growth of the Church. It was firmly established with the characteristics of faith, piety, holiness, and humility. The Pastoral Epistles teach that, in order for the church to be the light and the salt for the world, the church leaders should be equipped with the qualifications listed in the epistles and they should serve the church with the principles taught in the epistles. It is absolutely necessary that the works of the Spirit should continue in the life of the Church;

---

71) Sinclair B. Ferguson, *The Holy Spirit: Contours of Christian Theology* (Downers Grove: IVP, 1996), pp. 86-87.: "It is an event in redemptive history (*historia salutis*), and should not be squeezed into the grid of the application of redemption (*ordo salutis*)."

yet, the Pastoral Epistles show us the importance of the Church's reliance on the Word of God instead of in miracles or special works of the Spirit.

In addition, we must always keep a humble attitude as we study the New Testament. Humility can build a church, while pride can destroy one. The Holy Spirit works continuously to unite the Church (Eph. 4:3). In the last stages of his life, Paul said, "I am the worst sinner" (I Tim. 1:15). As we read and study the Bible, we must always have a humble mind. Rather than simply relying on our thoughts and experiences, we must judge and filter our thoughts and experiences according to the Bible.

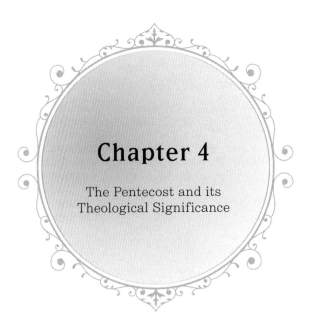

Chapter 4

The Pentecost and its
Theological Significance

The Pentecost is an epochal event in the progress of the redemptive history. Since this is a unique event in history, how is it related to individual believers? In view of the Old Testament prophesies and Jesus' testimonies in the Gospels, one cannot think of Jesus' death, resurrection, and ascension separately from the Pentecostal event. As a matter of fact, Jesus' death, resurrection, ascension and the Pentecost is one entire unit of redemptive history.

The atoning death of Jesus is applied to believers as their salvation and justification. Although Jesus' redemptive death was accomplished 2000 years ago, whoever confesses Jesus as their Savior and believes in Him, they will be justified and obtain salvation. "If you confess with your mouth, 'Jesus is Lord,' and believe in your heart that God raised him from the dead, you will be saved. For it is with your heart that you believe and are justified, and it is with your mouth that you confess and are saved" (Rom. 10:9-10, NIV). Once a person truly believes in Christ, from that moment on, one becomes a child of God (John 1:12). This is biblically confirmed truth.

Here, we cannot overlook another aspect of truth. The Scriptures maintain that sinners cannot confess Jesus as their personal Savior by themselves. Without the help of the Holy Spirit, no one can confess Jesus as the Savior, nor can anyone accept Him as God's Son. "Therefore I tell you that no one who is speaking by the Spirit of God says, 'Jesus be cursed,' and no one can say, 'Jesus is Lord,' except by the Holy Spirit" (I Cor. 12:3, NIV). It means that people can confess Jesus as the Savior only by the work of the Holy Spirit. The Spirit applies the events of Jesus' death and resurrection of two thousand years ago to those who personally confess Jesus as their Savior. The efficacy of Jesus' death and resurrection applies in the same way to both the people of the Old Testament and of the New Testament. Likewise, the Spirit helps to apply the effects of Jesus' redemption to all believers.

Yet, the Pentecostal event is intimately connected to the redemptive events of Jesus' death and resurrection. Jesus' death, resurrection, ascension, and the Pentecost remain as one unit of redemptive history that cannot be distinguished separately from each other. As Jesus' death and resurrection begins a new covenant era (Luke 22:20; I Cor. 11:25), the outpouring of the Holy Spirit at Pentecost allows the believers to be clothed in the power of the Spirit, so that they may accomplish an appropriate works for that period. To each believer the Spirit distributes appropriate gifts that are needed for the ministry of the gospel (Acts 2:16-18; I Cor. 12:4-11; I Peter 4:10). These gifts are not to be used for personal gain but for the building of Christ's church (I Cor. 12:7, 12-26; 14:12; Eph. 4:12).

On the day of the Pentecost, the New Testament Church was established. When Peter preached on the Pentecost, they accepted his message and were baptized, and about three thousand were added to their number that day (Acts 2:41). The fact that the New Testament Church was established during the Pentecost and that its disciples were filled with the Holy Spirit allows us to see how God empowered the church to be His witness for Christ. The New Testament Church was built to spread the news about how Jesus accomplished redemption and reconciliation through His death and resurrection. Therefore, if there had been no death and resurrection of Jesus Christ, the New Testament Church would not have been established. If the New Testament Church had not been established, the Pentecost would not have been needed. Hence, the Pentecost is a unique once-for-all event. Now, let us summarize the theological aspects of the Pentecost in light of the redemptive history.

1. The Baptism of the Holy Spirit and the Expansion of God's Kingdom

The Pentecostal event is not unrelated to the expansion of the Kingdom of God. The New Testament Church, which was established during the Pentecost, works to expand the Kingdom that began with Christ. Jesus began His earthly ministry declaring that "The time has come. The kingdom of God is near. Repent and believe the good news!" (Mark 1:15, NIV). During His life on earth, Jesus worked to expand the Kingdom of Heaven by spreading the gospel, driving out demons, healing the sick, and raising people from the dead. Even after His resurrection, Jesus appeared to His disciples over a period of forty days and spoke "about the kingdom of God" (Acts 1:3). Jesus Christ began to expand the Kingdom of God during His public earthly ministry and the forty days after His resurrection. After the Pentecost, the responsibility of expanding God's Kingdom was passed onto the New Testament Church. The New Testament Church always remembered that they were in the ministry of expanding God's Kingdom as they spread the gospel (see Acts 8:12; 19:8; 20:25; 28:31).[72]

Yet, in order to give the responsibility of this Kingdom ministry to the Church, the redemptive events of Jesus' death and resurrection are needed. The expansion of the Kingdom by the New Testament Church must be carried out between Jesus' death and resurrection on one side and Jesus' Second Coming on the other. Hence, all the ministries of the New Testament Church can be characterized as the Kingdom work, and the Church must continue to accomplish these works until the day of Jesus' return. In the words of John the Baptist,

---

72) Park, Hyung Yong, *An Exposition of the Acts of the Apostles* (Korean) (Suwon: Hapdong Theological Seminary Press, 2007), pp. 341-342.

we realize the significance of Jesus' ministry being fulfilled through the Church. In Luke 3:16-17, John the Baptist says, "I baptize you with water. But one more powerful than I will come, the thongs of whose sandals I am not worthy to untie. He will baptize you with the Holy Spirit and with fire. His winnowing fork is in his hand to clear his threshing floor and to gather the wheat into his barn, but he will burn up the chaff with unquenchable fire" (NIV). He indicates that Jesus' ministry will be characterized as "baptism of the Holy Spirit and fire" and will be eschatological in character. Moreover, this ministry correlates to the period that lies between the Pentecost and the Second Coming of Jesus. "The Holy Spirit means blessings, while the fire means judgments. The Holy Spirit provides baptisms for those who have been grafted onto the body of Christ. The purpose of the baptism by fire is to judge those who do not believe in Jesus at the time of Jesus' return." [73)]

John the Baptist said those words at the beginning of Jesus' ministry on earth, but those words implicitly refer to the period that lays between the Pentecost and the Second Coming of Jesus. The Church must continue in Jesus' footsteps in the Kingdom ministry during that period. In another words, after the Pentecost and before His Second Coming, Jesus, who resurrected and ascended into heaven, will use His Church to expand God's Kingdom. Hence, one cannot separate God's Kingdom from the Pentecost.

2. The Pentecost and Redemptive History

Luke portrays the Pentecost as the climax of redemptive history.

---

73) Park, Hyung Yong, *An Exposition of the Four Gospels,* vol. I (Korean)(Suwon: Hapdong Theological Seminary Press, 1994), p. 111. Park, Hyung Yong, *An Exposition of the Four Gospels,* Combined Volume (Korean)(Suwon: Hapdong Theological Seminary Press, 2009), p. 78.

If we contemplate on the Gospel of Luke and the book of Acts together, both written by Luke, the Pentecostal event plays a key role in the continuation of redemptive history.

Lampe believes that the Pentecost mentioned in Acts 2 is the turning point. He says, "The conviction that the Spirit-baptism, which in the Baptist's preaching had been no more than a part of the eschatological hope, had now, through the resurrection of Jesus, become a piece of 'realized eschatology,' is not confined to the Lucan writings."[74] We need to realize that the Pentecost is directly related to Christ's resurrection and ascension. As death and resurrection of Jesus were considered the climax of redemptive history, the Pentecost must also be included with those two as one unit of the climax. Although these events are different in the time of their occurrence, they are part of a well-knit unit. In another words, Christ's death, resurrection, and ascension along with the Pentecost are one unit of redemptive history.

Therefore, the Pentecostal event is also an epochal event that marks the new era in redemptive history. For, it too indicates the climax of Christ's ministry in the progress of redemptive history. Likewise, the Pentecostal event is not a secondary or a mere supportive event of redemptive history but a necessity. Hence, the Pentecostal event cannot be seen as the basis of "the second blessing" in the experiences of the believers as the Pentecostalists insist.[75]

---

74) G.W.H. Lampe, *The Seal of the Spirit* (London: S.P.C.K., 1976), p. 47.

75) Cho, Yong Gi (David Cho) distinguishes regeneration from the baptism of the Holy Spirit, believing that the Pentecostal event marks a second blessing for the believers. "One must experience regeneration to obtain new life, and baptism of the Holy Spirit must be experienced separately in order to obtain great power for rendering service in God's ministry." Cf. David Cho, *The Holy Spirit* (Seoul: Seoul Books, 1992), p. 143.

3. Jesus' Baptism at the Jordan and Baptism of the Church at Pentecost

Jesus' baptism at the Jordan and the Pentecost are closely related to one another. The Pentecostal event is considered the watershed of redemptive history where the old and the new era meet each other. The Pentecostal event occurred, not for Jesus, but for His disciples. As Jesus entered the New Covenant Era by being baptized by the Spirit in the Jordan River (Matt. 3:13-17; Luke 3:21-22), His disciples have also entered a new era by being baptized with the baptism of the Holy Spirit at Pentecost (Acts 2:1-4). Believers can only receive the Holy Spirit if the Messiah Himself has also received the Holy Spirit. Jesus' baptism at the Jordan and baptism of the Holy Spirit at Pentecost have an intimate relationship with one another. What the Jordan experience was to Jesus, the Pentecost experience was to the disciples. Jesus' redemptive death brought Messianic joy to many people in the new era. Now at the Pentecost, a greater enjoyment of the Messianic Age by virtue of Jesus' representative death was extended to embrace all those who remained faithful to Jesus and tarried at Jerusalem in obedience to His commands.[76]

The special historical and redemptive meaning of the Pentecostal event can only be seen when the relationship between what Jesus experienced at the Jordan and what the disciples experienced at the Pentecost is understood. Jesus' baptism at the Jordan proves Him to be the Messiah and empowers Him for the Kingdom Ministry, and the Pentecostal event not only establishes the new Messianic body or the body of the New Covenant but also empowers the New Testament Church to spread the gospel for the Kingdom.

The Pentecostal event proves that the New Testament Church

---

76) J.D.G. Dunn, *Baptism in the Holy Spirit* (Naperville: Alec R. Allenson, 1970), p. 40.

is the Messianic community. The New Testament Church was established on the Pentecost according to God's promises. Jesus clearly states that the Holy Spirit's baptism is the fulfillment of God's promise when He said, "I am going to send you what my Father has promised" (Luke 24:49, NIV)[77] and when He also said, "Wait for the gift my Father promised, which you have heard me speak about" (Acts 1:4, NIV).[78] Moreover, God was the One who poured the Spirit upon Jesus at His baptism at the Jordan. Looking at the two events together, Jesus' baptism at the Jordan and baptism of the Church at Pentecost are both a part of God's work and involve the pouring of the Holy Spirit.

4. The Presence of the Holy Spirit and Christ at Pentecost

The presence of Jesus should not be overlooked because of the important role of the Holy Spirit at the Pentecost. As John the Baptist has said, Jesus was the One who baptized at the Pentecost (Luke 3:16). In order to understand "the baptism of the Holy Spirit at Pentecost," it will be pertinent here to examine the Apostle Paul's lesson on the ministry of the Holy Spirit and on the ministry of Jesus. Paul's teaching proves that there is a clear Christological element in the Pentecostal event.

In I Corinthians 15:45 and in II Corinthians 3:17, Paul closely relates the Holy Spirit with Christ. He identified the function of Christ after the resurrection the same as that of the function of the Holy Spirit.[79] So, Paul could say that Christ, the Last Adam, is "the

---

77) ἐγὼ ἀποστέλλω τὴν ἐπαγγελίαν τοῦ πατρός μου ἐφ᾽ ὑμᾶς.

78) ἀλλὰ περιμένειν τὴν ἐπαγγελίαν τοῦ πατρὸς ἣν ἠκούσατέ μου.

79) Identifying Jesus with the Holy Spirit was an expression used after Jesus' resurrection. Paul does not identify Jesus and the Holy Spirit in the ontological sense, but in the experiences of the believers, the ministry of Jesus Christ after His Resurrection is

Life-giving Spirit."[80] In essence, the Incarnate Christ became one with the Spirit by His resurrection in the believers' experiences. However, they are one in their activities and in their redemptive significance and not in the ontological sense.

In examining from this perspective, the fact that Christ baptized with the Holy Spirit at Pentecost indicates that Christ Himself was present at the Pentecost. We might say that the Trinity was involved at the Pentecost. Christ carried out God's promise through the power of the Holy Spirit. In the redemptive historical perspective, the Pentecost was an event that cannot be considered without the presence of the exalted Christ. The exalted Second Adam came back as "the Life-giving Spirit." He came to his people to organize a body of the New Covenant, and He equips the body with His presence to continue in the Kingdom ministry.

John 14:18 also carries a similar Christological emphasis. In the context, Jesus tells his disciples, "I am going to the Father" (John 14:12). And by Jesus' request, God the Father will send a Counselor or the Holy Spirit (John 14:16, 26). To assure his disciples that He will not leave them, Jesus further says, "I will not leave you as orphans; I will come to you" (John 14:18) and also says, "On that day you will realize that I am in my Father, and you are in me, and I am in you" (John 14:20, NIV). One must understand the words of the resurrected Christ in the same sense when He says, "and surely I am with you always, to the very end of the age" (Matt. 28:20, NIV).

The words "on that day" (John 14:20) indicate the Pentecost and imply that He will send the Holy Spirit on that day. Here, it is

---

functionally identical with the ministry of the Holy spirit. cf. Park, Hyung Yong, "The Lord is the Spirit," *Presbyterian Theological Quarterly,* vol. 45, number 1 (1978, Spring Issue), pp. 28-39.

80) πνεῦμα ζῳοποιοῦν is translated as "the Life-giving Spirit" and is an appropriate expression used to describe the function of Christ after His resurrection.

clear that the ascension is linked to the Pentecost. In the progress of redemptive history, Jesus had to leave in his physical form to return in the form of the Spirit. In referring to the Holy Spirit, John 7:39 says that his disciples could not receive the Spirit because Jesus had not yet been glorified. This shows that Christ going to his Father was a prerequisite for the presence of the Spirit. John 14:28 is also used in the same sense. "You heard me say, 'I am going away and I am coming back to you.' If you loved me, you would be glad that I am going to the Father, for the Father is greater than I"(NIV).

The disciples need to be joyful for Jesus' departing because the Spirit can descend only when Jesus goes to the Father. The idea of Christ's physical resurrection and spiritual presence is included in the concept of the Lord's Supper in Reformed Theology. Christ may be separated from us physically, but he is present within us spiritually.

5. The Justification Aspect of the Pentecost

The Holy Spirit's pivotal role at the Pentecost must not be a reason to neglect the justification aspect of the Pentecost. The Pentecost can be understood as a legal pronouncement on the Church passed on from the Father through the Son. At the Pentecost, God declared and confirmed that the Church was a righteous community of His people. The Pentecost was an occasion in which God poured His power over the Church, but moreover, it effectively manifested that the Church was God's Church. As the New Testament clearly explains the unity between Christ and His Church, the Pentecost clearly explains the position of the Church in the New Covenant that was established through Christ's death and resurrection.

The fact that the Pentecostal event implies the justification aspect indicates that the Messiah must experience a legal course of trials.

In order for the Messiah's community or the Church of Jesus Christ to escape condemnation, the Messiah Himself had to experience the sufferings in place of His people (Luke 12:49-53). He Himself had to pay the penalty for our sins (Rom. 5:25). In other words, the Messiah has to receive the apocalyptic judgment and endure God's wrath. He has to receive a baptism of curses and condemnation and then triumph from that judgmental baptism through His resurrection (Matt. 16:21; Luke 12:49-53).[81]

When the Lord comes to baptize His people on the Pentecost, they are no longer under the judgment of condemnation and God's wrath because of the trials and triumph of their Savior. Hence, baptism in the Holy Spirit at Pentecost is a completely optimistic event for the Church and it only brings blessings to the Church. After His resurrection, Jesus referred to the Pentecostal event only as the baptism in the Holy Spirit. "For John baptized with water, but in a few days you will be baptized with the Holy Spirit" (Acts 1:5, NIV). Jesus dropped "fire" that symbolizes the element of destruction and condemnation from the words of John the Baptist (Luke 3:16). Therefore, the Pentecostal event means blessings for the Church and signifies only a positive meaning for those who believe in the Messiah.

However, one must not forget that the Pentecostal event included the concept of fire by the expression "tongues of fire that separated." In relation to what John the Baptist said in Luke 3:16, "He will baptize you with the Holy Spirit and with fire," the fire mentioned in Acts 2:3 was not used in a destructive manner. "They saw what seemed to be tongues of fire that separated and came to rest on each of them" (Acts 2:3, NIV). The scene reveals that "tongues of fire"

---

81) δεî in Luke 9:22 suggests that Christ must suffer before He is exalted.

was not destructive but came to rest. Judgment had already been eliminated, so the fire was not a fire of destruction.

We can, therefore, conclude that Jesus, not only empowered the Church to serve in the Kingdom ministry through the Holy Spirit's baptism at the Pentecost, but also showed that the Church was no longer under God's wrath. In other words, baptism in the Holy Spirit at Pentecost confirms that the Church was not under God's wrath but was declared righteous.

6. A Unique Unrepeatable Event

The Pentecostal event is the epoch-making event in redemptive history and a unique event. It is an unrepeatable event. The Pentecostal event is not the first of many incidences where the outpouring of the Spirit can occur, nor is it a baptism that can be repeated when necessary. The Pentecostal event is not a mere example, nor is it an event in which the effect of it can be replenished through another outpouring of the Spirit. Because of the diversity of the Spirit's ministry within the Church, we misunderstand to say that the Spirit diminishes in its power or that it withdraws for a while and then returns. However, the Pentecost is a unique work of the Spirit that happens only once in redemptive history.

The Bible depicts the Pentecostal event as one that occurred in relation to Jesus' death, resurrection, and ascension (John 16:7-13). "But I tell you the truth: It is for your good that I am going away. Unless I go away, the Counselor will not come to you; but if I go, I will send him to you" (John 16:7, NIV). When Jesus said, "Unless I go away," He clearly meant this phrase to refer to His death. His death is inseparably related to the coming of the Counselor, the Holy Spirit. Jesus' death and resurrection are historically unique events. And since Christ's death, resurrection, and ascension cannot be repeated, neither can the Pentecostal event, which is inseparably related to these events, be repeated.[82]

7. The Birthday of the New Testament Church

The Pentecost is an ecclesiastically significant event. The Pentecost occurred for the sake of the Church. We can say that the Christian Church had its beginning with the Pentecost. The Church did not exist before the Pentecost. Of course, this can cause a misunderstanding. God's people always existed. The people of the Old and the New Covenant that have been saved by faith in Messiah through God's grace existed always. However, the Holy Spirit was not given before the Pentecost, in which case, the New Testament Church could not have been established (John 7:37-39).

Moreover, if God had established the New Testament Church before Jesus' death and resurrection, the New Testament Church would have no message of reconciliation to proclaim that they were supposed to preach. God achieved salvation through the death and resurrection of his Son, Jesus Christ (Rom. 10:9-10) and thereafter, built the New Testament Church to spread the gospel of salvation, gospel of reconciliation, and gospel of love. If the New Testament Church had been built before Christ's death and resurrection, the New Testament Church would not have been any different from the Israelites of the Old Testament.

In addition, the New Testament Church could not have been established during the time of Jesus'ministry on earth. Of course,

---

82) The once-for-allness of the Pentecostal event was already discussed in chapter 1. For details, see chapter 1: The Pentecost and its Uniqueness and Significance.

Jesus anticipated the building of the New Testament Church at Pentecost (Matt. 16:18). Jesus called, taught, and trained the twelve disciples because they were going to be the secondary foundation for the New Testament Church (cf. Eph. 2:20). In truth, Christ is the only foundation for the Church, but Jesus wanted the apostles, who witnessed the redemptive events of his death and resurrection, to spread the gospel and start the New Testament Church. Therefore, the reason that Jesus picked out the apostles during his life on earth was not to build the New Testament Church at the same time, but to prepare the foundation for the Church. We do not consider "the foundation of a building" as the building itself. The foundation of a building helps to support the building that is built on top. Likewise, the apostles are the secondary foundation of the New Testament Church, not the Church itself. The New Testament Church was established during the Pentecost after Jesus' death and resurrection according to God's plan.[83]

The resurrected Christ laid an everlasting spiritual foundation to build a Church. Jesus as the Life-giving Spirit came at Pentecost and laid the foundation for the New Testament Church. Jesus promised to Peter that "on this rock I will build my church" (Matt. 16:18), and this was realized through the Pentecostal event.[84]

8. Baptism in the Holy Spirit at Pentecost and the Experience of the Disciples

Baptism in the Holy Spirit at Pentecost occurred as one of the

---

83) Park, Hyung Yong, *An Exposition of the Letter to the Ephesians* (Suwon: Hapdong Theological Seminary Press, 1998), pp. 140-144.
84) William Hendriksen, *The Gospel of Matthew* (*NTC*) (Grand Rapids: Baker, 1973), pp. 647-649.

events of God's redemptive history. Luke says, "When the day of Pentecost came" (Acts 2:1) to indicate that the Pentecostal event occurred on a specific day in which God pre-ordained. God planned it so that it would happen after Jesus' death and resurrection. Even if the apostles were unprepared, the Pentecost was meant to happen. When God permits a special event to occur in redemptive history, He guides the surrounding circumstances to support that event. The Pentecost celebrated the possession of God's promised land, and it is natural that He should bless the newborn New Testament Church by the empowering of the Holy Spirit. Hence, the disciples experienced the Holy Spirit in a special way during Pentecost. The reason that the disciples had the special experience on the Pentecost was because they were in the right place at the right time. When the Israelites crossed the Red Sea, they experienced something that believers of other generations could never experience. These Israelites could see and touch the walls made of water on either side of them (Exodus 14:22). Jesus' disciples experienced an unusual darkness "from the sixth hour until the ninth hour… over all the land" (Matt. 27:45) when Jesus died on the cross. Then when Jesus resurrected from the dead, the disciples saw that "the tombs broke open and the bodies of many holy people who had died were raised to life" (Matt. 27:52, NIV). In this way, believer or not, those who were present at that place and time of the Pentecost could witness the special manifestation of the Holy Spirit and those who believed could experience the outpouring of the Holy Spirit.

9. "Something Better" for the New Testament Believer

Can the ministry of the Holy Spirit be applied to those of the Old Testament and those of the New Testament in the same way?

Some assert that the Holy Spirit's ministry during the Old Testament was event-oriented, while the ministry of the Holy Spirit after the Pentecost was oriented towards a continual existence within the believers' hearts. There is a justification in this explanation when comparing the works of the Holy Spirit in the Old Testament with the works of the Holy Spirit in the New Testament. However, one cannot absolutely maintain that the Holy Spirit only worked outwardly during the Old Testament period and inwardly during the New Testament period. David's prayer, "Do not cast me from your presence or take your Holy Spirit from me," (Psalm 51:11, NIV) does not merely mean that he did not want the Holy Spirit to be taken away from His outward working. David is sincerely repenting of his sins and asking for forgiveness, which is a plea from the innermost depths of his person and an impossible task without the work of the Holy Spirit. This is a definite sign that the Holy Spirit was present within David.

The same can be said of Abraham. The faith of Abraham originates from no other source than from a regeneration experience by the work of the Holy Spirit. The Bible confirms this by saying that "We have been saying that Abraham's faith was credited to him as righteousness" (Rom. 4:9, NIV) and "He (Abraham) believed God, and it was credited to him as righteousness" (Gal. 3:6, NIV). The lives of those heroes in Hebrews chapter 11 also testify to the inner work of the Holy Spirit (cf. Exodus 31:3).

For believers in the Old Testament times, "these were all commended for their faith, yet none of them received what had been promised" (Heb. 11:39), and for believers in the New Testament era, "God had planned something better" (Heb. 11:40). Then, what is that "something better" that God had planned for the New Testament believers? It is the experience of being in union with the exalted

Christ, the Life-giving Spirit.[85] Jesus was exalted after his suffering, and in turn, the New Testament believers can experience being united with the exalted Christ. For the Old Testament believers, fellowship with God was preparatory and typological. The Old Testament believers' union with Christ was lacking in final character, and they could not experience the reality of the union with the exalted Christ.

A Closing word

The Pentecostal event was the turning-point in redemptive history and opened an era for the Church to spread the gospel. Luke describes the Pentecost as the point in which a new era of redemptive history began. This is seen in the fact that Luke records this event, not at the end of his first book, the Gospel of Luke, but in the beginning of his second book, the Book of Acts (compare the first part of Acts 1:1-3n and Luke 1:1-4). Even clearer is the fact that Luke distinguishes those events that finalize Jesus' ministry on earth, such as the time when Jesus appeared for forty days after his resurrection and his ascension, from those events that indicate the era of the Holy Spirit that began with the Pentecost. These two time periods are separated by a 10-day interim. During this interim, neither the resurrected Christ nor the inspiring work of the Holy Spirit are evident, but at this time, Matthias was chosen to be added as a disciple, using the old method of drawing lots (Acts 1:26).[86]

---

85) R.B. Gaffin, Jr., "The Holy Spirit," *The Westminster Theological Journal*, Vol. XLIII, No. 1 (Fall, 1980), pp. 71ff.

86) J.D.G. Dunn, "Feast of Pentecost," *The New International Dictionary of New Testament Theology*, Vol. II, pp. 786f.; J.D.G. Dunn, *Baptism in the Holy Spirit*, SBT 2nd series 15, 1970, pp. 44ff.; Henry E. Dosker, "Pentecost," *The International Standard Bible Encyclopaedia*, Vol. IV, p. 2318: "The almost universal opinion among theologians and exegetes is this: that Pentecost marks *the founding of the Christian church as an institution.* This day is said to mark the dividing line between the ministry of the Lord and the ministry of the Spirit."

A new era began with the coming of the Holy Spirit at Pentecost for the spreading of the gospel of Jesus Christ beginning from Jerusalem to the ends of the earth (Acts 1:8). The Pentecost is the baton touch event from the exalted Christ to the New Testament Church in expanding the Kingdom of God.

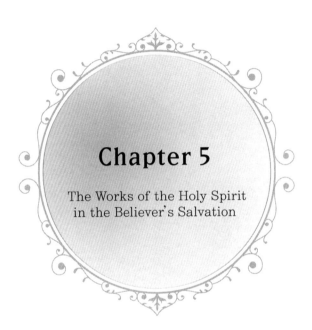

Chapter 5

The Works of the Holy Spirit
in the Believer's Salvation

The Holy Spirit is involved in all aspects of a believer's redemptive experience. Every experience of a believer, beginning from regeneration, indwelling of the Spirit, sanctification, and the seal of the Spirit, is related to the work of the Holy Spirit. In this chapter, we will concentrate on understanding the relationship between regeneration and baptism with the Holy Spirit, the relationship between baptism with the Holy Spirit and the fullness of the Spirit, the relationship between fullness of the Spirit and the Fruit of the Spirit, and the meaning of the fullness of the Spirit in a believer's life.

1. Regeneration and Baptism with the Holy Spirit

Pentecostal theologians do not distinguish between the "Holy Spirit's baptism" mentioned in Acts 1:5 and the one mentioned in I Corinthians 12:13. They differentiate between the believer's experience of regeneration and baptism with the Holy Spirit. They affirm that baptism with the Holy Spirit occurs after one's regeneration as a "special experience" that can be discerned by all "five senses." They also add that this experience can be recognized by the person in question as well as those around the person. Then what does the Bible say about this? I wish to find the answer to this question by looking at all the verses that mention baptism with the Holy Spirit.

It is inappropriate to use both Acts 1:5 and I Corinthians 12:13 on the same level to describe a believer's personal redemptive experience. When we try to interpret the meaning of a Bible verse, we need to look at the verses within the immediate context, the broader context, and the overall redemptive historical context. Acts 1:5 should be considered in relation to Jesus Christ's death, resurrection and ascension, and I Corinthians 12:13 must be considered as a believer's redemptive experience that comes by being grafted onto the body of Christ through faith. Yet, Pentecostal theologians muddle the issue by explaining regeneration and baptism with the Holy Spirit only in terms of an individual believer's experience.[87] Therefore, I Corinthians 12:13, rather than Acts 1:5, is more appropriate in explaining the relationship of baptism with the Holy Spirit to a believer's regeneration.

Even from a narrow perspective, one will agree that regeneration is the very first experience within an individual's redemptive experience. Regeneration marks the beginning of a new relationship with God, the first experience of a believer in becoming a child of God. Jesus witnessed this, when He says to Nicodemus: "I tell you the truth, no one can enter the kingdom of God unless he is born of water and the Spirit" (John 3:5, NIV). "Being born of water and the Spirit" in this verse indicates being "born again" (John 3:3, 7, 8) or regeneration. A believer is united with Christ by being born again and can become a citizen of heaven. So, the experience of regeneration is the very first redemptive experience of an individual believer.

Then what kind of a redemptive experience is baptism with the Holy Spirit for an individual believer? For the sake of convenience, we will quote I Corinthians 12:13 again which mentions baptism with the Holy Spirit. "For we were all baptized by one Spirit into one body – whether Jews or Greeks, slave or free – and we were all given the one Spirit to drink" (I Cor. 12:13, NIV). Paul uses this verse to compare the Church of Christ to the body of a human being. This is a body imagery to describe how the church functions. It indicates

---

87) R.A. Torrey says, " From this it is evident that regeneration is one thing, and that the baptism with the Holy Spirit is something different, something further. One can be regenerated and still not yet be baptised with the Holy Ghost." cf. R.A. Torrey, *The Baptism with the Holy Spirit* (Minneapolis: Bethany House Publishers, 1972), p. 16.

that, whether it be Jew or Greek, slave or free, once we are one in Christ, we have received the baptism by the Holy Spirit. In another words, one cannot go on to become a member of the Church without the Holy Spirit's baptism.[88]

Then why was the expression "baptism with the Holy Spirit" used in I Corinthians 12:13 instead of "regeneration" or "justification"? Two things need to be considered to answer this question.[89]

First, it is the unique work of the Holy Spirit that applies Christ's redemptive death and resurrection to an individual believer. Without the Spirit, no one can confess that Jesus is the Savior. That is why Paul said, "No one who is speaking by the Spirit of God says, 'Jesus be cursed,' and no one can say, 'Jesus is Lord,' except by the Holy Spirit" (I Cor. 12:3, NIV). The fact that a person, who died because of one's sins and faults, was deemed righteous and the fact that one can believe in Christ's death and resurrection of two thousand years ago are the results of the Holy Spirit's work. The Spirit gives faith to a believer who can confess Jesus as one's Savior, receive righteousness, and become a child of God, and from then on, the

---

88) Calvin interprets the first part of I Cor. 12:13, "For we were all baptized by one Spirit," as an indication of the believers' baptisms, but he interprets the latter part of the verse, "we were all given the one Spirit to drink," as an indication of Communion. Cf. John Calvin, *The First Epistle of Paul to the Corinthians,* trans. John W. Fraser (Grand Rapids: Eerdmans, 1973), p. 265. Grosheide explains that this verse is a symbolic language of the most intimate relationship among believers. (F.W. Grosheide, *Commentary on the First Epistle to the Corinthians (NICNT).* Grand Rapids: Eerdmans, 1968, p. 293). However, looking at the overall context of the verse, it is more reasonable to say that both the former and the latter part of I Cor. 12:13 refer to the baptism experienced by the believers once they become a member of Christ's Church (John A. Bengel, *Bengel's New Testament Commentary,* Vol. II (Grand Rapids: Kregel Publications, 1981, pp. 236-237). Even Calvin admits that he is not sure whether the latter part of I Cor. 12:13 symbolizes baptism or the Communion (Calvin, *op. cit.,* p. 265).

89) This has already been discussed in chapter 1 of this book under the sub-title of "The Pentecost and its Uniqueness and Significance."

Spirit dwells within the believers' souls (I Cor. 3:16; 6:19; Rom. 8:9-11). Likewise, it is the Spirit who initiates the first redemptive experience in the believer's life.

Secondly, "baptism" is the most appropriate word to describe someone who becomes a member of Christ's Church. Circumcision in the Old Testament corresponds to the baptism in the New Testament. Circumcision is a ceremony marking the Gentiles to become a part of God's people (Israel), and the New Testament Church provides baptisms to receive new converts into its community. Therefore, Paul does not use the terms "justification" or "regeneration," but rather, the term "baptism," to describe the process of an individual believer becoming a member of the Church.

Then at what point does an individual believer become part of the Church? It is the point at which the believer receives justification, experiences regeneration, obtains salvation and receives baptism with the Holy Spirit. Here we can see that in a believer's redemptive experience, regeneration occurs at the same time as "baptism with the Holy Spirit." Regeneration and baptism with the Holy Spirit explain the same experience from a different perspective.

This is not to say that one cannot experience the work of the Spirit after one's regeneration. But in all certainty, it is inappropriate to label the special work of the Spirit that follows one's regeneration as baptism with the Holy Spirit. Paul used the expressions "baptism with the Holy Spirit," regeneration, sealing of the Spirit, and justification, each in a different perspective to describe an individual's redemptive experience. Then how can we explain the special Pentecostal event that the disciples experienced? The disciples had already experienced regeneration before they experienced the special work of the Holy Spirit on the day of the Pentecost (Acts 2:1-4). We cannot doubt Peter's salvation during the period of the Lord's public ministry; otherwise, he could not have confessed, "You are the Christ, the Son of the living God" (Matt.16:16). Because Peter and the other disciples had experienced regeneration before the Pentecostal event and because Acts 1:5 points to the Pentecostal event as baptism with the Holy Spirit, regeneration and baptism with the Holy Spirit are considered two different experiences in the life of the disciples.[90] Such conclusions are made because the Pentecostal event is seen in light of an individual's experience and not in the perspective of redemptive history.

The disciples' experience during the Pentecost was a rightful and needed experience. When God allowed the redemptive event to occur, those, who were present, could not avoid experiencing special occurrences, ones that others of a different time period could not experience. The Israelites had a special experience when they crossed the Red Sea as if they were on dry land. They would have seen and touched a wall made of water for the first time in their lives (Ex. 14:21-25). When Jesus died on the cross, those who were present experienced three hours of darkness in daytime (Matt. 27:45). When Jesus rose from the dead, people living in that period could meet with those who were raised from their tombs. They could talk, shake hands, and have fellowship with the resurrected ones (Matt. 27:52-53). It is understood that the disciples experienced a special outpouring of the Spirit because they were present during the Pentecostal event. The Holy Spirit sealed the Church and empowered it during the Pentecost in order to give a testimony of Christ's redemptive history (Acts 2:1-4, 12-13). This does not mean that Christians of today should see walls of water in the Red Sea,

---

90) R. A. Torrey, *The Baptism with the Holy Spirit,* p. 16. Torrey proposes a pre-regeneration, post-baptism with the Spirit scheme because of the fact that Jesus' disciples had experienced regeneration separately from the Pentecostal event.

experience darkness in daytime, or meet with those who resurrect from the dead. Jesus' disciples experienced the Spirit's special work during the Pentecost, but this cannot be a set pattern for Christians of today.

2. Baptism with the Spirit and Fullness of the Spirit

When dealing with the work of the Holy Spirit, we must examine the differences between "the baptism with the Spirit" and "the fullness of the Spirit."[91] Before we do that, we should clarify the relationship between the two to understand each concept. "The fullness of the Spirit" is different from "the baptism with the Spirit." When we use the phrase "the baptism with the Spirit" to describe an individual's salvation experience (distinguished from the Pentecostal event), it refers to the individual's first acceptance of Christ as his or her Savior. Hence, "the baptism with the Spirit" coincides with regeneration, and the Bible clearly confirms this by saying that "For we were all baptized by one Spirit into one body—whether Jews or Greeks, slave or free—and we were all given the one Spirit to drink" (I Cor. 12:13). This verse clearly affirms that the union of a believer to the body of Christ is through the baptism of the Spirit. At the same moment that a believer unites with the body of Christ, regeneration

---

91) E. F. Harrison, *Acts: The Expanding Church* (Chicago: Moody Press, 1975), pp. 51-52. Harrison says, "Luke used the term 'filled' rather than baptized, for this was the actual effect. *Baptism* is the objective term, the theological reality, the Godward aspect of the matter. *Filling* is the manward, subjective aspect. *Filling* and *baptism* are not completely synonymous terms. *Baptism* is appropriate for the initial gift of the Spirit (1:5: 11:16-17), for it marks the beginning of a new relationship. Like water baptism, it belongs to Christian beginnings and is not repeatable (cf. I Co 12:13; see also the discussion of the apostles' situation regarding baptism, under Ac 1:5). One who has been baptized with the Spirit may be filled, not merely once (4:8) but again and again (4:31; Eph 5:18). But no one is reported to have been baptized with the Spirit more than once."(Italics are original)

occurs. Hence, "the baptism with the Spirit" is a unique once-for-all redemptive experience for a believer and one that occurs by accepting Christ as one's Savior.[92] From the time that an individual believes in Jesus, the Holy Spirit indwells the believer's heart. That is why Paul referred to the believer's body as the temple of the Spirit (I Cor. 3:16, 17; 6:19). Clearly, he testifies to the indwelling of the Spirit in the believer (Rom. 8:9-11).

"The fullness of the Spirit" can only occur within the heart of those who already believe in Jesus Christ. Therefore, a non-Christian cannot experience "the fullness of the Spirit." We need to remember that "the fullness of the Spirit" refers to the fact that the person of God the Spirit indwells the believer. The Holy Spirit is God, and yet, the Spirit shows His activity through the obedience of human beings. This is the testimony of the Bible and its teaching.

First, "the fullness of the Spirit" was used to portray a person's character. In choosing the seven deacons, the apostles said, "Brothers, choose seven men from among you who are known to be full of the Spirit and wisdom" (Acts 6:3). Among the seven, Stephen, in particular, is portrayed as one filled with "the Holy Spirit and wisdom" (Acts 6:10; 7:55). And Barnabas is described as one filled with "the Holy Spirit and faith" (Acts 11:24). Here, we need to turn our eyes to the method used in the Bible. The Bible indicates that along with Stephen and Barnabas seven deacons were full of "the

---

92) Here are Torrey's list of 7 steps to receiving the baptism with the Holy Spirit. 1) We need to change our minds about God and Christ. 2) We need to renounce all our sins. 3) When we receive a baptism in the name of Jesus Christ, we need to make an open confession. 4) We need to surrender completely to the will of God (Acts 5:32). 5) We must have "a real and intense desire" to receive the baptism with the Spirit (Luke 11:13). 6) To receive a special blessing, we must ask (Luke 11:13). 7) We must believe that we will receive whatever we ask (Mark 11:24). (See. R. A. Torrey, *The Baptism with the Holy Spirit,* pp. 40-65.) Torrey is one of the scholars who supports the "pre-regeneration and post-baptism with the Spirit."

Holy Spirit and wisdom" (Acts 6:3, 10) and "faith and the Holy Spirit" (Acts 6:5; 11:24). In these ways, the Bible illustrates the characters of specific persons with the term "fullness of the Spirit." It is clear from these verses that, when a person is described as "being full of faith, wisdom, and the Holy Spirit," the person's virtuous character is being revealed.

Secondly, "the fullness of the Spirit" can be a temporary and momentary phenomenon for a special purpose. Filled with the Holy Spirit, Peter stood in front of the high priest, and preached the gospel courageously, saying, "Salvation is found in no one else, for there is no other name under heaven given to men by which we must be saved" (Acts 4:12, NIV). Here, Peter's preaching of the gospel is directly linked to his fullness of the Spirit. After the apostles were released from the Sanhedrin, they gathered with the other believers to pray, and everyone in that place was filled with the Holy Spirit (Acts 4:31). The Bible then relates "the fullness of the Spirit" to the preaching of the gospel because those who were filled with the Holy Spirit "spoke the word of God boldly." "The fullness of the Spirit" was also seen in their daily lives in which "all the believers were one in heart and mind. No one claimed that any of his possessions was his own, but they shared everything they had" (Acts 4:32, NIV).

Another example of "the fullness of the Spirit" is found in Paul's preaching in Cyprus. While visiting Cyprus, Paul and Barnabas wanted to preach the word of God to the proconsul Sergius Paulus during their first missionary journey. However, when Elymas the sorcerer opposed the purpose of the Lord by opposing them, Paul was filled with the Holy Spirit and made Elymas temporarily blind (Acts 13:6-11). As such, the Scriptures show that "the fullness of the Spirit" is seen in relation to the preaching of the gospel.

These biblical examples teach that "the fullness of the Spirit" is used for the achievement of a special ministry. In the given verses (Acts 4:8, 31; 13:9), the word that describes "fullness" is used in an aorist tense to explain the once-for-allness of the action. Hence, "the fullness of the Spirit" occurred as a momentary experience for a special ministry.

Thirdly, the Bible proves that "the fullness of the Spirit" can be a continuing experience. The Scriptures say that Paul and Barnabas "were filled with joy and with the Holy Spirit" (Acts 13:52) when they were being thrown out from Pisidia Antioch after preaching the gospel. Moreover, Apostle Paul admonishes by saying, "Do not get drunk on wine, which leads to debauchery. Instead, be filled with the Spirit" (Eph. 5:18, NIV).

The imperfect tense in Acts 13:52 and the present tense in Ephesians 5:18 are used to illustrate the continuation of "the fullness of the Spirit" by emphasizing the on-going character of the action. Acts 13:52 shows that, though under persecution, the disciples were continuously filled with the Holy Spirit, and Ephesians 5:18 points out that believers need to be filled with the Holy Spirit continuously.

We saw that "the fullness of the Spirit" was used in three different ways. And, these three ways are eventually reduced to two main points.

First of all, "the fullness of the Spirit" can be used to portray a particular person's character, and secondly, "the fullness of the Spirit" is temporally categorized according to its duration. The temporal factor refers to how "the fullness of the Spirit" can either be a momentary phenomenon that accomplishes a special ministry or a continuous experience of the believers. As both are in the same category of time, it is only a matter of whether it is momentary or continuous. In fact, a momentary experience can be a part of a continuous experience. Believers should not be content with only a momentary phenomenon but should hope for a continuous filling. In conclusion, believers should strive for a continuous "fullness of the Spirit" in order to live in submission to the will of the Spirit.

3. A Life Filled with the Holy Spirit

A life filled with the Holy Spirit will be examined in detail. The Bible compares being filled with the Holy Spirit to being drunk (Luke 1:15; Acts 2:4, 15; Eph. 5:18). Why was this the case? There is a lesson for all believers to learn. Being a drunkard promotes a life of corruption and waste, pursuing vulgar and earthly pleasures. However, being filled with the Holy Spirit is a life benefiting both God and man, a life satisfied by a noble purpose.

After comparing the conditions of being drunk and being filled with the Holy Spirit, the Apostle Paul describes a life filled with the Holy Spirit in more detail. Alcohol controls the life of a drunkard but, thoughts, feelings, words, and the behavior of a person filled with the Spirit is completely ruled by the Spirit. Being filled with the Spirit doesn't mean a lack of self-control; rather, it means to understand oneself properly and to rely entirely on the Spirit's guidance. As a result, someone who is filled with the Holy Spirit has the wisdom to discern and make proper judgments in each circumstance.[93] The Apostle Paul explains several results that come from a life filled with the Holy Spirit.

---

93) In comparing the conditions of being filled with the Holy Spirit and being drunk, we must remember that their subjective experiences have nothing in common. The Bible does not support an irresponsible and uncontrolled emotional expression. Paul compares the two conditions simply to show the difference between the two. From a biblical perspective, an irresponsible subjective experience originates from a condition that lacks the Spirit's guidance. A person filled with the Holy Spirit is controlled by the Spirit and can refrain from committing those irresponsible acts. Donald T. Williams, *The Person and the Work of the Holy Spirit* (Nashville: Broadman and Holman Publishers, 1994), pp. 136-137.

First, a person filled with the Spirit maintains beautiful relationships with God and with other people (Eph. 5:19). "The fullness of the Spirit" allows a person to establish good relationships by speaking to each other in psalms, hymns, and spiritual songs. The first thing that needs to be properly established is a relationship with God and thereafter comes a proper relationship with fellow Christians. To God, we show this by giving him worship and to our brothers and sisters, by having good fellowship. A person filled with the Spirit worships God by remembering his omnipotence and mercy within the course of redemptive history. As a result, praise and joyful song exist within the heart of a person living in the Spirit.

Secondly, the fullness of the Spirit means to possess a grateful heart (Eph. 5:20). A person filled with the Spirit knows that God's will is to give thanks in all circumstances (I Thess. 5:18) and always has a grateful heart. The Bible does not dictate God's specific plan for an individual, but through Paul's letters, we can find God's general will for all believers. God's will is for the believers to be holy (I Thess. 4:3), pursue goodness and kindness (I Thess. 5:15), always be joyful (I Thess. 5:16), pray continually (I Thess. 5:17), and give thanks in all circumstances (I Thess. 5:18). Paul discloses that "this is God's will for you in Christ Jesus" (I Thess. 5:18). A person filled with the Spirit thanks the Lord in all situations.

Thirdly, a person filled with the Holy Spirit possesses an obedient heart towards others (Eph. 5:21). Obeying someone is a difficult task, and yet, being filled with the Spirit allows a person to act it out because the Holy Spirit resides in the person as the spirit of humility. The fullness of the Spirit, not only allows a person to obey Christ, but to obey one's fellow Christian brothers and sisters. As such, Paul explains the characteristics of a life filled with the Spirit; he then continues by giving specific examples from society. He uses the examples of a relationship between a husband and wife, parents and their children, and a master and his servant.[94)]

First, in a Spirit-filled relationship between a husband and wife, the wife must submit to the husband as one would to the Lord, and obey him as the Church obeys Christ. The husband should love the wife as Christ loves the Church and gave Himself for it (Eph. 5:22-28). This is the relationship in which both the husband and wife submit to the will of the Spirit. When both the husband and wife live under the control of the Spirit, their relationship becomes a relationship filled with the Spirit.

Next, Paul explains the second most important relationship within a life filled with the Spirit, that between parents and their children (Eph. 6:1-4). Children should obey their parents with love, thankfulness, and respect as they would obey the Lord. Unless their parents prevent them from believing in Christ or force them to commit a crime, children should obey their parents in full measure. On the other hand, parents must not exasperate their children and should raise them in the Lord (Eph. 6:4) through a discipline of love. If their discipline is inconsistent, too harsh, or abuses their position as parents, it will exasperate and anger the children. Moreover, parents should guide their children with encouragement and instruction and should become living models for their children. Likewise, a relationship between parents and their children is a relationship controlled by and filled with the Spirit.

The last relationship that Paul describes is the one between a

---

94) Calvin explains, "Society consists of groups, which are like yokes, in which there is a mutual obligation of parties. The first yoke is the marriage between husband and wife; the second yoke binds parents and children; the third connects masters and servants. So in society there are six different classes, for each of which Paul lays down its peculiar duties." cf. John Calvin, *The Epistles of Paul the Apostle to the Galatians, Ephesians, Philippians and Colossians,* trans. T.H.L. Parker (Grand Rapids: Eerdmans, 1974), pp. 204f.

master and servant (Eph. 6:5-9). Servants should serve their earthly masters as they would Christ, and they should do so, not just by action, but with a sincere heart. On the other hand, masters should treat their servants humanely in righteousness and fairness because the heavenly Master who rules over all earthly masters does not judge a person by their appearance (Eph. 6:9). To maintain a Spirit-filled relationship, both masters and servants should treat each other as they would to the Lord.

Paul uses these three relationships to testify that the daily lives of the believers are directly connected to the fullness of the Spirit. In short, being filled with the Spirit means, regardless of the circumstances, a believer must submit to and follow the will of the Spirit. The Bible mentions a few exceptions but in general, the fullness of the Spirit is directly linked to our daily lives. Hence, Christians should make the best effort to live a life that is full of the Spirit.

4. Fullness of the Spirit and the Fruit of the Spirit

(1) Imitation of Christ

"The fullness of the Spirit" is directly connected to a believer's daily life, and a life full of the Spirit naturally results in "the Fruit of the Spirit." Hence, here we will examine "the Fruit of the Spirit." "The Fruit of the Spirit" is a list of virtues that Christians, who are born again in Christ and under the Spirit's guidance, need, in order to live in imitation of Christ. The broader context of Galatians 5:22-23 explains how a born-again Christian can become more like Christ. Paul lists nine aspects of the Fruit of the Spirit, which were specifically needed by the Galatian church.

In addition to Galatians 5:22-23, many more virtues are

mentioned in Romans 5:3-5 (perseverance, character, hope, unashamedness), Romans 14:17 (righteousness, peace, joy), Ephesians 5:9 (goodness, righteousness, truth), I Timothy 6:11 (righteousness, godliness, faith, love, endurance, gentleness), II Timothy 3:10 (faith, patience, love, endurance), and II Peter 1:5-7 (goodness, knowledge, self-control, perseverance, godliness, brotherly kindness, love), and I Corinthians 13:4-7 (see bottom). Believers have not yet reached perfection, and their bodies are battlefields. "For the sinful nature desires what is contrary to the Spirit, and the Spirit what is contrary to the sinful nature. They are in conflict with each other, so that you do not do what you want" (Gal. 5:17, NIV).

To the battling Christians, Paul suggests three ways of living related to the Holy Spirit. They are: "walk[ing] in the Spirit" (Gal. 5:16), "[being led] by the Spirit" (Gal. 5:18), and "liv[ing] by the Spirit" (Gal. 5:25). We must note that these verses encompass the Fruit of the Spirit mentioned in Galatians 5:22-23.

The first of these verses, "walk[ing] in the Spirit," directs the behavior of the believers. The second, "[being led] by the Spirit" emphasizes the submission of the believers' wills to the guidance of the Spirit. The third, "liv[ing] by the Spirit" commands the believers to maintain an active spiritual relationship and mystical union with The Spirit.

The Holy Spirit resides within the believers, supplying them with motives, directing them and empowering them to be more like Christ. He quietly ministers to a believer with encouragements (Gal. 5:13) and admonitions (Gal. 5:26). Like a fruit whose growth process cannot be witnessed but nevertheless is verified when the fruit ripens, the Holy Spirit quietly and mysteriously ministers to a believer and produces the Fruit of the Spirit. The Fruit of the Spirit is a gift of grace from the Holy Spirit, but this does not mean that believers should be a passive. Christians are players, not spectators, in this spiritual battle.

Paul mentions in the passive tense in Galatians 5:18, "but if you are led by the Spirit, you are not under law" (NIV), while expressing in the active tense in Galatians 5:16, 25, "walk in the Spirit." This indicates a relationship between the Spirit's work and the believers' participation. This means that if believers live under the guidance of the Spirit, they will become more like Christ by producing the Fruit of the Spirit.

(2) The Fruit of the Spirit

Galatians 5:22 provides a catalog of virtues. Paul compares this catalog of virtues (Gal. 5:22-23) to one of vices (Gal. 5:19-21). The fruit of the Spirit is listed as the work of the Spirit that should be manifested in the new life of Christians: love, joy, peace, patience, kindness, goodness, faithfulness, gentleness, and self-control.

① Love (agape: ἀγάπη) – People use the term "love" very vaguely. Yet, the Bible discusses love in concrete terms. When God said He loves us, this was shown by the sacrifice of his only Son Jesus for our sins (John 3:16). When Christ said He loves us, this was shown by his death on the cross (Rom. 5:8; Phil. 2:5-11). The "love" in the Fruit of the Spirit is, not an act of human will, but the power of the Spirit that moves and shapes the human will and emotions. We can love only because God first loved us (I John 4:19). We find the perfect example of love in the life of Christ. Therefore, a spiritual person in imitation of Christ does not demand freedom to satisfy one's own needs but limits one's own freedom for others and shows love by serving others. The proof of a spiritual person is not seen in their spiritual gifts but in the love that they show.[95] Love is giving, sharing, sacrificing, and giving up of oneself. Love is throwing one's

---

95) James D.G. Dunn, *Jesus and the Spirit* (London: SCM Press, 1975), p. 295.

self away and serving others. The concreteness of love is shown here.

I Corinthians chapters 12, 13, and 14 concentrate on the gifts of the Holy Spirit. The fact that I Corinthians 13, which is "the love chapter," was placed between chapters 12 and 14 suggests a relationship between love and the gifts of the Spirit. In I Corinthians 12:31, Paul encourages the Corinthian church by saying, "Eagerly desire the greater gifts." This is immediately followed by "the love chapter," chapter 13, inferring that love may be one of the gifts of the Spirit. However, the Bible does not refer to love as one of the gifts of the Spirit. Paul clearly states that the "best way" in managing the gifts of the Spirit is through love. Therefore, love is indirectly considered one of the Fruits of the Spirit (Gal. 5:22).

Then does love have an equal standing as the other Fruits of the Spirit? Or is love set apart from and above the other Fruits of the Spirit? The Bible always gives more weight to love than the other fruits of the Spirit. Love is at the root of all the Fruits of the Spirit. Love must act as the catalyst for the other Fruits of the Spirit to take effect because "God is love" (I John 4:8). God does not allow the Fruit of the Spirit to be produced apart from Him. The amount of love a believer possesses shows to what capacity the believer allows God to live in and through one's life.

It will be beneficial to investigate the "song of love" in I Corinthians 13:4-7, which describes love in the greatest detail.

First of all, love is patient. Patience is a passive form of love. Patience means to wait and persevere. Patience is waiting on God's schedule. And patience is enduring those hardships when anger seems to overwhelm one's entire being (James 5:9). Patience is overlooking other people's weaknesses. These are concrete expressions of love. Saul, the first king of Israel was rejected by God because he could not wait for God's appointed time (I Sam. 13:8-14).

Saul should have waited until Samuel arrived, as an expression of his love for the Lord.

Secondly, love is showing kindness towards one another. In the Korean Bible, I Corinthians 13:4 says, "Love is meek," which is not the same as the 'meek' mentioned in Matthew 5:5, "Blessed are the meek." While the "meek" in Matthew 5:5 means "gentle, humble, considerate," the "meek" mentioned in I Corinthians 13:4 means "kindness." This is the only time Paul uses this word.[96]

Kindness is an active characteristic of love. Kindness gives a warm and comfortable feeling to the one receiving it. Henry Drummond said, "There is only one thing greater than happiness in the world, and that is holiness."[97] He was saying that holiness comes only from God, and that by serving one another in kindness, people can create happiness.

Thirdly, love is having a generous heart of mind. Jealousy arises in competitive situations. "Jealousy results from ambition of a person who considers himself superior than others and who always puts himself in a higher position. So, he hates the success of others and degrades it."[98] Paul describes the love that "has no jealousy." Love encompasses everything about the other person. "Love covers

96) In Matthew 5:5, the term "πραεῖς" (πραύς) is used and in I Corinthians 13:4 "χρηστεύεται" (χρηστεύομαι) is used. The Korean Version in I Corinthians 13:4, uses the term "meek," but it is more accurate to say "kindness" in this context. 'Mercy' which is mentioned as one of the Fruits of the Spirit (Gal. 5:22-23), represents kindness as in I Cor. 13:4. Among many translations, the Korean Version(Hangul Kaeyuk) and New Korean Revised Version(Hangul Kaeyuk Kaejungpan) use the term 'meek' for 'kindness.' Korean New Testament: New Translation(Saebunyuk Shinyak), Korea Standard Bible(Pyojoon Shinyakjunseo), Common Translation(Kongdongbunyuk), New Korean Standard Version(Pyojoon Saebunyuk), Revised New Korean Standard Version(Pyojoon Saebunyuk Kaejungpan), NIV (kind), NASB (kind), Novum Testament Latine (benigna est), Bijbel (goedertieren, merciful, clement), Die Bibel (freundlich) all use the term 'kindness.'

97) Henry Drummond, *The Greatest Thing in the World* (New York: Grosset and Dunlap, 1981), p. 21. This book is translated into Korean by Hyung Yong Park.

98) Sang Kun Lee, *I & II Corinthians* (Seoul: General Assembly Educational Committee, 1985), p. 181.

a multitude of sins" (I Peter 4:8). Without love, one cannot extend generosity to the other person.

Fourthly, love comes from humility. Humility means to forget one's accomplishments and to seal one's lips about the matter. While pride is the worst of all sins, humility is the best of virtues (Prov. 16:18). The Bible compares humility and pride side by side. "Before his downfall a man's heart is proud, but humility comes before honor" (Prov. 18:12). God belittles the proud and uplifts the humble to higher places. Paul describes Jesus' humility by describing Jesus' path to the cross as having "made himself nothing" and "humbled himself" (Phil. 2:7-8). Such humility shows Christ's love for us, sacrificing Himself on the cross.

Fifthly, love is shown by courtesy. If someone says they love others but behave rudely towards them, they do not know the real meaning of love. Good behavior is a characteristic of love that appears in one's daily life. Using public facilities as if they were one's own is an expression of love. Standing in line without cutting in front of others is an expression of love for others who are also standing in line.

Sixthly, love does not seek even that which is her own. Love does not pursue personal profit. If a person denies himself to obtain greater personal gain, his act of denying himself has no meaning. However, Christ's act of bearing the yoke of the cross was an act of true selflessness because He loved us.[99] True happiness lies in giving, not in taking or possessing (Acts 20:35).

Seventhly, a characteristic of love is meekness. A quick-temper is one of the most destructive characteristics in human nature. In

---

99) Drummond (*op. cit.*, p. 26) said, "Nothing is a hardship to Love, and nothing is hard. I believe that Christ's 'yoke' is easy. Christ's 'yoke' is just His way of taking life. And I believe it is an easier way than any other. I believe it is a happier way than any other," to explain Christ's suffering on the cross as an act of His selflessness.

just split seconds, even the most wonderful person can destroy one's lifetime of accomplishments and reputation when he cannot restrain his anger.

In the Parable of the Prodigal Son, the attitude of the eldest son on the return of his brother is a combination of jealousy, anger, ruthlessness, cruelty, self-righteousness, and stubbornness. A quick-temper tests the extent of love and reveals the loveless instincts of a human being. A quick-tempered person makes misery for all those who are in heaven and acts as an obstacle for those who are not yet in heaven from entering heaven. Loving another person holds back the anger.

Eighthly, a characteristic of love is honesty. Honesty represents pure motivations and looks on the positive side of things to act in the best manner. People are comfortable, happy, relaxed, and encouraged around an honest person.

Ninthly, a characteristic of love means to take joy in truth. Loving another person does not mean to use the other person for one's own benefit. Love does not pick on other people's weaknesses but rather, maintains proper relationships with others in goodness. Love and truth always walk together. Love can never be neutral. Love always takes sides and inevitably, takes the side of truth. Loving someone means to act on the principles of truth.

We examined the nine characteristics of love in detail. Realistically, it may appear to be focused too much on the virtues of love, but since faith produces love and love produces the other eight fruits of the Spirit, there is no harm done in this application (See John 17:13-26; I Peter 1:5-7).[100]

② Joy (chara: χαρά) – Paul states that the Fruits of the Spirit is

---

100) Grosheide (*op. cit.*, p. 313) explains the role of love by saying that "Love is basic for

joy or happiness. To understand joy, let us contemplate sadness, the opposite of joy. There are two types of sadness, includes one that is worldly and one that is god-fearing. The intensity of the two types of sorrow may be equal, but as a matter of importance, their motivations differ.

Paul mentions the hopeless sadness felt by a person on the verge of death (I Thess. 4:13). Paul says, "...worldly sorrow brings death" (II Cor. 7:10). Such sadness or sorrow goes against God's providence and relies on oneself to find the solutions to all spiritual concerns. Such worldly sorrow differs tremendously from godly sorrow.

Godly sorrow results from godly motivations. Godly sorrow is manifested in incidences, such as in the sorrow shown by the Ephesian Church elders when they knew that they would never see Paul again (Acts 20:38), the sorrow of Paul when he was concerned about Epaphroditus' condition during his illness (Phil. 2:7), the sorrow of Jesus when He cried because of the faithlessness of those within Jerusalem (Luke 19:41), and the sorrow of Paul when he worried about the faithlessness of the Jews (Rom. 9:2).

Godly joy and godly sorrow should be manifested alternately within the lives of the believers (Rom. 12:15). Joy is a Fruit of the Spirit created within us by the Holy Spirit. In Paul's letters, joy and faith run parallel (II Cor. 1:24; Phil. 1:25), joy and prayer are intimately connected (Phil. 1:4; Col. 1:11f.), and joy and righteousness go together side by side (Rom. 14:17; Phil. 2:18f.). "The Spirit generates joy, along with righteousness and peace, as its fruit (Gal. 5:22; Rom. 14:17). It enables a person to endure joyfully

---

it does not just refer to a certain relation, but it governs and sustains all relations, because it indicates a direction of life. Love will enable a person to do many things, such as to believe and to hope (vs. 7) but it will make it impossible for him to hate anything else except sin. Love is the root of all good actions."

the suffering and trials of Christian existence (I Thess. 1:6)."[101] The confidence that is gained after accepting Christ as the Savior and after becoming a member of the Church brings forth this godly joy (I John 1:4). This joy relies on the unchangeable character of God's existence and promise. Joy is the subjective component of appropriation of the eschatological salvation promise.

③ Peace (eirene: εἰρήνη) – Peace can be examined in two ways. First, there is that peace that exists within an individual because Christ placed himself on the cross to reestablish our relationship with God. "Therefore, since we have been justified through faith, we have peace with God through our Lord Jesus Christ" (Rom. 5:1, NIV).[102] The second is the peace that is found within a community of people. The Holy Spirit gives us peace as one of the Fruits of the Spirit, allowing us to keep the peace that saves us from God's wrath against sin (Rom. 5:1, 9) and also allowing us to co-exist in peace with other brothers and sisters (Eph. 4:3). Peace cannot be created by the passive wait-and-see attitude. A peaceful man does not retreat from participating. Rather, peace represents the self-sacrificing, self-forgetting, and self-giving love of God that encompasses all conditions of life. Despite the insult and hatred, a peaceful man stands firm in love. A peaceful man does not fail easily. A peaceful man is not easily angered.

Two hands are necessary to make a clapping sound. We must make peace with one another because we are God's workmanship

---

101) K. Berger, "χαρά," *Exegetical Dictionary of the New Testament,* Vol. 3 (Grand Rapids: Eerdmans, 1993), p. 454.

102) There is a textual problem in this verse. Manuscripts אᵃ, B³ and P support ἔχομεν (We have peace.) and manuscripts א*, A, B*, C, D, and K support ἔχωμεν (Let us have peace.). The authority and weight of the supporting manuscripts are balanced enough such that choosing to read either will not be a problem, but when looking at the overall context, instead of saying, "Let us have peace" in a hortatory subjective tense, the present indicative tense of "we have peace" is the one to choose. A believer who has become righteous is someone who already possesses peace with God (Eph. 2:14-18).

(Eph. 2:10). God called each believer to be a great being. He wants each believer to become calm, firm, and strong in his will. We must remember the old saying, "He who throws dirt only loses ground." To gain a peaceful spirit, we must do the following.

First, we must acknowledge that our natural tendency is to fight and argue with each other. We must remember that we are, not only aggressive and full of hatred, but possess a selfish, egotistical character, an old self that we cannot cast off.

Secondly, we must sincerely ask for God's help through prayer. When we admit our weaknesses and ask God for help, the Great Gardener will pull out the weeds from our lives and allow us to bear good fruit. Then we must rely on God and submit our lives to Him completely.

Thirdly, once we admit our weaknesses, God works within us. But we are afraid that God might expose the worst of our sins. Sometimes we even interfere in God's dealing in us. God wants to expose our selfish pride and make us see the hatred that we possess with a self-reflecting mirror. Yet, we hesitate in facing and exposing the self-demeaning aspects of our lives. True peace can find its place within us only when pride disappears. Peace flourishes only when arrogance is laid to rest. Peace grows with humility as its fertilizer.

We can obtain such peace when we rely solely on the Lord (Isa. 26:3), put our faith in the Bible (I John 3:19-20), and offer our prayers and praise to the Lord (Phil. 4:6-7).

④ Patience (makrothymia: μακροθυμία) – Patience was already mentioned as a character of love. Patience is both an attribute of Jesus Christ (and God) and a characteristic of the Christian. Thus, it is fitting to say that as God showed his patience toward us through Christ, we must have patience for those people who aggravate us (Rom. 2:4; I Tim. 1:16; James 1:19). Paul clearly shows that patience is a characteristic of the Christian by associating the term with a special word group. Patience is found with "mercy" (I Cor. 6:6; Gal. 5:22; Col. 3:12), "meekness" (Eph. 4:2; Col. 3:12), "love" (II Tim. 3:10),[103] "goodness" (I Thess. 5:14-15), and with "endurance" (Col. 1:11; II Tim. 3:10). All these occurrences indicate that patience is a good virtue of the Christian.

⑤ Kindness (chrestotes: χρηστότης) – As one of the Fruits of the Spirit, mercy has the same meaning as kindness. Kindness is an attribute of God that is recreated within a person when they experience regeneration. Kindness can be found in the story of the Good Samaritan. The Good Samaritan was useful and kind and a source of joy for the person beaten by a group of thieves (Luke 10:25-37).[104] Kindness does not allow someone to continue sinning. Kindness pays a price. Kindness requires courage, faithfulness, and selflessness. A kind doctor will clean out the puss from a patient's wound for it to heal better, but a fake doctor will cover up the wound with just a simple treatment. Kindness means the willingness to suffer for the sake of others. Kindness is a character trait or virtue manifesting itself in a gentle disposition and behavior toward others. It is manifested in the behavior of uprightness, mildness, and graciousness toward others.[105]

⑥ Goodness (agathosyne: ἀγαθωσύνη) – Only God is absolutely good. Jesus revealed this fact in the conversation with the rich man (Luke 18:18-19). Man is relatively good. Barnabas was a good man (Acts 11:24). Goodness has two meanings. The first type of goodness means not to have any blemishes, and the second type

---

103) Harm W. Hollander, "μακροθυμία," *Exegetical Dictionary* of *the New Testament*, Vol. 2 (Grand Rapids: Eerdmans, 1991), pp. 380-81.

104) I have discussed the nature of kindness in the early part of this chapter.

105) J. Zmijewski, "χρηστότης," *Exegetical Dictionary of the New Testament*, Vol. 3 (Grand Rapids: Eerdmans, 1993), p. 475.

means to be assertive in acting out goodness. Goodness originates from God, and goodness can be revealed through us only when the Holy Spirit lives inside of us.

⑦ Faithfulness (pistis: πίστις) – Faithfulness means fidelity. God is the source of absolute faithfulness, and human faithfulness is only a reflection of God's faithfulness. Christians build their faithfulness by obeying God's Word. Obedience, in and of itself, helps to strengthen faithfulness, but in essence, obedience to God's Word is the means of receiving grace and building faithfulness.

When Christians have reverence for the Lord, their faithfulness is developed. By honoring God, we can be his faithful stewards (I Cor. 4:1-5). Christians can also build their faithfulness by becoming more aware of Christ's Second Coming. In truth, Christians must follow the Spirit's lead in becoming more faithful.

⑧ Gentleness (prautes: πραΰτης) - As a Fruit of the Spirit, gentleness does not represent being weak. Rather, a strong person who controls his strength and acts gently towards others shows true gentleness. Courage displays true gentleness. Trusting in God's faithful promise brings out true gentleness. A gentle person can be compared to a tamed wild horse that is full of energy. Gentleness does not represent powerlessness, nor is it fragile. Rather, gentleness signifies a person who is full of the Spirit and power and who submits completely to the Holy Spirit and lives life under the Spirit's control. It is as if the wild, energetic horse been tamed and obeys the master's commands.

⑨ Self-Control (engkrateia: ἐγκράτεια) – As one of the Fruits of the Spirit, self-control does not mean asceticism. Jesus also does not teach asceticism in the sense of renouncing possessions, sexual activity, and food restrictions. Self-control does not mean avoiding the responsibilities of a daily life but to set proper visions and objectives, to have the proper mindset in accomplishing those tasks, and to march forward until one accomplishes those tasks. Self-control fashions one's life in the way God desires.[106]

We have examined each Fruit of the Spirit from Galatians 5:22-23. One thing to remember is that the Fruit of the Spirit must be understood through our relationship with God and with other people.

The gifts of the Spirit and the Fruit of the Spirit are not given solely for the use of the receiver but for the receiver to use for other people. The gifts of the Spirit can be applied more effectively when used for the benefit of other people. Likewise, the Fruit of the Spirit is borne not for its bearer but for others, which indicates that they are necessary for building Christ's church.

The variety present in the gifts of the Spirit is a source of energy to the church, while the Fruit of the Spirit creates unity within the church by following Christ's example. When we think about the Gifts of the Spirit or the Fruit of the Spirit, we must always relate to the building of Christ's church.

5. Can we categorize people as first and second-class Christians?

The Pentecostal scholars differentiate between a regenerated Christian and a Christian who has received the baptism with the Holy Spirit. They state that a regenerated Christian cannot experience a well-rounded, happy life as much as a Christian who has received the Holy Spirit's baptism, dividing Christians into first-class and second-class Christians. However, it is not right to divide Christians into classes. If someone receives Jesus as their Savior, they have received the Holy Spirit as well. We cannot separate Jesus and the Holy Spirit

---

106) H. Baltensweiter, "ἐγκράτεια," *The New International Dictionary of New Testament Theology,* Vol. 1 (Grand Rapids: Zondervan, 1975), p. 495.

in the redemptive experience of a believer. Hence, when we consider "the baptism with the Holy Spirit," we must do so in relation to the regeneration of Christians and the union of believers with Christ. In Christ's church, there is no distinction between a believer who has only experienced regeneration and a believer who has received the baptism with the Holy Spirit in addition to regeneration.

Through his Pentecostal sermon, Peter indicates that the advent of the Holy Spirit during the Pentecost fulfilled both the prophecy of John the Baptist in Luke 3:16 and Jesus' prophesy in John 7:38-39. "Exalted to the right hand of God, he has received from the Father the promised Holy Spirit and has poured out what you now see and hear" (Acts 2:33, NIV). Near the end of his sermon, Peter mentions how we should react towards the outpouring of the Holy Spirit at the Pentecost. "Repent and be baptized, every one of you, in the name of Jesus Christ for the forgiveness of your sins. And you will receive the gift of the Holy Spirit" (Acts 2:38, NIV). One must note that the Scripture explains repentance, forgiveness of sin, baptism in the name of Jesus, and the gift of the Holy Spirit all together as a single package. Peter does not say, "After you repent and have been forgiven, wait for the baptism with the Holy Spirit."[107] We must realize that the lifestyle presented by the Pentecostals of today is not the way in which people in the early Church lived in obedience to Peter's sermon (Acts 2:42-47). Therefore, people in Christ's church cannot be distinguished as first and second-class Christians.

Paul states that God the Father "blessed us in the heavenly realms with every spiritual blessing in Christ" (Eph. 1:3, NIV). This blessing applies, not only to those believers who experience the special works of the Holy Spirit some time after regeneration, but to all those who are united with Christ through their confession and

---

107) Donald T. Williams, *The Person and the Work of the Holy Spirit*, pp. 129-130.

belief in Christ. Of course, the believers who experience the works of the Holy Spirit will have a clear confirmation of their faith in Christ. This experience, however, does not justify the distinction of believers within the church as first-class and second-class Christians.

Because all those who believe become united with Christ, everything that Christ accomplished becomes their own. In as much, Paul can say that believers live with Christ (Rom. 6:8), suffer with Christ (Rom. 8:17), are nailed on the cross with Christ (Rom. 6:6), die with Christ (II Cor. 7:3), are resurrected with Christ (Col. 2:12, 3:1), are glorified with Christ (Rom. 8:17), become heirs with Christ (Rom. 8:17), and rule with Christ (II Tim. 2:12). When we believed, we became united with Christ, and the Spiritual blessings that Christ achieved became ours. This means that believers who receive the "Holy Spirit's baptism" in Pentecostalistic sense are not the only ones with an abundant life. Rather, those who live the same life that Christ lived, live abundantly.

In this chapter, we examined "the believer's experience and the baptism with the Holy Spirit" by dividing it into several topics. We proposed that the Pentecostal event should be seen, not in the perspective of an individual believer's redemptive experience, but in light of the death and resurrection of Jesus Christ, and the ascension of Christ into heaven. We also pointed out that differentiating regeneration and the Holy Spirit's baptism within an individual believer's redemptive experience was not the teaching of the Bible. Likewise, the Bible does not teach that a believer who experiences regeneration and also receives the "Holy Spirit's baptism," will live a more abundant life than the believer who only experiences regeneration. Rather, we acknowledge that a believer can have a special spiritual experience after regeneration and that such an experience will be a confirmation to the believer on how the Holy

Spirit is guiding his every step. And with the Gifts and the Fruit of the Holy Spirit, we must discover ways to build up the Church and live for others. Neither the Gifts of the Spirit nor the Fruit of the Spirit are to be used for our selfish desires. Believers who have experienced the special works of the Holy Spirit after regeneration must also remember that their experience bears the meaning of building up the church and living for others as Christ did on earth. Nothing can come from a spiritual experience that deviates from imitating Christ. The reason God gave the Gifts of the Spirit to believers and causes the believers to yield the Fruit of the Spirit is to build up the church as the body of Christ and to attain "the whole measure of the fullness of Christ" (Eph. 4:13, NIV).

We must always try to understand the works of the Holy Spirit with a humble heart. And we must use the objective truth of the Bible written by the inspiration of the Spirit to study the works of the Spirit, thereby reducing the errors that come from an individual's subjective experience. We cannot avoid using the term "baptism with the Holy Spirit" to portray one aspect of an individual believer's redemptive experience, for the Bible also uses this term (I Cor. 12:13). Baptism with the Spirit that portrays an individual believer's redemptive experience and baptism with the Spirit that portrays the Pentecostal event should not be fused into one. To escape this confusion, a believer's baptism with the Spirit is identified as the same as the regeneration experience, whereas the special experience of the Holy Spirit after regeneration should be described in a different term. We simply suggest the term that the Bible uses: "the fullness of the Holy Spirit."

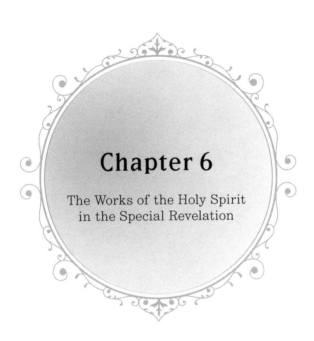

Chapter 6

The Works of the Holy Spirit
in the Special Revelation

When we study on the relationship between the Holy Spirit and special revelation, we can approach the subject matter in two directions. First, one can study on the subject as to what kind of a role the Holy Spirit had when the Scriptures were recorded. Second, one can direct his study as to how the 66 books of the Bible became accepted as the Bible that we read today and as to what was the role of the Holy Spirit in the process of accepting certain scriptures as Church's Bible. The former is called the "Biblical Inspiration," while the latter is considered the "Canonicity." Although it would be beneficial for the readers that we deal with both the "Doctrine of Inspiration" and the "Canonicity," we will confine ourselves to deal with the relationship between the Holy Spirit and special revelation due to the importance of the subject and time constraints. We will learn what the Bible teaches about the "Biblical Inspiration."

What role did the Holy Spirit have in recording the Bible? This question implies how we will understand "Biblical Inspiration." God the Spirit used human writers to create the Bible. The Spirit did not use people like robots or typewriters. He used the character and personalities of the people while they were writing the Bible. And the Spirit did not just use anyone but chose proper people for the task. While God reveals His Will and redemptive plan through the human authors, God the Spirit did not distort the humanness of the authors. Hence, the authors were not used as mere machinery in the writing of the Bible. They wrote the Bible as though they were recording their own thoughts.

The authors did not think that they were being forced or controlled against their will in writing the Bible. Likewise, the Spirit used the character and personalities of the authors as they were but led them to record the Bible without any errors. Revelation occurs because God wills it to occur. This is God the Spirit's mysterious work and wisdom.

1. The Self-consciousness of the Bible authors in recording the Bible

Did the authors think that they were recording God's Word when they were writing the Bible? The Bible does not answer this question directly. However, for a couple of reasons, we can affirm that the authors of the Bible recognized that they were writing God's Word.

Firstly, when Paul writes his letters to the church, he emphasizes the fact that he is the apostle for the church. Verses such as, "Paul, a servant of Christ Jesus, called to be an apostle" (Rom. 1:1; see I Cor. 1:1; Eph. 1:1; Col. 1:1; I Tim. 1:1; II Tim. 1:1; Tit. 1:1, NIV), "Paul, an apostle-sent not from men nor by man, but by Jesus Christ and God the Father, who raised him from the dead" (Gal 1:1, NIV) emphasize that Paul is the apostle of the church. An apostle is given an important role in the church, and Paul mentions that an apostle is in a position more important than a prophet for the New Testament Church (I Cor. 12:28). Paul says that the New Testament church was built on the foundation of the apostles and prophets (Eph. 2:20). Although Paul wrote his letters as an individual person, he sent them to the church as an Apostle. He also wanted the church to understand that he has exercised apostolic authority over the church.

Secondly, the apostle John wrote, "But the Counselor, the Holy Spirit, whom the Father will send in my name, will teach you all things and will remind you of everything I have said to you" (John 14:26; see 16:13, NIV). This means that what apostle John wrote (the Bible) was recorded according to the guidance of the Holy Spirit. John believed that God the Holy Spirit allowed him to remember the works of Jesus Christ and the meaning and the significance of Christ's

sayings and that the Holy Spirit inspired him to record what would be beneficial for the next generation. "The task of the Paraclete-Spirit then is to '*teach* you everything and *remind* you of everything' that Jesus has said."[108] When Apostle John wrote, "the Holy Spirit will teach you all things and will remind you of everything I have said to you" (John 14:26), he wanted to reveal "the Spirit's role to the first generation of disciples, not to all subsequent Christians."[109] The evangelist did not want to explain how "readers at the end of the first century may be taught by the Spirit, but to explain to readers at the end of the first century how the first witnesses, the first disciples, came to an accurate and full understanding of the truth of Jesus Christ."[110] The Spirit's role is not to bring new revelation, but to complete the revelation brought by Jesus himself. The Spirit helps the first witnesses and disciples of Christ remember His Truth wholly and accurately. It is clear that "the Evangelist thus indirectly gives an important clue to the character of his own Gospel." So, John believed that his writings were recorded through the inspiration of the Spirit.[111]

Thirdly, Peter writes concerning Paul's letters, "He (Paul) writes the same way in all his letters, speaking in them of these matters. His letters contain some things that are hard to understand which ignorant and unstable people distort, as they do the other Scriptures, to their own destruction" (II Pet. 3:16, NIV). Peter says that some of Paul's writings are hard to understand, so that some people who are ignorant have twisted his letters around to mean something quite different

---

108) George R. Beasley-Murray, *John: Word Biblical Commentary,* Vol. 36 (Waco: Word Books, 1987), p. 261.

109) D. A. Carson, *The Gospel According to John* (Grand Rapids: Eerdmans, 1991), p. 505; Leon Morris, *The Gospel According to John* (*NICNT*) (Grand Rapids: Eerdmans, 1971), p. 657.

110) Carson, *The Gospel According to John,* p. 505.

111) Herman Ridderbos, *The Gospel of John: A Theological Commentary* (Grand Rapids: Eerdmans, 1997), p. 511.

from what he meant, just as they do the other parts of Scripture. Here Peter placed Paul's letters on the same level as "the other Scriptures."

There are two ways to interpret "the other Scriptures" (*tas loipas graphas*: τὰς λοιπὰς γραφάς) in this verse.

1). The first opinion is that Peter was comparing Paul's letter to the Old Testament Scriptures and did not consider Paul's letters as part of the Scriptures. In other words, Peter mentions "the other Scriptures" to distinguish Paul's letters from the Old Testament Scriptures which were considered part of the Bible.[112] In this case, though Paul's letters were not considered as part of the Scriptures, Peter did approve of Paul's letters quite highly. Then the verse meant that just as "those who were ignorant and those who were weak" invited destruction because they interpreted the Old Testament inappropriately, so they also perished because they interpreted Paul's letters in an improper way. Then, it is notable that Peter considered Paul's letters very highly to the extent he compared Paul's letters with the Old Testament.

2). The second opinion is that Peter included Paul's letters as part of the Scriptures. "The other Scriptures" (II Pet. 3:16) refer to writings that were not included in the New Testament canon but have been accepted as belonging to the holy writings by the Church in due time. Such was not an uncommon case. Even before 60 A.D., holy writings were read with the Old Testament in the Church, and these same writings were included in the New Testament Scriptures at a later date. Therefore, by comparing Paul's letters with "the other Scriptures" which were later canonized and included in the New Testament, Peter was validating Paul's letters as part of the New

---

112) Cf. In the paragraph "the rest of men, who have no hope"(οἱ λοιποί) in I Thess. 4:13, λοιποί is used to distinguish Christians from non-Christians. Peter used the same word in II Pet. 3:16 to distinguish Paul's letters from the other Scriptures.

Testament. Like the Old Testament prophets, the apostles were aware of the fact that they were spreading the Word of God (I Thess. 2:13).[113] In this case, Peter was comparing Paul's letters to the Old Testament Scriptures on the same level.

Looking at the context, this second interpretation appears to be more suitable in its explanation. However, both interpretations value Paul's letters highly. Hence, Peter appears to write this verse while acknowledging Paul's letters to have the same authority as the Old Testament Scriptures.[114]

The contents above prove that the New Testament authors believed their writings to have the same authority and characteristics as the Old Testament. While writing the Scriptures, the New Testament authors did not think that they were merely writing personal letters or private literatures but believed to write the Word in God's authority.

2. Biblical Evidence for Biblical Inspiration

Though there are many Biblical verses that support for Biblical inspiration, we will deal with only two important verses here. They are II Timothy 3:16 and II Peter 1:20-21.

(1) II Timothy 3:16

"All Scripture is God-breathed and is useful for teaching, rebuking, correcting and training in righteousness" (II Tim.

---

113) "And we also thank God continually because, when you received the word of God, which you heard from us, you accepted it not as the word of men, but as it actually is, the word of God, which is at work in you who believe" (I Thess. 2:13).

114) Michael Green, *2 Peter and Jude* (*Tyndale New Testament Commentaries*) (Grand Rapids: Eerdmans, 1987), pp. 160-161; D.A. Carson, *The Farewell Discourse and Final Prayer of Jesus: An Exposition of John 14-17* (Grand Rapids: Eerdmans, 1980), p. 149.

3:16, NIV). "All Scripture is given by inspiration of God, and is profitable for doctrine, for reproof, for correction, for instruction in righteousness" (II Tim. 3:16, NKJV). "All Scripture is breathed out by God and profitable for teaching, for reproof, for correction, and for training in righteousness" (II Tim. 3:16, ESV).

When we explore the context of II Timothy 3:16, we note that Paul is teaching Timothy the realistic and functional value of the Scriptures. Paul reminds Timothy how much of an advantage he has over the false teachers by being armed with the Truth. Timothy learned about the Scriptures ever since he was a child (II Tim. 3:13-15). Hence, Paul introduces the essential nature of the Scriptures to explain its priceless value (II Tim. 3:16).

At this point, it is beneficial to look at the structure of the passage on biblical inspiration for the rest of the study. In translating "*pasa graphe theopneustos*,"[115] New International Version renders, "All Scripture is God-breathed" and New King James Version translates, "All Scripture is given by inspiration of God." And English Standard Version translates, "All Scripture is breathed out by God." We can ask several questions about the passage. First of all, when Paul used the word "scripture" (γραφή) in the passage, to what book was he referring? Secondly, what meaning does the term "all" (πᾶσα) have in the phrase "all scripture"? Thirdly, how should we understand the expression "is God-breathed" (θεόπνευστος)? If we answer these three questions in detail, we would be able to discover what Paul has in mind regarding biblical inspiration.

First of all, to what book does the "scripture" (γραφή) refer? The term "scripture" in the passage can be ascertained as referring to the Old Testament. The term *graphe* emphasizes the unity of

---

115) Πᾶσα γραφὴ θεόπνευστος

the Old Testament and is used in the New Testament in particular to refer to the Old Testament as a whole (Matt. 21:42; 22:29; Luke 4:21; 24:27, 32, 45; John 2:22; 10:35, etc.). In this passage, Paul uses *graphe* without an article (he: ἡ). It is uncommon that the term *graphe* is used without an article within the Pauline epistles.[116] There are three verses in the Pauline epistles that do not use definite article with *graphe*. They are Romans 1:2, 16:26, and II Timothy 3:16. As we study the context of Romans 1:2 and 16:26, it is obvious that this term certainly refers to the Old Testament. But II Timothy 3:16 uses the term *graphe* in a slightly different way. II Timothy is the last of the epistles that Paul wrote, and it is significant that this last epistle includes the very important verse, such as II Timothy 3:16 which teaches an important meaning about biblical inspiration. Therefore the absence of a definite article before the word *graphe* in II Timothy 3:16 must have had a special purpose.

When the word *graphe* is used without an article, the word *graphe* connotes "quality" in itself.[117] It suggests that all records that have "quality of *graphe*" are the writings inspired by God. When Paul uses "*graphe*" in II Tim. 3:16, he uses the term to refer to all records of *graphe* quality. This signifies that the term *graphe* refers

---

116) J. B. Smith, *Greek-English Concordance to the New Testament* (Scottdale, PA: Herald Press, 1947), p. 74. calculated the occurrence of the term *graphe* in the New Testament as 51 times, but in Pauline epistles only as 14 times. Among the 14 occurrences, three verses (Rom. 1:2; 16:26; II Tim. 3:16) do not have an article with the word *graphe*. The absence of the article in these verses is because of the technical character of the expression. Cf. W. F. Arndt and F. W. Gingrich, *A Greek-English Lexicon of the New Testament and Other Early Christian Literature* (Chicago: The University of Chicago Press, 1979), p. 164 (γράμμα, 2c).

117) See, Maximilian Zerwick, *Biblical Greek* (Rome: Biblical Institute Press, 1985), p. 57 (sec. 176, 177). Regarding II Tim. 3:16, Zerwick writes, "Hence in Πᾶσα γραφὴ θεόπνευστος 2 Tim 3, 16 it is correct to insist on the absence of the article as showing that inspiration belongs to Scripture as such (<<all Scripture...>>), whereas with the article (<<all the scripture...>>) it would simply register the fact that the existing Scripture was inspired, without establishing a formal principle." (p. 61-sect. 189).

not only to the Old Testament, but to the New Testament and to the writings in the process of being written with *graphe* quality.

Secondly, what does "all" (pasa) in the phrase "all scriptures" mean? One could understand the meaning of "all" in terms of a collective sense referring to "a whole" or "all." Others may see it referring to "a whole" made up with an individual. In this case the term is used in the sense of "every." Both the collective sense and individual sense consequently indicate "all" and causes no huge problem in the use of one or the other.[118] However, some people who view *pasa* as an individual sense (every) intentionally imply that some parts of the Bible were inspired and other parts were not.[119] Hence, it may be more appropriate to consider the word *pasa* referring to "all" as a collective sense. All authors of the Bible believe that all the books of the Bible could not have been written without God's inspiration.[120] Hence, this passage states that because all parts of the Bible were written through God's inspiration, the Bible is beneficial to fulfill the God's purpose.

Thirdly, how can we understand the expression "inspired by God" or "God-breathed" (θεόπνευστος) in the passage? First of all, determining whether "*theopneustos*" (θεόπνευστος) is used in the predicate sense or in the attributive sense in this sentence would be beneficial in answering this question. If the expression "inspired by God" is used in the predicate sense in the sentence, we can

---

118) B. B. Warfield (*The Inspiration and Authority of the Bible*. Philadelphia: The Presbyterian and Reformed Publishing Company, 1948, p. 134) takes this word to mean in an individual sense. He translates, "Every Scripture, seeing that it is God-breathed, is as well profitable." Warfield did not eliminate any part of the Bible when he said that every Scripture is God-breathed.

119) Cf. Hyung Yong Park, *A History of Criticism on the Gospels* (Korean) (Seoul: Sung Kwang Pulbishing Co., 1995), p. 25; L. Berkhof, *Manual of Christian Doctrine* (Grand Rapids: Eerdmans, 1973), pp. 43-44.

120) I. Howard Marshall, *Biblical Inspiration* (Grand Rapids: Eerdmans, 1983), p. 25.

translate the passage to mean "all scriptures are inspired by God."[121] If the same expression is in the attributive sense in the sentence, the passage can be interpreted as "all scriptures that were inspired by God." In the latter case, the phrase "inspired by God" directly modifies the term "scriptures." However, it is more appropriate to interpret "*theopneustos*" to be used in the predicate sense because, if "*theopneustos*" is interpreted as an attributive sense, "*ophelimos*" (ὠφέλιμος) also needs to be interpreted as an attributive sense since "*theopneustos*" and "*ophelimos*" are linked together by the simple word "and (καί)." Yet, when "*ophelimos*" is interpreted as an attributive sense, the meaning of the passage would be unnatural. Moreover, if "*theopneustos*" is considered as an attributive sense to say "all scriptures that were inspired by God," some parts of the Bible would be considered as inspired by God, while others would not be. Only the portion of the 66 books of the Bible that are qualified by "*theopneustos*" would be thought of as "inspired by God." Then only that portion of the Bible would be considered as "all scriptures" that were "inspired by God." In sum, the sentence structure and the underlying content supports "*theopneustos*" as used in the predicate sense.

Then what does "inspired by God" mean? This term is mentioned only once in the New Testament (*hapax legomenon*) and is a verbal adjective. Here, we need to decide whether "*theopneustos*" was used in an active sense or passive sense in the context. Interpreted in an active sense, it signifies "God-breathing," while in a passive sense, it signifies "God-breathed." When we apply these two meanings to biblical inspiration, the active sense means, "Scripture is inspiring," and the passive sense means, "Scripture is God-breathed."

---

121) "All Scripture is God-breathed" (N.I.V.); "All Scripture is inspired by God" (N.A.S.B.); "All Scripture is breathed out by God" (E.S.V.).

The active sense emphasizes how the Scripture is inspiring to the reader or the listener. And the passive sense stresses the inspiredness of the scriptures. At a glance, no huge problem seems to exist. But our position on biblical inspiration changes depending on the meaning of *"theopneustos."* If *"theopneustos"* is in the active sense, the Scripture will lose its ultimate inspired state and be used as a mere tool for inspiring. This will disregard the purpose and origin of the Scripture and focus on the inspiring functions of the Scripture. If *"theopneustos"* is understood in the passive sense,[122] however, the Scripture will have possessed its ultimate inspired state and its divine origin will become clear. In this case, the Scripture is the product of God-breathed. "'*Theopneustos*' points to an essential relationship between the breath of the Spirit and the *grape* (γραφή)."[123] Such a mysterious nature of the Scripture distinguishes it from other records in history. Calvin interprets II Timothy 3:16 that Paul teaches Biblical authority in view of the scriptures being inspired by God the Holy Spirit.[124]

The Scripture is the product of God's living breath,[125] thus, the Scripture is a record "inspired by God." The whole of the Scripture and its content originate from God's breath or His Spirit. Since the

---

122) In general, verbal adjective has an ending with –τος, it has passive sense. Ἀγαπητός means "beloved" (Matt. 3:17). Warfield underlies that "compounds of verbals in –τος with θεός normally express an effect produced by God's activity." He supplies such examples as θεόγραπτος, θεόδοτος θεοδίδακτος, θεομακάριστος and he asserts that "some eighty-six compounds of this type, of which, at least, seventy-five bear quite simply the sense of a result produced by God." Cf. B. B. Warfield, *The Inspiration and Authority of the Bible*, pp. 281-282.

123) G.. C. Berkouwer, *Holy Scripture* (Grand Rapids: Eerdmans, 1975), p. 140.

124) John Calvin, *The Second Epistle of Paul to the Corinthians, and the Epistles to Timothy, Titus and Philemon*, trans. T. A. Smail (Grand Rapids: Eerdmans, 1973), p. 330.

125) The word "Inspiration" in English came from the Latin Vulgate: *Omnis scriptura divinitus inspirata*. This word implies a sense of "breathed in, but Greek has a sense of "breathed out." N.I.V. New Testament in 1973 translates θεόπνευστος to mean "God-breathed" though A.V. translates into "is given by inspiration of God" and N.A.S.B. "is inspired by God."

origin of the Scripture is God, the author of the Scripture is, therefore, God the Spirit Himself.

In summarizing the meaning of the phrase "all scripture was inspired by God," the 66 books of the Bible that all the churches possess today have originated from God's breath and are the content that God intended.

(2) II Peter 1:20, 21

"Knowing this first, that no prophecy of Scripture is of any private interpretation, for prophecy never came by the will of man, but holy men of God spoke as they were moved by the Holy Spirit" (II Pet. 1:20, 21, NKJV); "Above all, you must understand that no prophecy of Scripture came about by the prophet's own interpretation. For prophecy never had its origin in the will of man, but men spoke from God as they were carried along by the Holy Spirit" (NIV); "But know this first of all, that no prophecy of Scripture is a matter of one's own interpretation, for no prophecy was ever made by an act of human will, but men moved by the Holy Spirit spoke from God" (NASB); "Knowing this first of all, that no prophecy of Scripture comes from someone's own interpretation. For no prophecy was ever produced by the will of man, but men spoke from God as they were carried along by the Holy Spirit" (ESV).

The verses above are crucial when dealing with the biblical inspiration along with II Tim. 3:16. They emphasize that prophetic proclamations come from God. In addition, we can see several truths on biblical inspiration from these verses.

First of all, how much of the Scripture does "all prophesies" include in Peter's phrase, "all prophesies of the Scripture"? Does "all prophesies of the Scripture" (πᾶσα προφητεία γραφῆς) refer to only the prophesies in the Scripture or the entire Scripture itself? Of course, what Peter originally meant was the Old Testament. Yet, the passage is emphasizing, not the value of the Scripture, but the accuracy and reliability of the Scripture. II Peter 1:19 says, "We have greater confidence in the message proclaimed by the prophets," which illustrates Peter's emphasis on the reliability of the Scripture. If the passage had stressed the worth or value of the Scripture, we could have assumed that Peter was comparing the prophecy of the Scripture with other part of the Scripture. Then we would have to construe that Peter only recognized the value of the prophecy as worthwhile in comparison to the other parts of the Scripture. Such an interpretation, however, does not agree with the rest of the context. As a result, it is more reasonable to conclude that the passage is emphasizing the accuracy and reliability of the Scripture and that the phrase "all prophecies of the Scripture" is referring to the entire Old Testament rather than just the Old Testament prophecies. Warfield is correct in saying that "prophecy of Scripture" in the verse refers to "the entirety of Scripture."[126]

Secondly, what does the passage say about what can be part of the Scripture and what cannot? We can infer two views from the "no prophecy in Scripture ever came from the prophets themselves" (II Peter 1:20, NLT).

The first view is to interpret the verse as "no prophecy in Scripture should not be interpreted privately."[127] This view stands on reasons that the false teachers interpret the Scripture in their own way, not following the traditional interpretation. Therefore, Peter is purposely attacking this error by refuting the freestyle interpretation and supporting the traditional interpretation of the church which

---

126) B. B. Warfield, *op. cit.*, pp. 135-136.
127) Korean Kaeyuk Version translates the verse in the same perspective.

derived from the Holy Spirit's guidance. II Peter 3:16 strongly supports this view,[128] but this view also faces some obstacles.

One, if II Peter 1:20 is rejecting the wrong methods of interpretation of the false teachers, viewing the verse in the context, II Peter 1:21 needs to provide basis for that rejection. However, II Peter 1:21 gives a very weak explanation in terms of basis. If we proceed from this perspective, the Scriptures cannot be the object of human interpretation because they were recorded by the inspiration of the Holy Spirit. Therefore, the Scriptures require inspiring activity of the Holy Spirit for interpretation. If such was Peter's intentions, his logic would be losing its focus. Peter would not prohibit an individual from interpreting the Scriptures.

Two, in a broader context, II Peter 1:16-21, on the whole, takes a defensive stance, and II Peter 2:1 mentions "false prophets" and "false teachers" for the first time and dictates their sins in detail. This is a transition into an offensive stance. Thus, it is safe to say that II Peter 1:20-21 which belongs to a broader context of II Peter 1:16-21 take a defensive stance. Then we need to consider the trend of thought between II Peter 1:16-19 and II Peter 1:20-21. If II Peter 1:20-21 is considered to take a defensive stance, Peter would not write II Peter 1:20-21 in thinking of the false prophets and their erroneous interpretation in mind. Rather Peter wrote II Peter 1:20-21 in thinking of the origin and evidence of the Scriptures in mind.

Three, Peter did not simply accept the interpretation of the traditional church and forbade personal interpretation by the believers. Of course, the Holy Spirit, not only guides the church to interpret the Scriptures properly, but also guides individuals to properly interpret

---

128) "He writes the same way in all his letters, speaking in them of these matters. His letters contain some things that are hard to understand, which ignorant and unstable people distort, as they do the other Scriptures, to their own destruction" (II Tim. 3:16, NIV).

the Scriptures. However, it is wrong to accept that this verse forbids the individual believer from interpreting the Bible. This would be creating a taboo that does not exist within the Scriptures.

The second view would understand the Scriptures as saying, "no prophecy of Scripture came about by the prophet's own interpretation."[129] This view keeps the origin of the Scriptures in mind. Peter is asserting that the scriptural prophecies are not simply the product of the authors' human interpretation but words given by the inspiration of God. Peter is referring to the divine origin of the Scriptures.[130] In II Peter 1:20, if Peter was discussing the topic of what the proper interpretation of an individual was, a logical explanation as to why II Peter 1:21 has been written would be difficult to determine. Moreover, the usage of the word *epilyseos* (ἐπιλύσεως) in the context supports the second view.

In Aquila's translation, Joseph used the term *epilysis* (ἐπίλυσις / ἐπιλυᾶν) when he interprets the dream of the wine official (Gen. 40:8).[131] According to the context, the fact that the interpretation of the dream is from God is evident. Hermas also uses *epilysis* to refer

---

129) "No prophecy of Scripture came about by the prophet's own interpretation" (NIV); " No prophecy was ever produced by the will of man" (ESV). This translation would require the text ἰδίας to be interpreted as "the prophet's own," which has a grammatical difficulty. In another words, the word "prophet" should be supplied for the interpretation which can cause problems. Simon J. Kistemaker (*Peter and Jude.* Grand Rapids: Baker, 1987,pp. 271-272), Michael Green (*2 Peter and Jude: Tyndale New Testament Commentaries.* Grand Rapids: Eerdmans, 1987, pp. 100-103), R.H. Strachan (*The Second Epistle General of Peter: The Expositor's Greek Testament,* Vol. V. Grand Rapids: Eerdmans, 1980, p. 132) and Richard J. Bauckham (*Jude, 2 Peter: Word Biblical Commentary,* Vol. 50. Waco: Word Books, 1983, pp. 230-235) are those scholars who support the second interpretation.

130) γίνεται (to come about) of II Peter 1:20 refers to its origin. However, he uses the term with οὐ in the context to indicate that the Scriptures are not merely the words of the prophets themselves. In addition, ἐπιλύσεως is the genitive of definition, not the genitive of origin. Therefore, the prophecies are not merely the product of the prophets themselves. Cf. Strachan, *op. cit.,* p.132.

131) Ardnt and Gingrich, *op. cit.,* p. 295.

to a God-given interpretation.[132] The prophets, first, received a vision (Amos 7:1; Jer. 1:11, 13) or a dream (Zechariah 1:8; Dan. 7:2) from God and then also received the interpretation. In Ezekiel 37:1-10, God gives Ezekiel a vision of the dry bones, and in Ezekiel 37:11-14, God Himself directly interprets the vision of the dry bones. God directly interprets the vision that Daniel received by the river Ulai (Dan. 8:15-27). Hence, a true prophecy encompasses God's direct interpretation and not the interpretation of the prophet himself.

Many scholars have attempted to translate as some other than the meaning "interpret." R. M. Spence translated it as "revelation,"or "revealment,"[133] E. R. Andry translated it as "prompting,"[134] F. Spitta interpreted as "dissolution,"[135] while J. Louw translated it as "inspiration" and "ecstasy."[136] George Smeaton rendered it as "excitation."[137] These attempts were made to insert the word within the context so that the meaning would be appeared in a natural way. If "*epilyseos*" (ἐπιλύσεως) has the meaning of "inspiration," the text would interpret as "all the prophecies of the Scriptures are not made by mere inspiration (ecstasy); prophecies were not given by humans alone but by those who were filled with the Holy Spirit who received the Word directly from God Himself" (II Peter 1:20, 21). This would fit the context well. If "*idias epilyseos*" is interpreted as "the interpretation of the prophet himself," the text would translate as "all the prophecies of the Scriptures did not come from the interpretations of the prophet

---

132) Hermas, *The Shepherd* (Parable 5.3:1, 2; 5.5:1; 5.6:8; 8.11:1; 9.11:9).

133) R. M. Spence, "Private Interpretation," *Expository Times* 8 (1896-1897), pp. 285-286.

134) E. R. Andry, *Journal of Biblical Literature,* 70 (1951), x vii.

135) See A. C. Thiselton, "Explain," *The New International Dictionary of New Testament Theology,* vol. 1 (Grand Rapids: Zondervan, 1975), p. 578. F. Spitta translated II Peter 1:20 as "No prophecy of Scripture is of such a kind that it can be annulled."

136) J. Louw, "Wat wordt in II Peter 1:20 gesteld," *Nederlands Theologische Tijdschrift,* 3 (1965), pp.202-212.

137) George Smeaton, *The Doctrine of the Holy Spirit* (Carlisle: The Banner of Truth Trust, 1974), p. 149.

himself; prophecies were not given by humans alone but by those who were filled with the Holy Spirit who received the Word directly from God Himself." This also fits within the context and ascertains a divine origin of the Scriptures.

Peter states that the Scriptures are not the result of human research, product of religious experiences, nor insight on spiritual matters. He adds that the Scriptures are not just a professional book of advice, admonishment and encouragement. If some of the content of the Scripture was written by the prophets without the inspiration of God, Peter states that it cannot be part of the Scriptures.[138] The Scriptures were not made by "human intention." Likewise, this text states what cannot be part of the Scriptures and describes the Scriptures as the Words which "[were given] by those who were filled with the Holy Spirit who received the Word directly from God Himself" (II Peter 1:21). By stating that the Scriptures were "written by people,"[139] the text does not exclude the role of the people in recording the Scriptures.

Then how is the Scripture different from other books? The text emphasizes that the Scriptures were not "mere interpretations of the human writers" but "were Words given by God directly."[140] Here, "Words given by God directly" were the Words that were written down by the Scriptural authors. In other words, the recorded Scriptures are the Words given directly by God (Eph. 3:3, 4). The text explicitly states that the origin of the Scriptures is God Himself. Peter clearly defines that fact that the Scripture does not derive from

---

138) L. Berkhof, *Principles of Biblical Interpretation* (Grand Rapids: Baker Book House, 1952), p. 45: "*It (The whole O.T.) is not of private interpretation, i.e. not the result of human investigation, nor the product of the writer's own thinking.*" Italics original.
139) ἐλάλησαν........ἄνθρωποι
140) ἀπὸ θεοῦ underlies that the words of the human writers are trustworthy in a particular way. It indicates the divine origin of the Scriptures.

humans but from God.

Thirdly, in what way did God reveal the Scriptures? The word "filled" within the text "being filled with the Holy Spirit" gives a clue as to the method of God's unveiling of the Scriptures. Peter uses *pheromenoi* (φερόμενοι) that has the meaning of "filled," "moved by," "were carried along" in a special way in this text. It is the only text in the New Testament that *pheromenoi* and the Holy Spirit appear together in the same context. Hence, it is clear that Peter used this word in this context for a special purpose. In order to understand the meaning of *pheromenoi* in this context, it is necessary to find another example where the same word *pheromenoi* is used in connection to the work of the Holy Spirit.

Luke portrays the descent of the Holy Spirit during Pentecost as "a sound of a strong rushing wind." From the phrase "strong rushing wind," (φερομένης πνοῆς βιαίας) the term "rushing" (φερομένης) is the same term as "filled" or "carried along" that Peter used. This illustrates the Holy Spirit as descending like "a strong rushing wind" to fill the disciples. The Holy Spirit was in complete control of the disciples. And Luke uses the same term (ἐφερομεθα) when describing the northeast wind, Euraquilo (hurricane force) that came upon the ship carrying Paul across the Mediterranean to Rome (Acts 27:14, 15). The New Revised Standard Version (NRSV) translation renders that "We gave way to it (northeaster) and were driven" (carried along by the wind). And New International Version (NIV) translates the verse, "So we gave way to it and were driven along." Luke wished to describe how the ship could not do much than to move as the wind blew. The ship had everything intact and everyone aboard but could not control its course or destination and had to follow the wind's course.

Generally, the work of the Holy Spirit can be seen through the lives of the believers. However, the meaning of the Holy Spirit's work in II Peter 1:21 goes beyond what can be seen in the lives of the believers.[141] The term "filled" (*pheromenoi*) indicates that the authors of the Scriptures are messengers of God. As a ship with sails move in the direction of the wind (See Acts 27:15, 17), the writers of the Scriptures are filled with the Holy Spirit and move in the direction of the Spirit's intentions. Therefore, what were written by human hands were the Words of the Holy Spirit, and that, in turn, became the Scriptures.[142]

Peter makes it clear to us that the Holy Spirit is the primary writer and that the human writers are the secondary writers of the Scriptures. Kistemaker explains, "The Holy Spirit employed men, not instruments, for the composition of Scripture. The Spirit used human beings with their talents and insights, their peculiarities and characteristics, keeping them from sin and error. The Holy Spirit is in control of man. Therefore, the text is clear on this point: in the writing of Scripture, man is passive and the Spirit active."[143] Smeaton says, "He (the Holy Spirit) so moved them that they could not but speak or write what the Spirit enjoined them to declare."[144] The Scriptures do not contain the words of human beings about God. Rather the Scriptures are God's Words that are revealed to human

---

141) Carl F. H. Henry. "Inspiration," *Baker's Dictionary of Theology* (Grand Rapids: Baker, 1960), p.287: "The word translated 'moved' is *phero* (literally, 'to bear along,' 'to carry'), and implies an activity more specific than mere guidance or direction."

142) Whether it be a dream, vision or ecstasy, the form in which the Holy Spirit sends a message to the human heart, Smeaton (George Smeaton, *The Doctrine of the Holy Spirit*, Carlisle: The Banner of Truth Trust, 1974, p. 150) indicates that we should not try to analyze it. He states two reasons for his argument. First of all, it is because we have never had such an experience that could be a model for comparison, and secondly, it is because our powers cannot function in deciphering the meaning of such messages. Cf. B. B. Warfield, *op. cit.,* p. 137.

143) Kistemaker, *op.cit.,* p. 273; Green, *op.cit.,* p. 103.

144) George Smeaton, *op.cit.,* p. 149.

beings concerning God's plan of salvation.

One thing to point out here is that, when the writers of the Scriptures are filled with the Holy Spirit, such a state is not maintained forever. The authors of the Scriptures recorded the contents through a special inspiration of the Holy Spirit. Yet, such an inspiration remained with them only while they were writing the Scriptures and not all the time. The inspiration of the Holy Spirit came upon the authors solely to achieve the goal of recording the Scriptures.

In summarizing the contents of II Timothy 3:16 and II Peter 1:20, 21, the Scriptures that we own today resulted from the activity of God's breathing out. Therefore, when A. J. Gordon says, "As the Lord breathed the Spirit into certain men, and thereby committed to them his own prerogative of forgiving sin, so he breathed his Spirit into certain books and endowed them with his infallibility in teaching truth,"[145] he is correct. In the same vein, he continues to say, "What Jesus said in justification of his doctrine of the new birth is equally applicable to the doctrine of inspiration: 'That which is born of the flesh is flesh, and that which is born of the Spirit is spirit' (John 3:6, AV)."[146] The Lord God used the authors of the Scriptures as His tools through the inspiration of the Holy Spirit and guided them to record what He wished to record. As a result, the recorded Scriptures are 100% divine and 100% human. The Scriptures that we hold in our hands are God's special revelation that is made particularly through God's wisdom.

---

145) A. J. Gordon, *The Ministry of the Spirit* (Grand Rapids: Baker, 1964), p. 168.
146) *Ibid.*, p. 169.

Chapter 7

The Role of the Holy Spirit in
Interpreting the Scriptures

Biblical interpretation is a new activity given to the New Testament church by the Holy Spirit. The Holy Spirit has equipped the New Testament church with the special ability to interpret the Bible. Thus, the churches in the New Covenant period must continuously engage in interpreting the Bible. Through the church's activity of Biblical interpretation, the Holy Spirit expands and strengthens Christ's church. Both the theological activities of the theologians and the preaching of pastors are results of Biblical interpretation. Here we will study the role of the Holy Spirit in Biblical interpretation from the redemptive-historical perspective.

1. The Holy Spirit and the Text

The most important aspect of Biblical interpretation is to understand how the original text of the Bible was recorded. The Bible was written by the inspiration of the Holy Spirit (II Tim 3:16, II Peter 1:19-21). Because the authors of the Bible were inspired by the Holy Spirit, the Bible contains not only what the human authors wanted to include but more importantly what the Holy Spirit chose to include.[147] Through a 100% guidance of the Holy Spirit, God used the authors to record what He wanted to include as the contents of the Bible. The Holy Spirit moved the human authors that they could not but write what the Spirit enjoined them to declare. "The prophetic Spirit imparted a supernatural illumination in virtue of which they understood fully what they were commissioned to announce, -- whether things past, present, or to come, -- beyond the range of the unaided human faculties."[148] Hence, the Bible is simultaneously the

---

147) Hyung Yong Park, *Biblical Hermeneutics* (Suwon: Hapdong Theological Seminary Press, 2002), pp. 102-117.

148) George Smeaton, *The Doctrine of the Holy Spirit* (Carlisle: The Banner of Truth Trust, 1974), p. 149

product of God and man. The Bible, unlike any other book, occupies a special place in the Church of Jesus Christ.

J. I. Packer states, "evangelicals stress that Scripture is a mystery in a sense parallel to that in which the incarnation is a mystery – that is, that the identifying of the human and the divine words in the one case, like the taking of manhood into God in the other, was a unique creative divine act of which we cannot fully grasp either the nature or the mode or the dynamic implications. Scripture is as genuinely and fully human as it is divine. It is more than Jewish-Christian religious literature, but not less, just as Jesus was more than a Jewish rabbi, but not less. There is a true analogy between the written Word and the incarnate Word. In both cases, the divine coincides with the form of the human, and the absolute appears in the form of the relative."[149]

It is our belief that each of the 66 books of the Bible is the inerrant word of God inspired by the Holy Spirit. Therefore, it is natural that the Bible records the activities of the Holy Spirit. Without the Holy Spirit, the authority of the Bible cannot be sustained, and without the Bible, one cannot understand the specific activities of the Holy Spirit. The close relationship between the Holy Spirit and the Bible is such that one cannot deal with one without involving the other.

2. The Holy Spirit and the Interpreter

A Biblical interpreter must be a born again Christian by the work of the Holy Spirit. An unbeliever will be incapable of interpreting the Bible correctly. This is because the central theme of the Bible, the sufferings of Christ on the cross and His resurrection thereafter,

---

149) J.I. Packer, "Biblical Authority, Hermeneutics, Inerrancy," *Jerusalem and Athens* (Philadelphia: The Presbyterian and Reformed Publishing Co., 1971), pp. 144-145.

cannot be comprehended with worldly wisdom. Only those who have been given God's wisdom through the Holy Spirit can understand the Bible. Simply stated, only the believers are capable of understanding the Bible. The knowledge of God cannot be attained by human endeavor. "All knowledge of God must be mediated to us by the Spirit, who searches the deep things of God and reveals them to believers."[150] Paul states, "But God has revealed it to us by his Spirit. The Spirit searches all things, even the deep things of God" (I Cor. 2:10, NIV) to say that only the Holy Spirit understands God's will. Thus, the first condition for interpreting the Bible is to believe in Christ and become a spiritual man (I Cor. 2:15). That is to say, when one becomes a Christian one can accept the Bible as God's word and from then may proceed to interpret it.

However, when the Holy Spirit and the interpreter are compared in their interpretive functions, one can see that the functions of both are in agreement in the context of Biblical interpretation. Jesus promised to send the Holy Spirit who would reveal what Jesus did and said. In John 14:26, Jesus says, "But the Counselor, the Holy Spirit, whom the Father will send in my name, will teach you all things and will remind you of everything I have said to you" (NIV). In John 16:13, Jesus says, "But when he, the Spirit of truth, comes, he will guide you into all truth. He will not speak on his own; he will speak only what he hears, and he will tell you what is yet to come" (NIV). According to these verses, the function of the Holy Spirit, according to Jesus, is to be a facilitator in understanding the contents of Jesus' teachings, in remembering the contents, in witnessing to the redemptive events, and in expounding upon the meaning of the contents. In other words, one vital element of the Holy Spirit's work

---

150) Michael Green, *I Believe in the Holy Spirit* (Grand Rapids: Eerdmans, 1977), p. 183.

is the interpretation of Christ's events and teachings.

The Holy Spirit's interpretive function, previously announced by Jesus, is identical to the function of the interpreter. An interpreter also expounds upon the meaning of the Bible in order to facilitate in its understanding. When an interpreter interprets, his ultimate interest should lie in analyzing and explaining the biblical events concerning Jesus Christ's death, resurrection and the Second Coming. This is where one discovers the similarity between the Holy Spirit's function and that of the interpreter's. In reality, the Holy Spirit carries out His interpretive function through the interpreter, and the interpreter could not function as a biblical interpreter without the Holy Spirit's guidance. Therefore, within the activity of biblical interpretation, the Holy Spirit and the interpreter are inseparably related to each other.

One can also see that the object of interpretation by the Holy Spirit and the interpreter coincides. The Holy Spirit only speaks what He hears from Jesus but never speaks on His own (John 16:13). That which the Holy Spirit heard from Jesus was what Jesus spoke about Himself (John 15:26, Luke 24:44). The Holy Spirit's function will be to rebuke about sin, to prove righteousness, and to announce judgment (John 16:8-11).[151] These verses indicate that the Holy Spirit's rebuke is effective due to Christ's death and resurrection. The Holy Spirit does not speak about abstract truth or speculative matters but about what He received from Jesus (John 16:14) and what was given to Jesus by God the Father (John 16:15). The Holy Spirit will focus on the death, resurrection, and the Second Coming of Jesus Christ, which are the culmination of God's revelation.[152]

---

151) The term "ἐλέγχω" used in John 16:8 literally means "to convict or convince someone of something or to point something out to someone." The Holy Spirit is responsible for explaining the redemptive events of Jesus Christ. Cf. Hyung Yong Park, *Biblical Hermeneutics* (Korean) (Suwon: Hapdong Theological Seminary Press, 2002), p. 154.
152) "The Spirit's ministry in this respect was not to bring qualitatively new revelation,

Then where are these redemptive events of Jesus recorded? These events were recorded in the Bible and passed down to us. Thus, the interpreter's interpretive interest is to clarify the meaning of these events. Through Biblical interpretation, the interpreter hopes to disclose the meaning of Jesus' redemptive events.

One can see that just as the Holy Spirit's interpretive interest lies in the redemptive, historical, and Christological perspective, the interpreter's ultimate interest also lies in the same redemptive, historical, and Christological perspective. In short, through the interpreter, the Holy Spirit carries out His interpretive function.

3. The New Testament Church equipped with a New Function of Interpretation

It is no exaggeration to say that the Christian church's history is the history of biblical interpretation. Then who equipped the Christian church with the ability to interpret the Bible? Was it a chance that the church received the ability to interpret the Bible, or is it attributable to God's wise and meticulous planning?

The Bible testifies that Jesus equipped the New Testament church with the new function of interpreting the Bible. This can be clarified by a comparative study of Jesus' interpretive function and the interpretive activity of the early Christian Church. Jesus promised to send the Holy Spirit, and He confirmed that when the Holy Spirit, another Counselor, came He will have the interpretive function (John 14:16, 26; 15:26; 16:7-14). Jesus demonstrated His interpretive function after His resurrection as the Life-giving Spirit (Luke 24:27;

---

but to complete, to fill out, the revelation brought by Jesus himself." See, D.A. Carson, *The Gospel According to John* (Grand Rapids: Eerdmans, 1991), p. 505.

I Cor. 15:45; II Dor. 3:17). The early Church was known to be involved in interpreting the redemptive events of Jesus Christ (Acts 8:29-39).

Jesus promises to send the Counselor, the Holy Spirit, after His death and resurrection by saying, "But I tell you the truth: It is for your good that I am going away. Unless I go away, the Counselor will not come to you; but if I go, I will send him to you" (John 16:7, NIV). Jesus also explains that when the Counselor comes, the Counselor will guide us in truth and will reveal the contents of the Bible (John 14:26, 16:13).

It is significant to note that Jesus foretells of the Holy Spirit's interpretive function after His departure and then follows the path of the cross to fulfill His redemption as planned by God. Jesus willingly walks through the path of the cross. After Peter's confession of faith in the region of Caesarea Philippi, Jesus "began to explain to his disciples that he must go to Jerusalem and suffer many things at the hands of the elders, chief priests and teachers of the law, and that he must be killed and on the third day be raised to life" (Matt. 16:21, NIV). At this time, Peter, who had previously professed his well-known confession of faith, rebukes Jesus, "Never, Lord! This shall never happen to you!" (Matt. 16:22, NIV). Hearing this, Jesus severely scolds Peter, "Get behind me, Satan! You are a stumbling block to me; you do not have in mind the things of God, but the things of men" (Matt 16:23, NIV). This exchange between Jesus and Peter is evidence that Jesus willingly accepted his path of the cross as God's plan, and thus, he cheerfully followed it though it was a painful and difficult one.

After His resurrection, Jesus interprets "all the Scriptures concerning Himself" for His two disciples on the road to Emmaus (Luke 24:27).[153] Jesus is testifying by using "all the Scriptures concerning Himself," that the entire Old Testament, in various ways, points to Himself (Acts 10:43). The disciples on the road to Emmaus were in a state of confusion because they doubted that after Jesus was persecuted and died, He rose again from the dead and reappeared to many people. Therefore, Jesus had to expound for the disciples on the road to Emmaus all the events concerning himself as it was written "in the Law of Moses, the Prophets and the Psalms" (cf. Luke 24:27; 24:44-48). It is notable that Jesus' interpretation focuses on the redemptive, historical, and Christological perspective.

Here, we can see that Jesus, after His resurrection, demonstrates His interpretive function and by doing so, He is demonstrating that His interpretive function is identical to that of the Holy Spirit's. He had announced, while He was on earth, that the Holy Spirit would exercise the interpretive function. And Jesus, as the Life-giving Spirit after the resurrection, demonstrated the same interpretive function. Thus, the Bible uses an expression that regards Jesus' function after His resurrection as being identical to the function of the Holy Spirit. The Bible says that not only are Christians to be justified by the Spirit of God (I Cor. 6:11) but Christians are also to be justified by faith in Jesus Christ (Gal 2:17). Also, concerning sanctification of the saints, the Bible clearly states that Christians have been sanctified by the Holy Spirit (Rom 15:16) or that Christians have been sanctified in Jesus Christ (I Cor. 1:2). Thus, Paul freely alternates between expressions such as "the Spirit living in you" (Rom. 8:9, 11) and "the Christ in you" (Rom. 8:10). After the resurrection Jesus personally exhibited His interpretive function by interpreting the Bible.

---

153) W. Hendriksen, *The Gospel of Luke* (*NTC*) (Grand Rapids: Baker, 1978), p. 1065. Hendriksen expounds that "there are four lines, which, running through the Old Testament from beginning to end, converge at Bethlehem and Calvary: the historical, typological, psychological, and prophetical." Cf. Gottlob Schrenk, "γράφω," *TDNT*, Vol. I, p. 752.

The New Testament Church was established after the Pentecost, where there was a special outpouring of the Holy Spirit. We must note at this juncture that not only do the apostles interpret Jesus' death and resurrection but Philip also interprets the Bible through the Holy Spirit's guidance (Acts 8:29-39). The Ethiopian eunuch had read Isaiah 53 but could not understand it. The Holy Spirit sent Philip to the scene who proceeded, with the Holy Spirit's guidance, to interpret the chapter for the Ethiopian eunuch by explaining that the passage refers to Jesus Christ. Philip's interpretation also indicates that it is focused on the redemptive, historical, and Christological events. This is evidence that after Jesus' death and resurrection, God equipped the New Testament Church with the ability to interpret the Bible as a part of the church's new function. The reason for this is because as a member of the Early Church, Philip interpreted the Bible with the Holy Spirit's guidance. Also, we must note that after Jesus' death and resurrection, the Holy Spirit continued to exercise His interpretive function for the Church.

It is a real blessing for the New Testament Church to be equipped with the interpretive function of the Bible. When the church is challenged by an ambiguous theological stance or by untruths, it has an appointed task to undauntedly protect the truth through its interpretive function. This is because the church's interpretive function of the Bible was given by Jesus Christ, the head of the Church, and by the Holy Spirit, who is also the guide for the Church. God the Holy Spirit, through the church's interpretive function, strengthens the church, always challenges the church's purity, and guides the church to be faithful to Christ. The Holy Spirit, in His sovereignty, leads the church to maintain its integrity in the matter of biblical interpretation. The church's activity involving biblical interpretation organically continues toward completion.

Here, we will summarize the main points of the role of the Holy Spirit in biblical interpretation.

First, biblical interpretation must be centered on the Bible. The reason for this is that since the Bible was written by the Holy Spirit's inspiration, the Bible presents the Holy Spirit's activities and the Holy Spirit speaks through the text of the Bible.

Secondly, the Holy Spirit's interpretive function is ultimately manifested by the interpreter's actual interpretation of the Bible. Accordingly, an interpreter cannot interpret the Bible without the Holy Spirit's help. This teaches us that the interpreter must always rely on the Holy Spirit and humbly carry out the duties of biblical interpretation.

Thirdly, it is a real blessing for the New Testament Church to be equipped with the interpretive function of the Bible. God's people of the Old Testament times were not blessed with this interpretive function. Only the New Testament Church that began on the Pentecost received this special blessing. Accordingly, we must realize that Jesus Christ equipped the New Testament Church with this interpretive function as a part of the newly given order to the church. The church should make the utmost effort to properly exercise this new ability so that the church, which is the body of Christ, attains "to the unity of the faith and of the knowledge of the Son of God, to mature manhood, to the measure of the stature of the fullness of Christ" (Eph 4:13, ESV).

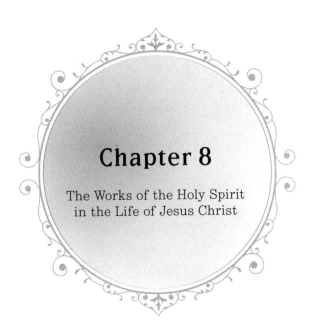

Chapter 8

The Works of the Holy Spirit
in the Life of Jesus Christ

Christ and the Holy Spirit are inseparably related to each other. When we ponder the relationship between Christ and the Holy Spirit, we are reminded of the relationship between the second and third person in the Trinity. But we are not attempting to investigate this relationship from an ontological perspective. Rather, the study lies in illuminating Christ's relationship with the Holy Spirit following the progress of His life on Earth and identifying its significance.

Let's begin with the fact that the Gospels do not contain as many accounts of people filled with the Holy Spirit compared to, say, the Book of Acts and Paul's Letters. One can argue that this discrepancy can be attributed to the Holy Spirit's dynamic activity after the Pentecost. But in reality, the Gospels were also written after the epochal Pentecost (Acts 2:1-4). Therefore, there is a possibility that the authors of the Gospels recorded the Holy Spirit's activity as if they had heard Jesus speak about it. Confusion may arise because of the time lapse between the actual event and the recording. On further consideration, because they had to resolve complicated issues of their time, such as that of circumcision, the relationship between law and grace, and of receiving the Holy Spirit, the disciples could have written the Gospels as a solution manual to these challenges, much as if Jesus had provided them for that purpose. However, the disciples were not swayed by either of these possibilities when writing the Gospels.

1. Why the Gospels lack more accounts of people filled with the Holy Spirit?

The authors of the Gospels recorded exactly what they heard and observed. Using the materials at hand and with the inspiration and guidance of the Holy Spirit, they faithfully recorded the Gospels. If this was the case, why is there so little written about those people who were filled with the Holy Spirit in the Gospels? The answer to this question can be addressed in three parts.

First, the reason why the Gospels lack more accounts of people filled with the Holy Spirit is because during Jesus' public ministry, with the exception of Jesus, the Holy Spirit did not often work through others.[154] This fact is proof that the Gospels we presently possess are the exact and truthful accounts of biblical history. The authors of the Gospels did not record the events that took place after the Pentecost as if they had occurred during Jesus' life on earth, but instead, accurately reported them as they happened. Thus, the lack of documentation of more people filled with the Holy Spirit increases the reliability of the Gospels.

Second, the lack of more testimonies of people filled with the Spirit clearly manifests the significance of the Pentecost. After the Pentecost, the Holy Spirit actively works through many people. However, the Holy Spirit is not observed to work in the same, active way in the Gospels, as in the Book of Acts. The reason for this is because under God's plan, the Holy Spirit's activity was to be directly connected to Jesus' crucifixion and especially His resurrection. Consequently, the lack of more accounts of the Spirit's activity in the Gospels has the effect of increasing the significance of the Pentecost.

Third, the Gospels lack more accounts of people filled with the

---

154) The Gospels record that only a few people were filled with the Holy Spirit before the birth of Jesus Christ. John the Baptist was "filled with the Holy Spirit from birth" (Luke 1:15), Elizabeth "was filled with the Holy Spirit" (Luke 1:41), and John the Baptist's father, Zechariah "was filled with the Holy Spirit" (Luke 1:67) also. Furthermore, Simon was "moved by the Spirit" (Luke 2:27) and instructed by Him. Therefore, the activities of the Holy Spirit in history is as follows: only a few were filled with the Spirit before the birth of Jesus, then the Spirit's activity was concentrated on Jesus during His lifetime, and finally after the Pentecost, many more were filled with the Spirit (i.e., Peter, Acts 4:8; believers, Acts 4:31; Stephen, Acts 6:5, 10; 7:55). This highlights the meaning of the progress of redemptive history.

Holy Spirit because He mainly dwelled within Jesus Christ during His lifetime. Hence, rather than directly working in the lives of the believers, the Holy Spirit worked through Jesus' ministry in the Gospels. The Holy Spirit who was promised to the people of God on the Last Day depended on the completion of the Messiah's appointed task. The Messiah must be crucified to cleanse us of our sins and rise again from the dead before the Spirit who dwelt within Jesus could be released to guide the disciples (Luke 24:49; Acts 1:4-5). Therefore, the lack of more accounts of people filled with the Holy Spirit in the Gospels can be attributed to the Spirit's fidelity to Jesus Christ during His lifetime.

2. The Holy Spirit and the Announcement of Jesus' Birth

Paul says, "But when the fullness of time had come, God sent forth his Son, born of woman, born under the law, to redeem those who were under the law, so that we might receive adoption as sons" (Gal. 4:4-5, ESV). Paul is explaining when and how Jesus the Son of God was incarnated. This is a fulfillment of God's promise. God's messenger, Gabriel, relates to Mary that, "The Holy Spirit will come upon you, and the power of the Most High will overshadow you; therefore the child to be born will be called holy – the Son of God" (Luke 1:35, ESV; cf. Matt. 1:18-21). The birth narratives of Jesus provide hints of the significance of the Spirit's role in the incarnation.

With these words, God promised ahead of time, the birth of Jesus that the holy one will be born when the time was right. John the Baptist's father, Zechariah's prophecy (Luke 1:67-69) concerns the Messiah's birth and therefore has a great significance. Zechariah begins his prophecy with a song, very much "filled with the Holy Spirit" (Luke 1:67). "The praise of God can also be inspired by the

Spirit (cf. I Cor. 14:26). What we have here is initially a psalm of praise giving a divinely inspired commentary on the significance of the events which have begun to take place."[155] Zechariah's Spirit-inspired psalm clearly delineates two aspects.

The first aspect is that the Messiah came as the horn of salvation in the house of David to save His chosen people, just as the holy prophets foretold of Jesus' coming (Luke 1:67-75; cf. Rom. 1:3). Through Zechariah, the Holy Spirit plainly discloses who Jesus Christ is and what He will do as the Messiah.

The second aspect concerns the relationship between Jesus Christ, the Messiah, and Zechariah's son, John the Baptist. Zechariah understood that the Holy Spirit promised him a child because he was childless in his old age. But he also understood that the child's main purpose in life was to prepare the way for a much greater and holy One; he was to be "a prophet of the Most High" (Luke 1:76). The Holy Spirit clearly defines the relationship between the presently unborn Jesus and John the Baptist, through Zechariah's psalm.

3. The Holy Spirit and the Birth of Jesus

The special role that the Holy Spirit plays, concerning the birth of Jesus, is observable in the fact that He was born of a virgin. From the conception of Jesus until His birth, the Holy Spirit's activity is visible. At that time, Mary and Joseph were engaged to each other. Even before they lived together, the Holy Spirit brought about the conception of Jesus in Mary (Matt. 1:18). And through Mary's conversation with Elizabeth, the Holy Spirit confirmed that Mary's child was truly God's Son (Luke 1:39-45). It should be noted that the

---

155) I. Howard Marshall, *Commentary on Luke* (*NIGTC*) (Grand Rapids: Eerdmans, 1978), p. 90.

Holy Spirit led Joseph and Mary in Nazareth to travel to Bethlehem so that the Messiah would be born in the town that He was prophesied to be born (Micah 5:2; Luke 2:1-20).

Therefore, the birth of Jesus was inseparably related to the special guidance of the Holy Spirit. When Joseph discovered that Mary was pregnant, he decided to divorce her quietly. However, an angel intervened and persuaded Joseph to stay with her; the angel told him, "Joseph son of David, do not be afraid to take Mary home as your wife, because what is conceived in her is from the Holy Spirit" (Matt. 1:20, NIV). The angel's words inform us that Mary's unbelievable conception of Jesus is indeed under God's supervision.[156] Therefore, all these evidences leave no room to doubt that Jesus' identity as God's Son is confirmed from His birth. Unlike Christians who join God's family as His children through adoption (John 1:12), Jesus was God's Son in nature from birth. As a result, we find that Jesus calls God "Abba Father" (Mk. 14:36), a title that indicates the most intimate relationship between a father and son. There is no indication of any other person calling God by such an intimate title as "Abba Father" before Jesus. Only Jesus had the privilege of using this title as God's very own Son because He was set apart by the Holy Spirit as God's Son beginning from Mary's conception.

The work of the Spirit in the conception of Jesus "preserves both the reality of his union with us in genuine human nature, and his freedom from the guilt and curse of Adam's fall (Rom. 5:12-21). Since his person is not of Adamic stock, he does not share in the

---

156) Hyung Yong Park, *An Exposition of the Four Gospels* (I) (Korean) (Suwon: Hapdong Theological Seminary Press, 1994), p. 73. Joseph's act of accepting Mary as his wife served two roles. First, it preserved Mary's honour. Second, it served to hide God's honour. The reason for the latter was because Jesus, as God, was brought up as if He was Joseph's son. Even from the beginning of the redemptive event, God's infinite wisdom in His planning is evident.

guilt and condemnation of Adam (Rom. 5:12-14). Since he assumed human nature through the Spirit who sanctified this union from the moment of his conception, he was one of us and was capable of bearing others' guilt as one who was not personally liable for it."[157] Jesus Christ is God and man from His conception.

4. The Holy Spirit and Jesus' Baptism

Jesus' baptism by John the Baptist was an important turning point in His life because His baptism initiated His public ministry (Matt. 3:13-17; Mk. 1:9-11; Luke 3:21-22). Jesus was not baptized by John the Baptist because He had any sins of which He had to repent or because He needed to practice the cleansing ritual. Jesus did not have to repent because He was God's Son, perfect and pure. Jesus explains why He received John the Baptist's baptism by saying that "Let it be so now; it is proper for us to do this to fulfill all righteousness" (Matt. 3:15, NIV). Nonetheless, the significance of Jesus' baptism can be further elucidated with several points.

First, through His baptism, Jesus identified Himself with the believers. In essence, God/Man manifested a humility by placing Himself as an equal to His people. It was necessary to make Himself equal to human beings in all areas because Jesus came in human form to solve the problem of human sin. Therefore, His baptism was one step in the direction of equalizing Himself with His people so that He could properly perform His role as the Savior.[158]

---

157) Sinclair B. Ferguson, *The Holy Spirit: Contours of Christian Theology* (Downers Grove: IVP, 1996), p. 42.

158) G. Vos, *Biblical Theology* (Grand Rapids: Eerdmans, 1948), p. 344: Here, Vos states that, "for if Jesus bore sin vicariously, and received forgiveness vicariously, then there can be no objection on principle to saying that He repented for the people vicariously" to explain the profound significance of Jesus' baptism.

Second, Jesus was publicly manifested as the Messiah by receiving John the Baptist's baptism. Before He was baptized, Jesus was a Messiah hidden in His private life. But His baptism officially announced to the whole world that He, Jesus, is the Messiah. God's voice from heaven, "This is My Son, whom I love; with Him I am well pleased" (Matt. 3:17, NIV; cf. Luke 3:22) is the confirmation that Jesus is the Messiah. The voice from heaven combines the words from Psalm 2:7 and Isaiah 42:1. Psalm 2:7 refers to a king's coronation ceremony, whereas, the words of Isaiah 42:1 prophesy the coming of the Servant-Messiah. The words of the voice from heaven indicate that Jesus is a "servant-king," and testifies to the kind of life that Jesus will lead, for Jesus' life was to be a life of service. In short, Jesus, the manifested Messiah, is a "servant-king" (Matt. 12:15-21). In a way, Jesus' baptism foreshadows His death on the cross.[159]

Third, from His baptism by John the Baptist as the starting point, Jesus is commissioned to the work of the kingdom of God and empowered by the Holy Spirit to fulfill His task. Why did Jesus, who is wholly God as well as Man, require the Holy Spirit's powers? To properly understand the answer concerning this question, we must remember the fact that Jesus, who is God, came in the body of man to solve the problem of sin. If Jesus had dwelt on earth as God only, He would not have needed the power of the Holy Spirit. However, because He came as a perfect man, He needs to be empowered by the Holy Spirit. During His lifetime on earth, which lasted 33 years, Jesus did not exhibit His powers as God but rather led a life similar to ours. Therefore, with the power of the Holy Spirit, Jesus began the work of the kingdom and continued it with the power of the Holy Spirit.

---

159) Chester K. Lehman, *Biblical Theology, Vol. 2, New Testament* (Scottdale: Herald Press, 1974), p. 95.

Jesus' baptism by John the Baptist is significant because of God the Father's commissioning of Jesus Christ for the work of His kingdom, God the Son's dedication for Messianic work, and the establishment and progress of the kingdom of God by God the Holy Spirit's power. The Trinity was actively involved in the first creation (Gen. 1:26); likewise, the Triune God's presence and involvement is attested to in the establishment of God's eschatological Kingdom.

And, one of the important reasons for the Holy Spirit's presence with Jesus during His baptism was that, in accordance with John the Baptist's prophecy, Jesus, in turn, could baptize others in the name of the Holy Spirit (Luke 3:16). Jesus will fulfill the redemption and will pour out the Holy Spirit's baptism of blessing on those who call out His name (Luke 12:49-53; cf. Acts 1:5, 2:14-21). This indicates that Jesus' ministry, which began with John the Baptist's baptism, began not only through the Holy Spirit but was also a ministry controlled by the Holy Spirit.

5. The Holy Spirit and Jesus' Ministry

When we examine Jesus' public ministry in several areas, it becomes evident that the ministry was carried out through the Holy Spirit.

First, we can know that Jesus' announcement of the Gospel of the Kingdom is attributed to the Holy Spirit. Luke tells us that Jesus' ministry began in the synagogue of Nazareth (Luke 4:16-21). At that time, Jesus read the book of Isaiah and said, "The Spirit of the Lord is on me," (Luke 4:18) and also said, "Today this scripture is fulfilled in your hearing" (Luke 4:21, NIV). This fact that Jesus brings the Gospel to the poor and proclaims the year of the Lord's favor supports the fact that everything is accomplished through the Holy

Spirit's activity.

Second, Jesus exorcised the demons from people through the Holy Spirit. It is of great significance that Jesus drove away demons. It has great significance because the order of the first creation, which was corrupted by Satan, was restored by Jesus, the second Adam. Jesus said, "But if I drive out demons by the Spirit of God, then the kingdom of God has come upon you" (Matt. 12:28, NIV). Luke uses "the finger of God" (Luke 11:20) instead of "the Spirit of God." Scholars believe that "the Spirit of God" is closer to the original text than "the finger of God." But apparently Luke used "the finger of God" instead of "the Spirit of God" to emphasize God's direct intervention.[160]

The fact that Jesus exorcised the demons is evidence of the destruction of Satan's kingdom and the commencement of God's kingdom. The kingdom of God appearing in the world with the coming of Jesus Christ, signifies none other than the accomplishment of the prophecy (Matt. 11:13; Luke 16:16), the binding of Satan (Matt. 12:28), the wonderful and all-inclusive salvation (Matt. 11:5; Luke 4:18, 19), the Son of Man's authority and power (Mk. 2:10), and the blessedness of the poor in spirit.(Matt. 5:3).[161] God's kingdom is expanded and preserved by the power of the Holy Spirit. "For the kingdom of God is not a matter of eating and drinking, but of righteousness, peace and joy in the Holy Spirit" (Rom 14:17, NIV).

Third, the miracles performed by Jesus, as symbols of redemption, are more than just instructional character. Jesus' miracles are a reality of salvation in themselves and a realization of God's

---

160) J. Jeremias, *New Testament Theology: The Proclamation of Jesus* (New York: Charles Scribner's Sons, 1971), p. 79.

161) H. Ridderbos, *The Coming of the Kingdom* (Philadelphia: The Presbyterian and Reformed Publ. Co., 1962), pp. 105-106.

kingdom. When we read about the healing of the sick, it is recorded that Satan is the cause of the physical illnesses (Matt. 12:22). This does not mean that Satan causes all illnesses. Illnesses are a direct consequence of the disruption of the order of the first creation. And Satan is responsible for this disruption. Therefore, Satan is depicted as the cause of all sicknesses (Luke 13:16). Thus, when Jesus healed these illnesses, He healed with the power of the Holy Spirit. From this, we can see that every area of Jesus' ministry was carried out by the Holy Spirit.

6. The Holy Spirit and Jesus' Resurrection

The Gospels simply recount Jesus' resurrection. However, a sufficient account of the Holy Spirit's role in Jesus' resurrection can be found in the Pauline epistles. The Holy Spirit is God's primary instrument in the resurrection of Jesus Christ and the resurrection of the believers. The idea found in Paul's Letters and in Acts does not demonstrate that Jesus resurrected by Himself but rather that God raised Jesus from the dead (Acts 4:10, 5:30; Rom. 10:9; I Cor. 15:15). God the Father is the author of the resurrection, and Jesus is the passive object of the resurrection. In addition, when God raised Jesus from the dead, He used the Holy Spirit as an instrument. "And if the Spirit (*Pneuma*) of Him who raised Jesus from the dead is living in you, He who raised Christ from the dead will also give life to your mortal bodies through His Spirit, who lives in you" (Rom. 8:11, NIV).

These words are a promise with a great significance that reveals that just as God raised Jesus from the dead through the Holy Spirit, He will bring about the resurrection of the believers through the Holy Spirit as well (I Cor. 3:16-17, 6:19). It is significant to note that the

Spirit that God the Father used for the resurrection of Jesus Christ is one and the same as the one used in the resurrection of the believers. And the fact that the same Spirit dwells within the believers today is reassurance of their resurrection. The great drama of the resurrection is in the hands of God the Father. God used the Holy Spirit as an instrument to resurrect Jesus; in the same way, the Holy Spirit that dwells within the believers will be used to bring each believer back to life. In other words, the event that occurred with the firstfruits (I Cor. 15:20) will be replayed with the rest of the fruits.[162] The Spirit that dwells within the believers acts as a bridge that ties their present life and future eternal life. In truth, those who have faith in Jesus Christ are living even today in the resurrection-life. Thus, in the Gospels, the Holy Spirit's role is unclear in the resurrection of Jesus Christ, but we can clearly see the Holy Spirit's role in the resurrection of Jesus in the Pauline epistles.

7. The Holy Spirit and the Life-giving Spirit

Through His resurrection, Jesus became the Life-giving Spirit (I Cor. 15:45).[163] Therefore, the apostle Paul said, "the Lord is the Spirit" (II Cor. 3:17), identifying Jesus Christ with the Holy Spirit. Paul did not deny the doctrine of the Trinity here. The fact that the apostle Paul identified Jesus with the Spirit is not from the ontological

---

162) G. Vos, *The Pauline Eschatology* (Grand Rapids: Eerdmans, 1961), pp. 163-164: Because of the reality of the intimacy of the union of the believers and the resurrected Jesus, Paul could express that the two are one in spirit (*hen pneuma*) (I Cor. 6:17).

163) The following scholars believe that Jesus became the Life-giving Spirit at His Resurrection: D.M. Stanley, *Christ's Resurrection in Pauline Soteriology* (Romae: E Pontifico Instituto Biblico, 1961), p. 124; J.A. Schep, *The Nature of the Resurrection Body* (Grand Rapids: Eerdmans, 1964), p. 176; J.D.G. Dunn, *Jesus and the Spirit* (London: SCM Press, 1975), p. 322; E. Schweizer, "πνεῦμα, πνευματικός," *Theological Dictionary of the New Testament*, Vol. VI, pp. 419-420.

perspective but shows that the role of the Spirit and Jesus' role after His resurrection are very similar in the experiences of the believers.

Due to the resurrection, Jesus transformed to become a spiritual body (I Cor. 15:44). The spiritual body is suitable to the spiritual world. The activities of Jesus with a spiritual body and the Holy Spirit are similar. This is all because Jesus was resurrected through the Holy Spirit. The contents of Jesus' words after His resurrection, "All authority in heaven and on earth has been given to me. Therefore go and make disciples of all nations, baptizing them in the name of the Father and of the Son and of the Holy Spirit, and teaching them to obey everything I have commanded you. And surely I will be with you always, to the very end of the age" (Matt. 28:18-20, NIV) must be understood from the redemptive-historical perspective, that Jesus became the "Life-giving Spirit." Had Jesus not become the "Life-giving Spirit," He could not have been with His people always.

Here, we have examined the relationship between the Holy Spirit and Jesus Christ from the time when Jesus was conceived until His exaltation. No part of Jesus' life existed without the presence of the Spirit. Jesus' life was lived through the Holy Spirit and with the Holy Spirit. The Holy Spirit was always with Jesus, from His virgin birth, growth in His childhood, private life, public ministry, His death and resurrection, and even until His exaltation.

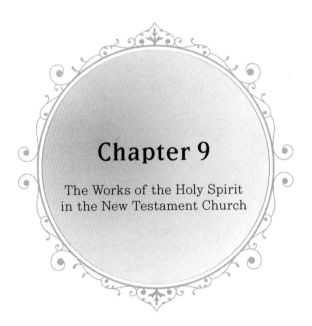

Chapter 9

The Works of the Holy Spirit
in the New Testament Church

The redemptive events of Jesus Christ are of an eschatological order. That is, the birth of Jesus is an eschatological event, and the death and resurrection of Jesus is an eschatological event as well. Furthermore the coming of the Holy Spirit on the Pentecost and the establishment of the New Testament Church are the eschatological events, also.

The New Testament Church as a community of faith is responsible for preaching to the end of the earth the message of salvation which is accomplished in the death and resurrection of Jesus Christ. Thus, the proclamation of the Gospel of salvation by the New Testament Church is an eschatological event. All the redemptive events which were accomplished in the first Coming of Jesus Christ are eschatological events. So it is only appropriate to deal with the relationship between the Holy Spirit and the New Testament Church from an eschatological perspective.

1. Jesus' Consciousness toward the Pentecost

It is well attested that the four Gospels and the Acts show that Jesus is consciously moving toward the Pentecost in His ministry. Jesus affirmed that His disciples will understand His suffering on the cross and the resurrection after the Coming of the Holy Spirit at Pentecost. "But I tell you the truth: It is for your good that I am going away. Unless I go away, the Counselor will not come to you; but if I go, I will send him to you. When he comes, he will convict the world of guilt in regard to sin and righteousness and judgment" (John 16:7-8, NIV).[164] "Going away," or "departure" here means the

---

164) What Jesus is saying in this passage does not mean that Jesus and the Spirit cannot simultaneously minister to God's people. Rather, the thought is eschatological. The saving reign of God cannot be fully inaugurated until the death, resurrection, and glorification of

death of Jesus Christ and "the promise of the Comforter" makes the disciples look forward to the Pentecost (John 14:16; 15:26; 16:13). When Jesus says that "It is for your good that I am going away," He means that He is returning to where He has come from. "This return does not mean the end of his work on earth but rather a new beginning that will by the sending of the Spirit bring Jesus' work to full manifestation. It is not enough to say that the disciples will fully understand the true identity of Jesus only through the internal presence of the Spirit."[165] At the time the disciples heard these words of Jesus' departure, they could not understand what he meant. But Jesus, facing His death, was looking forward to the special activity of the Holy Spirit on the Pentecost that will be beneficial to the disciples. When Jesus lived in the state of Incarnation, He was unable to be omnipresent, but when He died and rose again from the dead, He was to be omnipresent as the Life-giving Spirit (I Cor. 15:45). And the disciples did not have to depend on the visible and physical presence of Jesus any more. Furthermore, the Holy Spirit would not come at the Pentecost when the incarnate Jesus was still alive. John says, "Up to that time the Spirit had not been given, since Jesus had not yet been glorified" (John 7:39, NIV). Jesus, facing His death, says to His disciples that His death will be beneficial to them.[166]

Jesus Christ. Cf. D.A. Carson, *The Gospel According to John* (Grand Rapids: Eerdmans, 1991), pp. 533-534; Herman Ridderbos, *The Gospel of John: A Theological Commentary* (Grand Rapids: Eerdmans, 1997), pp. 530-531.

165) Herman Ridderbos, *The Gospel of John: A Theological Commentary,* p. 530. The phrase συμφέρει ὑμῖν ("it is better for you") was uttered by the high priest Caiaphas as the Jews plot to kill Jesus (John 11:50). God is using the actions of an evil man to fulfill His purpose. Caiaphas in his evil intention was saying that the Crucifixion of Jesus will be beneficial to the people, but in reality the death of Jesus was beneficial to the believers. The usage of "it is better for you" in John 11:50 and John 16:7-8 reveals that His departure means His death.

166) Leon Morris, *Commentary on the Gospel of John* (Grand Rapids: Eerdmans, 1971), pp. 696-697.

After the resurrection, Jesus explains the events of the Pentecost more clearly. The disciples should not leave Jerusalem until they receive the power from above. "I am going to send you what my Father has promised; but stay in the city until you have been clothed with power from on high" (Luke 24:49, NIV). It is evident that the consciousness of Jesus was revealed as looking forward to the Pentecost.

Then what was the reason why Jesus, facing His death, was looking forward to the Pentecost beyond His death? And why did Jesus say that the disciples should not leave Jerusalem until they received the power of the Spirit? The answer lies in the uniqueness of the Holy Spirit coming upon the disciples at the Pentecost, and during this unique time that the Spirit is given, the New Testament Church will be established.

2. The New Testament Church established on the Pentecost

The birth of the New Testament Church goes back to the Pentecost. On the day of the Pentecost, people who repented, hearing the gospel proclaimed by the Apostle Peter, were numbered three thousands (Acts 2:41). This gathering of the believers is the beginning of the New Testament Church.

It should be noted that Jesus began His public ministry with a view to the establishment of the New Testament Church on the Pentecost. This can be seen particularly in the intention of Jesus when He began to select His disciples. When we read John 1:40-42, we notice that Jesus met Peter by introduction of Andrews. When Jesus first saw Peter, He says to Peter, "You are Simon son of John. You will be called Cephas (which, when translated, is Peter)" (John 1:42, NIV). Jesus says these words during the beginning stages of His public ministry. He is announcing in the early part of His public ministry that the son of John will become Peter (stone). What was the reason why Jesus could not say at that time, "You are Peter" in the present tense? It is because "becoming Peter (stone)" has a fundamental relationship with the establishment of the New Testament Church which is constituted with people who confess Jesus as their Lord and the Son of God. When Peter met Jesus for the first time, he could not confess Jesus the Son of God. So, when Jesus saw Peter by introduction of Andrews, Jesus, using the future tense, said to him, "You will be called Cephas" (John 1:42).

Let us examine the conversation between Jesus and Peter during the latter part of Jesus' ministry. During His earthly ministry, Jesus taught His disciples directly or indirectly concerning who He is. When Jesus was anticipating the Cross in the near future, He went to the region of Caesarea Philippi with his disciples. There, He asked them two questions. The first question was, "Who do people say the Son of Man is?" (Matt. 16:13, NIV) and the second question was, "Who do you say I am?" (Matt. 16:15, NIV).

Concerning the first question, the disciples' answer was not satisfactory to Jesus. But, regarding the second question, Peter, representing the other disciples, answers Jesus with his famous confession of faith, "You are the Christ, the Son of the living God" (Matt. 16:16, NIV). Upon hearing his confession of faith, Jesus was very pleased. So, Jesus responded to Peter, "Blessed are you, Simon son of Jonah, for this was not revealed to you by man, but by my Father in heaven. And I tell you that you are Peter, and on this rock I will build my church, and the gates of Hades will not overcome it" (Matt. 16:17-18, NIV).[167]

---

167) Attempts have been tried to solely connect the establishment of the New Testament Church with Peter's confession. This is based on the Greek grammar that the person Peter

Here we note the change from what Jesus said to Peter in the early part of His ministry to what He said to Peter after Peter's confession at Caesarea Philippi. The change was from "You will be called Cephas" (John 1:42) to "You are Peter" (Matt. 16:18). The change was from the future tense to the present tense. What makes this change happen? This change is due to the process of redemptive activities of Jesus Christ. The saying of "You are Peter" was not a possibility during the early part of Jesus' ministry when Peter could not confess Jesus as Lord and the Son of God (John 1:41-42), but when Peter eventually was able to confess Jesus as the Lord and the Son of God, the present tense declaration was a possibility (Matt. 16:16-19).

Now we need to notice the timing of the establishment of the New Testament Church. At Caesarea Philippi, Jesus said to Peter, "You are Peter" using the present tense, but He did not say that I am now establishing the Church on this rock. Instead, Jesus said, "on this rock I will build my church," using the future tense. Why was Jesus not able to say, "I am building my church"? It was because the redemptive events of the death and resurrection of Jesus remain in the future when He said these words. It was not possible and not in the plan of God to establish the New Testament Church which is responsible for proclaiming the gospel of redemption prior to the accomplishment of redemptive events. When the New Testament Church was established prior to the death and resurrection of Jesus Christ, the Church has no message to proclaim at that moment in

---

(*Petros*) is a masculine noun, but stone (*petra*) is feminine. However, it is appropriate to consider the Apostle Peter who confessed Jesus the Lord and the Son of God as the foundation or the stone on which the Church was to be established. It is not right to disconnect the Apostle Peter from his confession. Cf. Hyung Yong Park, *An Exposition of the Four Gospels, II* (Korean) (Suwon: Hapdong Theological Seminary Press, 1994), pp. 95-96; Edmund P. Clowney, *The Church* (Downers Grove: IVP, 1995), pp. 39-41.

redemptive history. These words of Jesus in the future tense implied that He thought of the Pentecost as the time of establishment of the New Testament Church.

Here we note the interrelationship of the death and resurrection of Jesus, the outpouring of the Holy Spirit on the Pentecost, and the establishment of the New Testament Church. When Jesus said, "I am going to send you what my Father has promised; but stay in the city until you have been clothed with power from on high" (Luke 24:49, NIV), He was testifying the closeness between the Pentecost and the establishment of the Church. The Pentecost was the event which the Holy Spirit outpoured with power on the Church. Thus, the New Testament Church was a redemptive community which was established on the basis of the redemptive events of Jesus Christ.

3. Redemptive Community established only by the Holy Spirit

There are many different kinds of community in the world. Outwardly, the Church looks the same as other communities, but in its characteristics it is a quite different community. For one, all other communities are constituted with human efforts, but the Church can only be constituted by the Holy Spirit. The Scriptures emphasize this fact clearly (I Cor. 12:13; Eph. 4:4). "For we were all baptized by one Spirit into one body -- whether Jews or Greeks, slave or free -- and we were all given the one Spirit to drink" (I Cor. 12:13, NIV). The phrase, "We were all baptized by one Spirit into one body," can be read in the context as "we were all baptized in one Spirit into one body."[168]

---

168) I Cor. 12:13 refers to the fact that all Christians have a common experience of the Holy Spirit in Christ. This verse supports not only the unity of Christian community but also "the baptism of the Holy Spirit" as all the believers' first experience of the Spirit. Cf.

The Holy Spirit separates believers from non-believers (I Cor. 2:10-14). The Holy Spirit initiates the beginning of the Christian life (Gal. 3:2-3). Paul says, "Are you so foolish? Having begun by the Spirit, are you now being perfected by the flesh?" (Gal. 3:3, ESV). Furthermore, the Holy Spirit makes one to become the child of God (Rom. 8:14-17). It is absolutely necessary for non-believers to be aided by the Spirit to enter into the community of faith. If one wants to be saved and to be a member of the community of faith, he should confess, "Jesus is Lord," and believe in his heart that God raised Jesus from the dead (Rom. 10:9-10).

Who, then, has given the faith with which the believer confesses, "Jesus is Lord," and believes in the death and resurrection of Jesus Christ? The Scripture clearly testifies that our faith is not from us, but from God. "For it is by grace you have been saved, through faith—and this not from yourselves, it is the gift of God" (Eph. 2:8). It is only by the Holy Spirit that people are able to confess, "Jesus is Lord." When we believe in Jesus, the Spirit begins to abide in us (Rom. 8:9-10), and for that reason, the believer is called "the temple of God" (I Cor. 3:16; 6:19).

The Spirit creates in the believer the personality of Jesus Christ. Christ enters into the life of the believer by the Spirit. The New Testament Church is the community of God's children who confess, "Jesus is Lord." Therefore, the Church is the redeemed community constituted only by the Holy Spirit.

David John Lull, *The Spirit in Galatia* (SBL Dissertation Series 49, Ann Arbor: Edwards Brothers, Inc., 1978), pp. 61-62; James D.G. Dunn, *Jesus and the Spirit,* p. 261; Gordon D. Fee, *The First Epistle to the Corinthians* (*NICNT*) (Grand Rapids: Eerdmans, 1987), pp. 603-604.

4. The Holy Spirit and Evangelism of the Church

The Holy Spirit prepares the Church and equips her to fulfill her purpose which is to proclaim the gospel of redemption accomplished by the death and resurrection of Jesus Christ.

First, the Holy Spirit provides courage to the Church for Gospel proclamation. The disciples of Jesus were afraid of persecutors prior to the Pentecost. The attitude of the disciples before the Pentecost is shown when they denied Jesus on the scene of the trial and the cross and fled from the scene for their safety (Luke 22:54-62). However, the New Testament Church was established on the Pentecost with the disciples being empowered by the power of the Holy Spirit. Just as Jesus promised that "the Holy Spirit will teach you at that time what you should say" (Luke 12:12, NIV) and "the Counselor, the Holy Spirit, whom the Father will send in my name, will teach you all things and will remind you of everything I have said to you" (John 14:26, NIV), so Peter and John, standing before the council of the rulers, elders and teachers of religious law, proclaimed the gospel of Jesus with boldness (Acts 4:13, 31). When the disciples were told "never again to speak or teach about Jesus" (NLT) by the council (Acts 4:18), Peter and John replied to them with boldness that "Judge for yourselves whether it is right in God's sight to obey you rather than God. For, we cannot help speaking about what we have seen and heard" (Acts 4:19-20, NIV). Luke was emphasizing that when Peter was speaking to the council of the rulers and the elders, he was filled with the Holy Spirit (Acts 4:8). It is clear that the Holy Spirit gives to the disciples in all circumstances courage to proclaim the Gospel of Jesus Christ.

Second, the Holy Spirit promotes the community consciousness in the Church. The book of Acts provides sources from two different perspectives regarding community consciousness of the New Testament Church. The records show that the Holy Spirit promotes community consciousness from the positive angle on one hand, and on the other hand the Holy Spirit maintains community consciousness from the negative angle.

Positively, the Acts records in 2:42-47 and 4:31-37 the Holy Spirit's promotion of the Church's community consciousness. The life of the early New Testament Church described in the above two passages shows their commitment to the community rather than to an individual and the Spirit-filled life with an exceeding joy and care for one another. They were "one in heart and mind" (Acts 4:32). They shared "everything in common" and "every day they continued to meet together in the temple courts" (Acts 2:44, 46, NIV). They were "praising God and enjoying the favor of all the people" (Acts 2:47, NIV). These are characteristics of one body filled with the Holy Spirit (Cf. Acts 2:38; 4:31; Eph. 5:18-6:9). The Holy Spirit causes in a positive sense every member of the Church to have community consciousness. The Holy Spirit enables every member of the Church to sacrifice himself for the community at the cost of giving up of his own benefits.[169]

The Holy Spirit keeps the purity of the Church's community in a radical way. The story of Ananias and Sapphira recorded in Acts 5:1-11 is a radical act of the Holy Spirit which maintains purity from hypocrisy in the Church. Ananias and Sapphira lied to the Holy

---

169) It is beneficial at this juncture to compare the High Priestly Prayer of Jesus (John 17:13-26) and the Life of the Early Jerusalem Church (Acts 2:42-47). Jesus prayed for the Church prior to the Crucifixion. He prayed that ones who belonged to Him would have ① joy ② sanctification: holy separation ③ truth: the word of God ④ missions ⑤ unity and ⑥ love. It is significant that the life of the Early Jerusalem Church clearly manifests these exact characteristics: ① joy: exhilaration (Acts 2:46), ② sanctification: holy separation (Acts 2:44-46), ③ truth (Acts 2:42), ④ missions (Acts 2:47), ⑤ unity (Acts 2:44-46), and ⑥ love (Acts 2:42-47).

Spirit when they, hiding part of their possession, told to the Church as if they offered the whole sum of their property (Acts 5:3). As a result, Ananias and Sapphira instantly "fell down and died" (Acts 5:5). The death of the couple appears to be heavy compared to their sin.

But the Early Jerusalem Church came to know the seriousness of false testimony before the Holy Spirit. Furthermore, the Early Church learned that the Spirit is in control of the New Testament Church. The mistake of Ananias and Sapphira was to think the Church not as the community of the Spirit, but merely as a community of human beings. They think that they can cheat the apostles and the community. In this incident, the Holy Spirit promotes community consciousness by eliminating impurity from the Church.

Luke explains the conditions of the Early Church after the incident of Ananias and Sapphira by saying that "great fear seized the whole church and all who heard about these events" (Acts 5:11, NIV), and that "all the believers used to meet together in Solomon's Colonnade" (Acts 5:12, NIV). This is evidence that the Early Church renewed community consciousness after the radical yet purifying incident.

One thing that is evident is that the Gospel was proclaimed widely as a result of the Spirit's activity that promotes community consciousness whether positively or negatively. Luke summarizes the *positive activity* of the Spirit in promoting the community consciousness which resulted in "the Lord add[ing] to their number daily those who were being saved" (Acts 2:47, NIV), and Luke also ends the story of Ananias and Sapphira by saying that "nevertheless, more and more men and women believed in the Lord and were added to their number" (Acts 5:14, NIV). This clearly reveals the responsibility of the Church that the Holy Spirit bestowed upon her. The Church must proclaim the Gospel of Jesus Christ from Jerusalem to the end of the world.

Third, the Holy Spirit eliminates the hindrances for Gospel proclamation. The Pentecost event overcomes the curse of the Tower of Babel (Gen. 11:7-9) for the proclamation of the Gospel. The event of Babel brought the curse from God that "come, let us go down and confuse their language so they will not understand each other" (Gen. 11:7, NIV). Now, the Pentecost event of the coming of the Holy Spirit removes the curse of confusion of language so that the Gospel may be proclaimed from Jerusalem to the whole world.[170]

The Apostles spoke different languages and "each one heard them speaking in his own language" (Acts 2:6). People present there said, "We hear them declaring the wonders of God in our own tongues!" (Acts 2:11, NIV). The Gospel, though originated from the Jews and began from Jerusalem, was proclaimed even to the Samaritans at whom the Jews looked with contempt in those days. The Bible states that the gospel was preached to the Samaritans by the Spirit-filled Philip (Acts 6:5; 8:4-25). "When they believed Philip as he preached the good news of the kingdom of God and the name of Jesus Christ, they were baptized, both men and women" (Acts 8: 12, NIV). The Jews do not mix with the Samaritans (Cf. John 4:1-26). However, the gospel of Jesus Christ makes no distinction between the Jews and Gentiles. The event in Samaria triggers many questions because it is written that they believed Philip as he preached and were baptized in the name of Jesus, but "the Holy Spirit had not yet come upon any of them" (Acts 8:16, NIV). When one is baptized, he should confess Jesus as Lord (Rom. 10:9-10). And moreover one is not able to confess Jesus as Lord without the guidance of the Spirit. The Bible clearly states that "no one can say, 'Jesus is Lord,' except

---

170) Park, Hyung Yong, *An Exposition of the Acts of the Apostles* (Korean) (Suwon: Hapdong Theological Seminary Press, 2007), pp. 58-61.

by the Holy Spirit" (I Cor. 12:3). Then it is true that when one is baptized in the name of Jesus, he is guided by the Holy Spirit.

What does it mean, then, in the case of the Samaritans, that "the Holy Spirit had not yet come upon any of them"? The Samaritans heard Philip preaching Christ and saw the miraculous signs he performed. The Simon the Sorcerer also believed and was baptized (Acts 8:13). When Peter and John arrived in Samaria from Jerusalem, they prayed for the Samaritans that they might receive the Holy Spirit (Acts 8:15). The reason that the apostles prayed for them is because "the Holy Spirit had not yet come upon any of them" (Acts 8:16). What does Luke want to convey when he contrast "the Holy Spirit had not yet come upon any of them" with "they had simply been baptized into the name of the Lord Jesus" (Acts 8:16)?

Luke, in these words, wants to convey the idea that while the confessing Samaritans accepted Jesus as Lord with the guidance of the Spirit, they did not experience the miraculous works of the Holy Spirit. The Samaritans were genuine believers excluding Simon the Sorcerer (Acts 8:20-21). Luke means by this phrase of "the Holy Spirit had not yet come upon any of them" to refer to the special extraordinary outward pouring of the Holy Spirit. Otherwise Simon the Sorcerer would not "follow Philip everywhere and [was] astonished by the great signs and miracles he saw" (Acts 8:13). It is evident that the obstacles between the Jews and the Samaritans were demolished by the extraordinary signs of the Holy Spirit for the gospel proclamation.

The Holy Spirit allows the gospel to be offered even to the Gentile Cornelius (Acts 10:3, 5, 19, 38). Peter was witnessing of Jesus Christ who was crucified on the cross in Jerusalem and raised from the dead on the third day. "While Peter was still speaking these words, the Holy Spirit came on all who heard the message" (Acts

10:44, NIV). The Spirit guides Peter to proclaim the gospel of Jesus to the family of Cornelius.

In Ephesus, Paul preached the gospel to those who only know John's baptism of repentance (Acts 19:4). After hearing the gospel, "when Paul placed his hands on them, the Holy Spirit came on them, and they spoke in tongues and prophesied" (Acts 19:6, NIV). The twelve men were baptized in the name of Jesus Christ. Thus, the Spirit removes obstacles for the Church to proclaim the good news of Jesus.

What is the work that the Holy Spirit does for the Church? The answer to this question is that the Spirit does everything for the Church. The Holy Spirit is the foundation of the Church, seals the Church, and empowers the Church to proclaim the good news to the ends of the world. The Holy Spirit provides power, method, and opportunity to the Church for gospel proclamation.

Chapter 10

The Role of the Holy Spirit
in the Resurrection

The doctrine of the resurrection is the most important teaching in the Christian Church. The resurrection is the hope of believers and ensures proper value to the life of Christians. So Paul says, "if only for this life we have hope in Christ, we are to be pitied more than all men" (I Cor. 15:19, NIV).

We pay much attention to the cross of Christ, but not enough attention to the resurrection. We should note that "for Paul, salvation reaches the whole man, not merely his soul; and hence will be attained only with the glorious resurrection of the body." ---"A lack of appreciation of this essentially eschatological character of Pauline soteriology has resulted in the modern, truncated theologies of the redemption, which are concerned only with Jesus' death, and neglect the function of his resurrection."[171] The resurrection is the most important and central teaching of the Bible. The Bible also teaches that the role of the Spirit is crucial in the resurrection. As God used the Holy Spirit to raise Jesus from the dead the third day, He will use the same Spirit to raise the believers in the future. Thus, as fish cannot live without water, we cannot discuss the resurrection without the role of the Holy Spirit. We will now study the role of the Holy Spirit in the resurrection on the basis of the teachings of the Bible.

1. The Role of the Holy Spirit in the Resurrection of Jesus

We presuppose the fact that Jesus, having a divine nature, is capable of raising Himself from the dead. Of course, Jesus who is God has power to raise Himself from the dead. However, the Bible records the role of Jesus Christ in His resurrection as passive. This

---

171) David Michael Stanley, *Christ's Resurrection in Pauline Soteriology* (Romae: E Pontificio Instituto Biblico, 1961), p. 195.

provides us with a new perspective regarding the resurrection of Jesus Christ.

As we study the Gospels and the epistles, we find different perspectives on the role of Jesus in His resurrection. However, there is no conflict between the Gospels and the epistles. Rather the different perspectives provide a complete teaching about the resurrection of Jesus.

The Gospels record that Jesus Christ is capable of raising Himself from the dead. "The reason my Father loves me is that I lay down my life--only to take it up again. No one takes it from me, but I lay it down of my own accord. I have authority to lay it down and authority to take it up again. This command I received from my Father" (John 10:17-18, NIV). "Jesus answered them, 'Destroy this temple, and I will raise it again in three days'" (John 2:19, NIV). These two verses clearly attest to the fact that Jesus Christ had an authority and played an active role in His resurrection. This becomes manifested when we compare "destroy his temple, and I will raise it again in three days" (John 2:19) with "the temple he had spoken of was his body" (John 2:21). In response to the Jews, Jesus was clearly talking about His bodily resurrection.

Thus, the Gospels attest that Jesus not only lay down His life voluntarily but that He also takes His life back in His power (John 10:17-18). This is the way that the Gospels want to emphasize the authority and the power of Jesus Christ as God.[172]

On the contrary, the Pauline epistles emphasize the role of God the Father in the resurrection of Jesus. The Pauline epistles record that God is the One who raises Jesus from the dead, and Jesus is the

---

172) C. F. Evans, *Resurrection and the New Testament* (*Studies in Biblical Theology*, 2nd series, 12. London: SCM Press, 1970), pp. 21-22.

One who was raised by God the Father. Paul says, "he who raised the Lord Jesus will raise us also with Jesus and bring us with you into his presence" (II Cor. 4:14, ESV). Again Paul says, "if you confess with your mouth, 'Jesus is Lord,' and believe in your heart that God raised him from the dead, you will be saved" (Rom. 10:9, NIV). We see in these verses clearly that God is the active agent in the resurrection of Jesus and Jesus is the object of God's resurrecting power. The Acts and the Pauline epistles describe the resurrection of Jesus in the same way in many verses (Cf. I Cor. 15:15; Col. 2:12; I Thess. 1:9-10; Acts 4:10; 5:30, etc).[173]

For what reason is Jesus described as playing a passive role in His resurrection in the Pauline epistles, and how is this different from the Gospels? The Pauline epistles emphasize the union of Jesus with the believers in the resurrection. The epistles are concerned with emphasizing the continuity rather than the difference in the resurrection of Jesus and the believers. Paul does not want to manifest the power and divinity of Jesus, but the passive role of Jesus in His resurrection in becoming "the firstfruits of them that slept" (I Cor. 15:20, KJV).

The Pauline epistles, emphasizing the common aspect between the resurrection of Jesus and the resurrection of believers, stress the important role of the Holy Spirit in these two resurrections. God has used the Holy Spirit as an instrument to raise Jesus from the dead and He will certainly use the same instrument, the Holy Spirit, to raise the

---

173) The Pauline epistles use ἐγείρω and ἀνίστημι when describing the resurrection of Jesus. When the verb is active, God is always the subject of the sentence as the author of the resurrection, and Jesus is always the object of God's active role. And when the verb is passive, Jesus is always the subject receiving the action of God in the resurrection. Although I Thess. 4:14 describes the role of Jesus as active, the active verb is used in the quotation section in the sentence. Cf. David Michael Stanley, *Christ's Resurrection in Pauline Soteriology*, p. 261: "Only once does Paul say 'Christ rose' (1 Thes 4:14), a passage which appears to be a citation from an ancient creedal formula."

believers from the dead in the future. "And if the Spirit of him who raised Jesus from the dead is living in you, he who raised Christ from the dead will also give life to your mortal bodies through his Spirit, who lives in you" (Rom. 8:11, NIV).[174]

Here we come to know that just as God used the Holy Spirit to raise Jesus from the dead, He will also use the same Holy Spirit to raise the believers from the dead in the future.

2. The Holy Spirit who dwells in the believers

How do we know for certain that God will raise the believers from the dead? How are we convinced that God will raise us from the dead? Fallen mankind strongly depends on material possessions to find peace and certainty. However, God, who is the spirit, does not give us an assurance for the resurrection with material substance. God assures us of our resurrection in a more certain and spiritual way.

God's wisdom is manifested by how when one believes in Jesus as his Lord, soon thereafter, God causes the Holy Spirit to indwell the believer. That is the reason why Paul says, "Therefore I tell you that no one who is speaking by the Spirit of God says, 'Jesus be cursed,' and no one can say, 'Jesus is Lord,' except by the Holy Spirit" (I Cor. 12:3, NIV), and "Don't you know that you yourselves are God's temple and that God's Spirit lives in you?" (I Cor. 3:16, NIV; cf. I Cor. 6:19). The Holy Spirit begins to dwell in the believer the moment he confesses Jesus as Lord.

---

174) Rom. 8:11 must be interpreted in connection with Rom. 8:10. Rom. 8:10 describes the present state of the bodily presence of the believers and Rom 8:11 the future glorious state of the bodily form of the believers' resurrection. Paul in this verse does not deal with the contrast between the body and spirit of a man but rather between the present state of the bodily form of believers and the future state of the resurrected body of believers.

Paul warns, "Do not put out the Spirit's fire" (I Thess. 5:19, NIV) and "do not grieve the Holy Spirit of God, with whom you were sealed for the day of redemption" (Eph. 4:30, NIV) because the Spirit dwells in the believer. Therefore, the Holy Spirit who indwells the believers is the guarantee for the resurrection of the believers.

The Apostle Paul, on the basis of this thought, assures us of the fact that believers will be enclothed with the resurrection body. So, he says, "now we know that if the earthly tent we live in is destroyed, we have a building from God, an eternal house in heaven, not built by human hands" (II Cor. 5:1, NIV).[175]

Paul continues to prove that the Holy Spirit, who is dwelling in the believers, is the assurance for the resurrection of the believers in the future by saying that "Now it is God who has made us for this very purpose and has given us the Spirit as a deposit, guaranteeing what is to come (II Cor. 5:5, NIV; Cf. Rom. 8:23; II Cor. 1:22). Paul uses the term, "down payment," (ἀρραβών) to indicate the certainty of the believers' future.[176] This word is defined as paying a part of the purchase price in advance so as to secure a legal claim to the object in question. God assures the resurrection of the believer by the Holy Spirit, the down payment that dwells in the believer.

The Bible describes the various work of the Holy Spirit in the

---

175) We need to understand the phrase "Jesus is Lord" in the historical context of the first century. Believers distinguished themselves from the Jews and the Gentiles by confessing Jesus Christ as Lord. Therefore, to confess Jesus as Lord in the context of the first century means to believe Jesus as God and commit one's life to Him absolutely. Cf. Gordon D. Fee, *The First Epistle to the Corinthians* (*NICNT*) (Grand Rapids: Eerdmans, 1987), pp. 581-582.

176) Arabon(ἀρραβών) is a commercial word which comes from the Hebrew word erabon(עֵרָבוֹן) (Gen. 38:17ff.). This word means to make a downpayment as a pledge and assurance of legal ownership. Therefore, this word makes the covenant legally effective. Cf. J. Behm, "ἀρραβών," *Theological Dictionary of the New Testament,* Vol. I (Grand Rapids: Eerdmans, 1972), p. 475; A Sand, "ἀρραβών," *Exegetical Dictionary of the New Testament,* Vol. I (Grand Rapids: Eerdmans, 1990), p. 158.

life of the believer.

One, the Holy Spirit is the One who inspires (John 14:26, 16:13-15; II Tim. 3:16).

Two, the Holy Spirit is the One who teaches (John 14:26).

Three, the Holy Spirit is the One who testifies (John 15:26).

Four, the Holy Spirit is the One who prophesies (John 16:13; I Tim. 4:1).

Five, the Holy Spirit is the One who convicts (John 16:8).

Six, the Holy Spirit is the One who baptizes (Matt. 3:11; Mark 1:8; John 1:33).

Seven, the Holy Spirit is the One who regenerates (John 3:1-8).

Eight, the Holy Spirit is the One who comforts (John 14:16, 26, 15:26, 16:7; I John 2:1).

Nine, the Holy Spirit is the One who dwells in the believer (John 14:17; I Cor. 3:16, 6:19).

Ten, the Holy Spirit is the One who gives the resurrection life (II Cor. 3:6; Rom. 8:11).

Thus, the Holy Spirit, who has a direct relationship with the life of the believer, gives assurance for the resurrection of the believer in the future.

3. The Role of the Spirit in the Resurrection of the Believer

The Holy Spirit dwells in the believer as an assurance of resurrection. The indwelling Spirit becomes a bridge that conveys what Jesus Christ accomplished in His death and resurrection for the believers.

The believer is living a resurrection life by having faith in Jesus Christ. Thus, the believer's life is a spiritual life because the Spirit is dwelling in him. Some teach that the earthly life of the believer is a physical life and the life in heaven with the Lord is a spiritual life. This kind of teaching is not Biblical and is alien to the teachings of Paul. The believer begins to live a spiritual life when the Spirit begins to dwell in him. And the Spirit begins to dwell in the believer when he confesses Jesus as Lord. The difference between the earthly life of a believer and life in heaven with the Lord is that the former is the period during which the believer lives with a mortal body under the plan and providence of God, while the latter is the period when the believer, after death, lives eternally in heaven in the resurrection body with the Lord.

What is clear is that the one who does not have the Holy Spirit now is not a recipient of the resurrection body and is not able to live a Spirit-filled life. And the believer who has the Spirit as an assurance will surely be enclothed with the resurrection body and will live a spiritual life eternally. No one will snatch away this blessing from the believer. It is confirmed here that the Spirit is the bridge between the present earthly life of the believer and the future life in heaven with the Lord. It is pertinent to quote here that "if the Spirit of him who raised Jesus from the dead is living in you, he who raised Christ from the dead will also give life to your mortal bodies through his Spirit, who lives in you" (Rom. 8:11, NIV). Paul wants to reveal that God raised Jesus Christ from the dead by His Spirit and the same God will raise the mortal body of the believer from the dead through His Spirit who is dwelling in the believer. The grand redemptive drama of God's raising Jesus through His Spirit, the Spirit's indwelling the believers, and God's raising the mortal body of the believer through His Spirit who indwells the believer is in the hand of the Almighty God. What God accomplished for Jesus Christ will be accomplished by God Himself for the believer.

In other words, what happened to the firstfruits will happen to the believer (I Cor. 15:20). The Savior is considered here as a Messiah in his representative capacity, which provides a guarantee that His resurrection must repeat itself in that of the believers. "What God did for Jesus He will do for the believer likewise."[177] That the Holy Spirit is the same instrument God used for the resurrection of Jesus and believers shows the certainty of the resurrection of the believers. The fact that the Spirit presently dwells in the believer is the proof that the resurrection principle is working in their lives and will certainly be accomplishing the future bodily resurrection.

Here, we find one principle as to how a believer can have the certainty of his own resurrection. The more strong assurance the believer has for his own faith in Jesus Christ, the more strong assurance he has for his own resurrection. If his faith in Jesus is weakened, his certainty for his own resurrection is also weakened, for the Holy Spirit dwells in the believer when he believes in Jesus which is an assurance for the resurrection.

4. The Resurrection Body is the Spiritual Body

The future resurrection body of the believers has a direct relationship with the works of the Holy Spirit. Paul, writing to the Corinthian church members who had some doubts about their bodily resurrection, poses a question, "With what kind of body will they come?" (I Cor. 15:35, NIV). He answers the question by comparing the characteristics of the natural body with those of the Spiritual body (I Cor. 15:42-45).

---

177) G. Vos, *The Pauline Eschatology* (Grand Rapids: Eerdmans, 1966), pp. 163-164.

The Natural Body	The Spiritual Body
The body is perishable.	The body is imperishable.
It is sown in dishonor.	It is raised in glory.
It is sown in weakness.	It is raised in power.
It is sown a natural body.	It is raised a Spiritual body.[178]

The left column describes the characteristics of a natural body and the right column the characteristics of a Spiritual body. The natural body refers to the present body of believers on earth, and the Spiritual body refers to the resurrection body of believers at the Second Coming. The natural body follows the order of the first man Adam, the living soul, while the Spiritual body follows the order of the last man Jesus Christ who becomes "the Life-giving Spirit" through His resurrection (Gen. 2:7; I. Cor. 15:45).

These verses teach that the resurrection body of believers in the future will be like the Spiritual body Jesus was enclothed at His resurrection. This spiritual body is a suitable body in the spiritual kingdom. The Spiritual body will be completely occupied by the Holy Spirit; it will be used as an instrument by the Holy Spirit; and it will be an appropriate body for the resurrected life Jesus Christ initiated through His resurrection. Therefore, the believers would understand what kind of resurrected body they will have by observing the activities of Jesus in the period between His resurrection and ascension.

---

178) Paul uses the phrase "it is sown" (σπείρεται) four times in this context. This means that Paul has the dead body in mind. However, the concept of a body prior to death is not completely excluded, for Paul describes the present body of believers as "the mortal body" (Rom. 8:10-11; II Cor. 4:10f.) and "this body of death" (Rom. 7:24). It must be noted here that Paul has the characteristics of a body prior to death in mind.

Jesus' resurrection body is a Spiritual body that surpasses the limits of time and space. After His resurrection, Jesus says, "see my hands and my feet, that it is I myself. Touch me, and see. For a spirit does not have flesh and bones as you see that I have" (Luke 24:39, ESV). This illustrates that His resurrection body is different from a spirit. Jesus even ate "a piece of broiled fish" (Luke 24:42; John 21:5-14) as if He wanted to prove His resurrection body to be a bodily form.

Thus, Jesus' resurrection body can be observed by the naked eye and can disappear suddenly from the sight of humans (Luke 24:31). And Jesus, with His resurrection body, came and stood among the disciples while the doors were locked (John 20:19-20). The resurrection body can take food though it does not need to have digestive organs in the body (Luke 24:39-43) and can be taken into heaven from us and will come back in the same way we have seen him go into heaven (Acts 1:11).

The resurrection body of believers will be like Jesus' resurrection body.[179] The Scripture confirms the continuity between Jesus' resurrection body and the believer's resurrection body by saying that "just as we have borne the likeness of the earthly man, so shall we bear the likeness of the man from heaven" (I Cor. 15:49, NIV). The continuity between Jesus' resurrection body and the believer's resurrection body is possible because the Holy Spirit is to be used as an instrument in the resurrection of Jesus as well as the believer's resurrection. The Holy Spirit will create the resurrection body suitable for the Spiritual world. Then, the Holy Spirit "will transform our lowly bodies so that they will be like his glorious body" (Phil.

---

179) Those who came alive from the dead before the resurrection of Jesus (Matt. 27:51-53; Luke 7:11-17; 8:49-56; John 11:38-44) were restored to their life again. They lived for a while and died again. But the resurrection body of believers will forever live.

3:21, NIV) and the believers will confess that "now we are children of God, and what we will be has not yet been made known. But we know that when he appears, we shall be like him, for we shall see him as he is" (1 John 3:2, NIV; Cf. I Cor. 13:12).

So far we have dealt with the role of the Holy Spirit in the resurrection. God the Father used the Holy Spirit as an instrument in Jesus' resurrection and He will use the same Spirit in the resurrection of believers at the Parousia. And the fact that the Holy Spirit presently indwells believers is evidence for the resurrection of believers. The Holy Spirit will make the believer's resurrection body to be a spiritual body suitable for the Spiritual world. The believers are currently living a resurrection life with these blessings.

Therefore, we should pay careful attention to the exhortation of Paul when he says, "Therefore, my dear brothers, stand firm. Let nothing move you. Always give yourselves fully to the work of the Lord, because you know that your labor in the Lord is not in vain" (I Cor. 15:58, NIV).

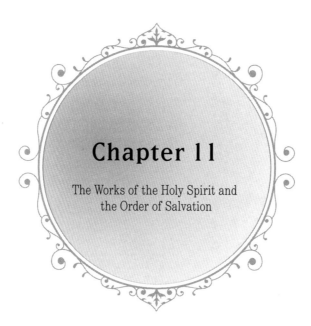

Chapter 11

The Works of the Holy Spirit and
the Order of Salvation

It is impossible to discuss the salvation of believers without the works of the Holy Spirit. The Holy Spirit guarantees the salvation of believers from the initial act to the last completion. The Holy Spirit begins to secure the salvation of believers and makes sure of it to the last moment. Therefore it is evident that the work of the Holy Spirit is manifested in every stage of a believer's salvation experience. We will not deal with *ordo salutis* (the order of salvation)[180] *per se* here but discuss the relationship between the work of the Holy Spirit and a believer's salvation experience.

1. The Holy Spirit and Grace

We were dead in our transgressions and sins. We were not able to please God on our own. Rather we followed the ways of this world and of the ruler of the kingdom of the air (Eph. 2:1-3). As a result, we were by nature objects of God's wrath. But God who is full of grace granted our salvation by His grace and through faith. The scripture says, "For it is by grace you have been saved, through faith--and this not from yourselves, it is the gift of God--not by works, so that no one can boast. For we are God's workmanship, created in Christ Jesus to do good works, which God prepared in advance for us to do" (Eph. 2:8-10, NIV). This graceful work of salvation was wrought by the Triune God, the Father, the Son and the Holy Spirit. Paul was unequivocally explaining this work of salvation in the beginning section of Ephesians. For the Triune God's work for our salvation,

---

180) *Ordo Salutis* in the Reformed tradition is as follows. ① God's election, ② Calling through the gospel, ③ Regeneration (being born again), ④ Conversion (faith and repentance), ⑤ Justification, ⑥ Adoption, ⑦ Sanctification, ⑧ Perseverance of Saints, ⑨ Death (going to the Lord), and ⑩ Glorification. John Murray, *Redemption Accomplished and Applied* (Grand Rapids: Eerdmans, 1955), pp. 79-87.

Paul revealed the work of our God the Father in Ephesians 1:3-6, the work of Jesus Christ in Ephesians 1:7-12 and the work of the Holy Spirit in Ephesians 1:13-14. It is impossible to achieve our salvation without the unifying work of the Triune God.

The work of the Holy Spirit is absolutely necessary to apply to us the accomplished redemption by Jesus Christ on the cross and resurrection. The Holy Spirit works to open the door for us, who "were separate from Christ, excluded from citizenship in Israel and foreigners to the covenants of the promise, without hope and without God in the world" (Eph. 2:12, NIV). It is also true that the Holy Spirit in His grace sent Peter to Cornelius and helped Peter proclaim the Gospel of Jesus Christ to Cornelius family (Acts 10:44-48; 11:15-18). And it is the Holy Spirit who opens the door for the Gentiles to enter into the believing community of the covenant. The Gentiles receive the Holy Spirit by faith, not by works (Gal. 3:1-5). This is clearly manifested in Paul's question to the Galatians saying, "Did you receive the Spirit by observing the law, or by believing what you heard?" (Gal. 3:2, NIV). It is the grace of the Holy Spirit that we are saved by faith only, not by our works. The Holy Spirit gives faith to those who hear the message of Jesus Christ and causes them to accept Jesus as Lord (Rom. 10:9-10, 17). There is "no one who is speaking by the Spirit of God says, 'Jesus be cursed,' and no one can say, 'Jesus is Lord,' except by the Holy Spirit" (I Cor. 12:3, NIV). No one can confess Jesus as Lord without the help of the Holy Spirit. Because there is no one who can keep the law completely and "there is no one righteous, not even one; there is no one who understands, no one who seeks God" (Rom. 3:10-11, NIV). Therefore it is by grace only that we are saved by faith and the Gentiles are saved without works. All these are the work of God.

2. The Holy Spirit and Regeneration

The most important experience of the believers in *ordo salutis* (the order of salvation) is regeneration. The regeneration is the once-for-all experience in the life of a believer by which he departs from the community of Satan and belongs to the community of God; he moves from death to life; he transfers from a journey to Hell to a journey to Heaven. Calvin notes that "the most certain mark by which the sons of God are distinguished from the children of the world is their regeneration by the Spirit of God to innocence and holiness."[181] Therefore Jesus says to Nicodemus, "I tell you the truth, no one can see the kingdom of God unless he is born again" and "I tell you the truth, no one can enter the kingdom of God unless he is born of water and the Spirit. Flesh gives birth to flesh, but the Spirit gives birth to spirit. You should not be surprised at my saying, 'You must be born again'" (John 3:3-7, NIV).[182] The Lord used the water in this context to refer to "the ceremonial expression for the cleansing of our person by His own obedience or atoning sacrifice, proving the complete removal of guilt and of everything that could exclude us on the ground of law from the kingdom of God."[183] And the Spirit is "the personal Holy Spirit, who gives the inward capacity or fitness for the kingdom of God, who breaks the power of sin, and makes all things new."[184] The two conjoined elements, the water and the Spirit,

---

181) John Calvin, *The Epistles of Paul to the Romans and Thessalonians,* trans. R. Mackenzie (Grand Rapids: Eerdmans, 1973), p. 164.

182) For the interpretation of this verse from the Reformed perspective, see John Murray, *Systematic Theology,* II (Korean), trans. Park, Moon Jae (Seoul: Christian Digest, 1991), pp. 187-199.

183) George Smeaton, *The Doctrine of the Holy Spirit* (Carlisle: The Banner of Truth Trust, 1974), p. 184.

184) Smeaton, *The Doctrine of the Holy Spirit*, p. 184.

mean to refer to the meritorious cause (atoning sacrifice of Jesus) and the efficient cause (inward cleansing of the Spirit).[185] So, our Lord says to Nicodemus, "no one can enter the kingdom of God unless he is born of water and the Spirit" (John 3:5; cf. Ezekiel 36:25). No one can have an eternal life without being born again by the Holy Spirit. So, Paul confirms that "he saved us, not because of righteous things we had done, but because of his mercy. He saved us through the washing of rebirth and renewal by the Holy Spirit, whom he poured out on us generously through Jesus Christ our Savior, so that, having been justified by his grace, we might become heirs having the hope of eternal life" (*Titus 3:5-7*, NIV). And the most important aspect of the regeneration experience is to confess Jesus as Lord (Acts 2:36). "Therefore I tell you that no one who is speaking by the Spirit of God says, 'Jesus be cursed,' and no one can say, 'Jesus is Lord,' except by the Holy Spirit" (I Cor. 12:3, NIV). The Holy Spirit is the one who for the first time applies the redemption accomplished in the death and resurrection of Jesus Christ to individual believers.

3. The Holy Spirit and Repentance

Jesus Christ, during His public ministry on earth and even before the death on the cross, promises to send the Holy Spirit. During His earthly ministry, Jesus foretells of the work of "convincing the world concerning sin" among the many works of the Holy Spirit (John 16:8-13). Then after the Pentecost event (Acts 2:1-4), we notice the evident, convicting works of the Holy Spirit. When Peter proclaimed the gospel in the fullness of the Spirit, people responded by saying, "Brethren, what shall we do?" while repenting their sins (Acts 2:37-

---

185) Smeaton, *The Doctrine of the Holy Spirit,* p. 184.

38). The regenerated man ought not only to have faith in Jesus Christ but also to repent his sins. Faith and repentance are like two sides of a coin. They cannot be separated from each other. Faith is a positive response towards Christ, while repentance is a negative response of turning away from sins.[186] When people who heard Peter's sermon say, "What shall we do," Peter's reply is, "Repent and be baptized, every one of you, in the name of Jesus Christ for the forgiveness of your sins. And you will receive the gift of the Holy Spirit" (Acts 2:38, NIV). Here we notice the relationship among faith, repentance, and the Holy Spirit. Peter proclaimed the gospel as the apostle of the New Testament Church and as a member of the same Church. The Holy Spirit causes men and women to repent of their sins and accepts them into a new community of the Church through the Church's preaching of the gospel.

4. The Holy Spirit and Adoption as sons

A sinner cannot become a child of God. It is not possible for the most holy God to have sinners as His sons. Therefore before He adopted sinners as His sons, God made Jesus Christ who had no sin to be sin for the sinners, so that in Him the sinners might become the righteousness of God (II Cor. 5:21; Rom. 4:25). The death and resurrection of Jesus Christ is the foundation by which sinners can become children of God. The reason God adopts us as His children, is because we are justified by faith in Jesus Christ through the help of the Holy Spirit. Justification is the activity of God who reckons the justification of Jesus to be our justification. Adoption is the activity

---

186) Morton H. Smith, *Systematic Theology*, Vol. 2 (Greenville: Greenville Seminary Press, 1994), p. 454.

of God who accepts us as His sons on the basis of our justification earned only by faith in Jesus Christ. Adoption as sons means to move from an unredeemed family of Gentiles to a redeemed family of God.[187]

The Scripture clearly testifies that we are not born to be children of God. "Yet to all who received him, to those who believed in his name, he gave the right to become children of God, children born not of natural descent, nor of human decision or a husband's will, but born of God" (John 1:12-13, NIV). The status and privilege of a believer does not come naturally as a result of regeneration, but are given by God Himself (I John 3:1-2). It is now possible for us to call God the Father "Abba, Father" by the help of the Holy Spirit because God justified us and gave us the status of His sons (Rom. 8:15; Gal. 4:5-6). Without the Holy Spirit we are unable to call God "our Father." It is the Holy Spirit who works to make us children of God.

5. The Holy Spirit and Sanctification

The Scriptures describes the variety of activity of the Holy Spirit for the holy life of believers. The character of the works of the Holy Spirit is once-for-all as well as continual. From among the salvation experiences of believers, the calling, regeneration, justification, and adoption as sons are not repetitive in character but a once-for-all character of the Holy Spirit.[188] The New Testament explains in two ways the once-for-all character of sanctification (Cf. I Cor. 1:2; 6:11; II Tim. 2:21) as well as the progressive aspect of sanctification (Cf. Col. 1:19; Eph. 1:22; 4:10). As such the salvation experiences of believer are closely related with the works of the Holy Spirit. Let us

---

187) John Murray, *Redemption Accomplished and Applied,* p. 167.
188) John Murray, *Systematic Theology,* II (Korean), p. 289.

now consider briefly the relationship of the Holy Spirit with the life of believers.

First, the Holy Spirit in the life of believers

The important thing that the believer needs to confirm is the proper and right relationship with the Holy Spirit. Those without the right relationship with the Spirit cannot become Christians and are not able to live a sanctifying life. The Scripture reveals the relationship between the Spirit and the believer in many ways.

(1) The believer is regenerated by the Holy Spirit (John 3:5-8).

Regeneration is the beginning of the work of the Holy Spirit in the life of a believer. Without the regeneration experience there will be no other experiences. Without the work of the Spirit, man cannot know Christ Jesus, and without Jesus Christ, man cannot have eternal life (John 6:48, 54; 14:6).

(2) The believer is baptized by the Holy Spirit (I Cor. 12:13).

The Scripture testifies that "For we were all baptized by one Spirit into one body--whether Jews or Greeks, slave or free--and we were all given the one Spirit to drink" (I Cor. 12:13, NIV). This verse explains the regeneration experience of a believer from another perspective.[189] Regeneration is the first salvation experience in the life of the believer, so "Baptism of the Spirit" describes the first stage

---

189) Paul uses the term "Baptism of the Holy Spirit," for it is an appropriate expression for this context. I Corinthians 12 describes the Church as the body of Christ and therefore "the Baptism of the Spirit" is an appropriate term to describe the first experience of a believer who enters into a new community of faith. Just as in the Old Testament period, where the circumcision was the first experience the Gentiles needed to have when they came into the community of Israel, so in the New Testament period, it was necessary to be baptized when the believers came into the community of the New Testament Church.

through which the believer comes into the Church, the body of Christ. Therefore regeneration and the Baptism of the Spirit are the same experience explained from different perspectives.

(3) The Holy Spirit is indwelling in the believer (Rom. 8:9-11).

The Holy Spirit begins to indwell the believer the moment he confesses Jesus as Lord and continues to dwell in the believer until the time of the believer's death. Therefore the believers are God's temple where God's Spirit lives (I Cor. 3:16; 6:19; Eph. 2:21-22). Calvin rightly says, "For as by the Spirit He consecrates us as temples to Himself, so by the same Spirit He dwells in us."[190] It is in this sense that the Scripture says, "Do you not know that your body is a temple of the Holy Spirit, who is in you, whom you have received from God? You are not your own; you were bought at a price. Therefore honor God with your body" (I Cor. 6:19-20, NIV).

(4) The believer is sealed by the Holy Spirit (Eph. 1:13).

There is a dispute as to when the Holy Spirit sealed the believer. Martin Lloyd-Jones is of the opinion that in the individual Christian's salvation experience, the timing of the sealing of the Holy Spirit does not coincide with the time of regeneration. He says that "Sealing is an experience, something that God does to us, and we know it when it happens. You cannot say that about your sanctification which is a work of God down in the depths of the soul, convicting of sin, leading to better desires."[191] Lloyd-Jones stresses that the sealing is God's work in our lives in terms of experience so that we would know what

---

190) John Calvin, *The Epistles of Paul to the Romans and Thessalonians,* trans. R. Mackenzie, p. 165.

191) Martin Lloyd-Jones, *God's Ultimate Purpose: An Exposition of Ephesians One* (Carlisle: The Banner of Truth Trust, 1978), p. 262.

is happening. The sealing of the Holy Spirit comes after we have faith in Jesus Christ, that is, after we become Christians. It is clear that Lloyd-Jones distinguishes the time of regeneration from the time of sealing. Instead, he suggests that the "sealing with the Spirit" is the same as the "baptism with the Spirit."[192] In his use of the phrase, "baptism with the Spirit" should be understood in the sense of the Pentecostal movement.

However, the Scripture testifies that the time of sealing coincides with the time of regeneration. Paul mentions the sealing of the Spirit twice in Ephesians (Eph. 1:13; 4:30). And Paul states, "Do not grieve the Holy Spirit of God, with whom you were sealed for the day of redemption" (Eph. 4:30, NIV). This verse does not mean that an individual Christian is sealed from a certain moment after being saved to the day of redemption. Rather it means that a Christian is sealed from the moment when the Spirit dwells in him to the day of redemption.[193]

Therefore, it is right to support the opinion that regeneration and the sealing of the Spirit happens at the same time in the life of a believer. Just as regeneration and the Baptism with the Spirit are the same experience in the believer's salvation experience seen from different perspectives, so are the sealing of the Spirit and regeneration considered the same experience from different perspectives. The sealing of the Spirit is God's act of sealing for His ownership, saying that "this is mine," when He begins to dwell in the believer. Once one belongs to God, he cannot depart from the bosom of God the

---

192) *Ibid.*, p. 264.

193) Martin Lloyd-Jones makes clear that the sealing of the Spirit does not coincide with the time of regeneration. Lloyd-Jones emphasizes an experimental aspect of the sealing of the Spirit. He says that we will all recognize the sealing experience when it happens. Cf. Martin Lloyd-Jones, *God's Ultimate Purpose,* pp. 260, 262, 264, 266.

Father (John 6:37, 65; Rom. 8:31-39).

Second, the Spirit's exhortations toward the believer

    (1)A believer should act by the help of the Spirit (Gal. 5:16, 25;
        Rom 8:4).

The Scripture exhorts the believer to "live by the Spirit" (Gal. 5:16).
When the believer lives by the Spirit, it is possible for him not to live
according to his sinful nature but according to the Spirit (Rom. 8:4).
When we set our hearts on what our nature desires, we live according
to our sinful natures, but when we set our hearts on what the Spirit
desires, we live in accordance with the Spirit (Rom. 8:5-6). The
Scripture clearly testifies that the believer cannot continue to live a
Christian life without the help of the Holy Spirit.

    (2)A believer should ponder the works of the Spirit (Rom. 8:5; Col.
        3:1-4).

The believer is moved from earth to heaven by the Spirit (Col. 3:1).
"God raised us up with Christ and seated us with him in the heavenly
realms in Christ Jesus" (Eph. 2:6, NIV). The Holy Spirit is used as
an instrument for this work (Rom. 8:11). This is the reason why Paul
claims that "our citizenship is in heaven" (Phil. 3:20, NIV). Those
who have the citizenship of heaven should set their hearts on things
above, where Christ is seated at the right hand of God (Col. 3:1-2).
The believer cannot live outside of this world, but he should drive
away things of this world from his mind. He should put in the utmost
effort to set his mind on heavenly things.

    (3)A believer should be filled with the Holy Spirit (Eph. 5:18;
        Acts 2:4).

From Paul's expression of the statement, "Do not get drunk on wine, which leads to debauchery? Instead, be filled with the Spirit" (Eph. 5:18, NIV), we learn a few lessons. Paul uses the imperative, plural form, a passive voice, and present tense in this verse.

Firstly, Paul uses the imperative in this verse. This means the believer is commanded to be filled with the Spirit. When the believer is filled with the Spirit, the believer has an active responsibility to be filled with the Spirit. He needs to try to be filled with the Spirit in the activities of his life.

Secondly, Paul uses the plural form when he commands one to be filled with the Spirit. This means that being filled with the Spirit is not a matter that pertains to a certain group of Christians, but it is a matter for all Christians. All Christians should be filled with the Spirit. This is what Paul is aiming at when he uses the plural form.

Thirdly, Paul uses the passive voice in this verse. He says, "Be filled with the Spirit." This means that when the believer is filled with the Holy Spirit, it is the Spirit who fills the believer.

Fourthly, Paul talks about the "filling with the Spirit" in the present tense. The usage of the present tense implies a continual filling of the Spirit in the believer. And the present tense must indeed refer to the repetitive filling with the Spirit. Thus Paul wants the believer to be filled with the Spirit.

(4)A believer should yield the fruit of the Spirit (Gal. 5:22-23).

"But the fruit of the Spirit is love, joy, peace, patience, kindness, goodness, faithfulness, gentleness and self-control. Against such things there is no law" (Gal. 5:22-23, NIV). The gifts of the Spirit underscore the variety found in the Church while the fruit of the Spirit underscores the unity of the Church. The fruit of the Spirit witnesses to the oneness of the believer in Christ. The fruit of the Spirit is not innate to believers, but is manifested by the Spirit Himself in the life of the believer.

    (5)A believer should own the sword of the Spirit for his life (Eph. 6:17).

The sword of the Spirit is the word of God. The sword of the Spirit is an offensive weapon as well as a defensive weapon. When Jesus was tempted by Satan, He defeated Satan by the word of God (Matt. 4:1-11; Luke 4:1-13). And Jesus proclaimed the good news by using the word of God. In the same way the believer should have the sword of the Spirit in order to live a Spirit-led life. "For the word of God is living and active. Sharper than any double-edged sword, it penetrates even to dividing soul and spirit, joints and marrow; it judges the thoughts and attitudes of the heart" (Heb. 4:12, NIV). The fact that the sword of the Spirit is the word of God implies indirectly that the Spirit is always working with the word of God. The believer should be equipped with the sword of the Spirit, that is, the word of God, in order to gain victory in the battle against Satan. "To be equipped" means to know the word of God well.[194]

    (6)A believer must pray in the Spirit (Eph. 6:18; Rom. 8:26).

We do not know exactly what we ought to pray for. Oftentimes we express desires in our prayers that God does not want to hear. The Spirit helps us in our weakness and intercedes for us with groans that words cannot express. Paul says, "He who searches our hearts knows the mind of the Spirit, because the Spirit intercedes for the saints in accordance with God's will" (Rom. 8:27, NIV). Though we are weak, and do not know exactly what to ask for, we should pray to

194) Park, Hyung Yong, *An Exposition of the Letter to the Ephesians* (Korean) (Suwon: Hapshin Press, 2006), pp. 290-291.

God on all occasions. Thus Paul exhorts us to "pray in the Spirit on all occasions with all kinds of prayers and requests. With this in mind, be alert and always keep on praying for all the saints" (Eph. 6:18, NIV).

Third, the believer should not commit sin against the Spirit

(1)The believer should not put out the Spirit's fire (I Thess. 5:19).

It is quite certain that we cannot eliminate the indwelling Spirit from us. However, we are able to live not in accordance with the desires of the Spirit, but with the desires of our physical body. In the event that we are controlled by our physical desires, the Holy Spirit does not interfere with our activities. This does not mean that the Spirit has no power, nor authority over our actions. Rather the Spirit is silent because when we feel our freedom is interfered with, we do not have joy in our lives. This is a part of God's love that comes from the unlimited wisdom of the Spirit.

(2)The believer should not grieve the Holy Spirit of God (Eph. 4:30).

How do we grieve the Holy Spirit? Is it possible for man to grieve God? The Holy Spirit wants us to live in accordance with the desires of the Spirit, looking to things above, that is, the things of the heavenly realm. So, it is possible for man to grieve the Spirit by doing the things of this world. They are "bitterness, rage, anger, brawling, slander, and every form of malice" (Eph. 4:31). When we practice "sexual immorality, impurity, debauchery, idolatry, witchcraft, hatred, discord, jealousy, fits of rage, selfish ambition, dissensions, factions, envy, drunkenness, orgies, and the like" (Gal. 5:19-21, NIV), the Holy Spirit who is dwelling in us is seriously grieved. The Spirit who is always holy is grieved by our sinful lives.[195]

6. The Holy Spirit and Perseverance

There is a truth in the Reformed Theological tradition that says, "once believed, always believed." When one is truly saved, he cannot fall away from God's people. We are sure about this truth because our salvation is not achieved by our power or our credit, but by God the Holy Spirit Himself. The believer is sealed for the day of redemption and no one can nullify the Spirit's sealing of the believer. "In him you also, when you heard the word of truth, the gospel of your salvation, and believed in him, were sealed with the promised Holy Spirit" (Eph. 1:13, ESV). The Scripture testifies that we cannot lose our membership as God's people because the Spirit who indwells us is an assurance of our salvation (II Cor. 1:22; 5:5). The Holy Spirit assures us of the eternal character of our salvation.

7. The Holy Spirit and Glorification

The Scripture witnesses to the fact that the Spirit will achieve the glorification of our salvation. The Spirit will raise our mortal body at the second coming of our Lord (Rom. 8:11, 23). The resurrection body, in which we will be enclothed by the works of the Spirit, will be the Spiritual body appropriate for the Spiritual world (I Cor. 15:42-45). And the Spirit will assure the final rest for the ones who are asleep in Jesus Christ (Rev. 14:13).

---

195) Barnes lists the ways we grieve the Holy Spirit: ① publicly committed sin, ② all anger, ③ lustful thoughts and desires, ④ ungratefulness, ⑤ rejection of the Spirit's guidance, and ⑥ a resisting attitude against the Spirit. Cf. Albert Barnes, *Notes on the New Testament: Ephesians, Philippians and Colossians* (Grand Rapids: Baker, 1980), p. 93.

Thus far we have discussed the relationship between our salvation experiences in *ordo salutis* (the order of salvation) and the work of the Spirit. We come to a conclusion that when we are justified, our salvation is not partially achieved, as if it is being completed in the process of sanctification. Rather when God declares "you are justified," we are saved 100%. Then the Christian life in this physical body is a manifestation of a holy life that God made complete when we believed. What we are as saved people will be clearly revealed at the return of Jesus Christ. John illumines us of our future state that "now we are children of God, and what we will be has not yet been made known. But we know that when he appears, we shall be like him, for we shall see him as he is" (I John 3:2, NIV). The Holy Spirit is the major agent in all these processes of our salvation.

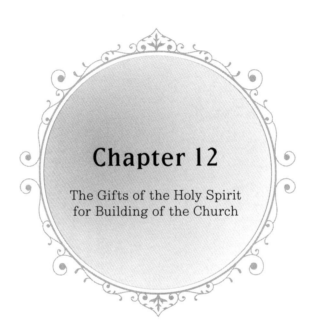

Chapter 12

The Gifts of the Holy Spirit
for Building of the Church

When we think about the gifts of the Holy Spirit, we recall the verses found in I Corinthians 12:8-10; 12:28-30; Romans 12:6-8, and Ephesians 4:11. To properly study the gifts of the Holy Spirit other verses from the Bible must be included. However, the four verses listed above allow one to easily list all the gifts of the Holy Spirit. Therefore, with the understanding that the gifts of the Holy Spirit have already been introduced by these four verses, we will delve into a deeper study of them.

1. The lists of the Gifts of the Holy Spirit

(1) I Corinthians 12:4-11[196]	(2) I Corinthians 12:28-30
Wisdom	Apostles
Knowledge	Prophets
Faith	Teachers
Healing	Miracle workers
Miraculous powers	Gifts of Healing[197]
Prophecy	Those that help others
Distinguishing spirits	Gift of Administration
Speaking in tongues	Speakers of different tongues
Interpreting tongues	Interpreters of tongues

---

196) The gifts of the Holy Spirit are listed in I Cor. 12:8-10, after God as the Trinity is mentioned in I Cor. 12:4-7. It can then be understood that Paul wrote about the gifts, conscious of the makeup of the Trinity, the Father, the Son, and the Holy Spirit. Cf. Michael Green, *I Believe in the Holy Spirit* (Grand Rapids: Eerdmans, 1977), pp. 52, 116-117.

197) The gift of healing is mentioned three times in I Corinthians chapter 12 (I Cor. 12:9, 28, 30). Each time the gift is expressed in plural form (χαρίσματα ἰαμάτων). This indicates that there are a variety of gifts within the gift of healing. It is a mistake to think that a person gifted with the power to heal is able to heal every illness or that the person is empowered with the gift at all times. Thus, setting up a ministry of healing by reason that the person was empowered to heal a specific illness at a specific time, is wrong. Cf. Gordon D. Fee, *The First Epistle to the Corinthians*, p. 594.

(3)Romans 12:6-8	(4)Ephesians 4:11
Gift of prophesy	Apostles
Gift of service	Prophets
Gift of teaching	Evangelists
Gift of encouragement	Pastors
Gift of generosity	Teachers
Gift of leadership	
Gift of mercy	

The gifts of the Holy Spirit can be condensed into a list of 20 items, provided as follows: ① apostles, ② prophets, ③ evangelists, ④ pastors and teachers, ⑤ gift of prophecy, ⑥ gift of tongues, ⑦ gift of interpreting tongues, ⑧ faith, ⑨ gift of miracles, ⑩ gifts of healing, ⑪ wisdom, ⑫ knowledge, ⑬ gift of distinguishing spirits, ⑭ gift of leadership, ⑮ gift of helping others, ⑯ gift of service, ⑰ gift of teaching, ⑱ gift of encouragement, ⑲ gift of generosity, and ⑳ the gift of mercy.[198] It is essential to note that not all the gifts are supernatural in nature but that the list includes a variety of gifts necessary for building up the church.[199] In addition, these gifts are not naturally obtainable but are priceless gifts given by God.

2. The gifts of the Holy Spirit are given according to the sovereignty of the Holy Spirit

The Holy Spirit works as He wills. His work cannot be

---

198) From the gifts of the Holy Spirit, ⑪ wisdom, ⑫ knowledge (I Cor. 12:8), ⑮ the gift of helping others, ⑯ the gift of service (Rom 12:7; I Cor. 12:28), ⑲ the gift of generosity, and ⑳ the gift of mercy, cannot be clearly delineated.

199) D.A. Carson, *Showing The Spirit: A Theological Exposition of I Corinthians 12-14* (Grand Rapids: Baker, 1987), p. 37.

interfered on by people (cf. John 3:8). Therefore, external influences do not affect or guide the Holy Spirit even when he imparts the gifts to people. The gifts are imparted in His sovereignty and to those who need them. This is verified in I Corinthians 12:11 where it states, "All these are the work of one and the same Spirit, and he gives them to each one, just as he determines."[200]

We may ask God for the gifts, but the decision to impart the gifts belongs to the authoritative power of the Holy Spirit. And it is the Holy Spirit's sole authority to determine whether or not a gift should be imparted and which gift should be imparted if He so decides the impartation necessary. Thus, those who have been gifted by the Holy Spirit cannot boast of or feel superior due to the gifts. As the gifts are not imparted as a reward by the Holy Spirit, we will not find any evidence of anything boastful in ourselves. We cannot receive the gifts by seeking or praying for them either. The gifts are given according to the Holy Spirit's will as stated in the following verse, "For who makes you different from anyone else? What do you have that you did not receive? And if you did receive it, why do you boast as though you did not?" (I Cor. 4:7, NIV). In short, the gifts of the Holy Spirit are given to each person in His sovereignty.

3. The person with the gifts of the Holy Spirit is not free from flaws

We expect those who have been given the valuable gifts of the Holy Spirit to be faultless and without flaw. On the contrary,

---

200) D.A. Carson, *Showing The Spirit,* p. 41: "These gifts, we are further reminded, are distributed to *each man*: no one is giftless, for the Spirit works with individuals. But a new thought is articulated: not only does the Spirit distribute these gifts to each individual, he does so 'just as he determines'."

those with the gifts cannot automatically become perfect, for the gifts coexist with the fallibility and weakness of humans. Hence, Christians continue to have faulty characters even after they receive the gifts of the Holy Spirit. In another sense, a Christian's faulty character is independent of his/her receipt of the gifts. Abraham, the faithful patriarch, twice lied that his wife, Sarah, is his sister (Gen 12:14-20; 20:1-18), and Isaac lied just as his father did (Gen 26:6-11). Like Abraham and Isaac, even leaders of great faith are sinful by nature.

In some cases, Christians misuse the gifts they have received. Some misuse the gifts for their selfish ambitions or vainglory, some pride themselves to be better people because of the gifts, and others misuse the gifts by seeing themselves in a more superior light. This is evidenced by the marks of extreme imperfections in the lives of great Christians.[201]

The church body is a community made up of incomplete and faulty believers. We must remember that the problem-filled Corinthian church was called "the church of God in Corinth" (I Cor. 1:2; II Cor. 1:1). Therefore, we cannot expect the church to be devoid of internal problems. On top of that, false prophets and spirits disrupt the harmony of the church, and some church leaders will lead with personal motives rather than those of God's in mind.

Hence, we can see that the lives of those who receive the

---

201) Here we include the contents of R.A. Torrey's exposition, "How to forfeit the gifts of the Holy Spirit." 1) When a Christian renounces his faith, all his/her God-given powers are taken away. Torrey uses the story of Samson as an example of this. 2) God-given powers are forfeited when sin enters one's life. An example of this is King Saul's life. 3) God-given powers are forfeited by one's debauchery. 4) God-given powers are forfeited by monetary greed. 5) God-given powers are forfeited by vanity or pride. 6) God-given powers are forfeited through the negligence of one's prayer life. 7) God-given powers are forfeited by neglecting God's Word. Cf. R.A. Torrey, *The Baptism with the Holy Spirit*, pp. 71-82.

valuable gifts of the Holy Spirit do not automatically become perfect and faultless. Having the gifts of the Holy Spirit does not mean that the Christian with the gifts are automatically transformed into the image of Christ. A person's Spirituality is not revealed from experiencing the gifts but rather, is revealed when he wholeheartedly lets the Holy Spirit work in his life.

4. Everyone is equipped with more than one gift of the Holy Spirit

In Christ's church, Christians are not categorized into first and second class believers. All Christians are children of God, bought by the blood of Christ (Eph. 1:7; John 1:12). The gifts of the Holy Spirit are given to believers for the building up of the church.

Paul says, "Now the body is not made up of one part but of many. If the foot should say, 'Because I am not a hand, I do not belong to the body,' it would not for that reason cease to be part of the body. ---- If the whole body were an eye, where would the sense of hearing be? If the whole body were an ear, where would the sense of smell be?" (I Cor. 12:14-15, 17, NIV). Paul uses the imagery of a human body to explain the diversity of the church and its rich unity due to this diversity.

All Christians are a necessary part of the church. Each believer is needed for the whole. The unity of the church is not obtained by the similarities of each of its members. Christian unity also is not like the unity created by the pebbles on the beach; it is not a unity arising from external organizations. The unity of the believers arises from the gathering of people with various gifts, working with the same motives and guiding principles to accomplish the same goal.

The Holy Spirit gives each Christian a different gift.[202] Thus, many diverse gifts are scattered about within the church. And although some Christians may have the same gifts, the gifts have been imparted each to a different degree. The gifts are given by the Holy Spirit in His sovereignty, so Christians should not envy the gifts of others but should make an effort to develop and use their own gifts.

5. The gifts of the Holy Spirit were given to build the church which is the body of Christ

The fact that each Christian receives more than one gift proves that the gifts were given to build the body of Christ. Here, we will study this fact from another perspective.

First, we must take note that the verses that specifically list the gifts, I Corinthians 12:8-10; 12:28-30; Romans 12:6-8; Ephesians 4:11, are all Paul's epistles. Paul's epistles, among all the New Testament books, were written for the church.

In particular, it is of great significance that these verses are found in I Corinthians, Romans and Ephesians. Romans, written prior to Paul's visit to the church in Rome, was a doctrinally oriented record about the Gospel of Christ (cf. Rom 1:1-4); the verses in Romans that specifically list the gifts are found within the section that describes the lives and activities of the Christians, in particular, within the verses that discuss the connection between the human body and the body of Christ.

---

202) This statement can be clarified by understanding how the Bible expresses it. By using expressions such as, "Now to each one the manifestation of the Spirit is given..." (I Cor. 12:7, NIV), "...and he gives them to each one, just as he determines" (I Cor. 12:11, NIV), "Now you are the body of Christ, and each one of you is a part of it" (I Cor. 12:27, NIV), and "But to each one of us grace has been given as Christ apportioned it" (Eph 4:7, NIV), Paul explains that God gives to each Christian the gifts they need for the good of the church.

Ephesians is known as the epistle that describes the kind of church the Christian church should be, and it is notable that the gifts of the Holy Spirit are mentioned in this epistle to support the idea that the gifts are for the building of the body of Christ. And because I Corinthians was written to the church in Corinth when they were struggling with the concept of the gifts and other problems, it is expected that this epistle concentrate on the gifts of the Holy Spirit.

These three epistles were written with the church in mind in one way or another. The fact that these three epistles specifically deal with the gifts of the Holy Spirit does not place more weight on the gifts themselves. Rather, it is implied that they want to point out the necessity of the gifts in the building up of the church.

Second, when the context of the verses that concentrate on the gifts of the Holy Spirit are studied, we can know that the gifts were given to build up the body of Christ.

For example, the verses (I Cor. 12:12-26) that explain how each member of the church can build up the body of Christ are specifically introduced between I Corinthians 12:8-10 and I Corinthians 12:28-30, which deal with the gifts of the Holy Spirit. Each member of the body must organically cooperate to help the body function harmoniously. Each member does not exist for himself but exists for the other members and also does not consider them as competitors. There must not be any jealousy or strife among the members, but they must all work together to facilitate the activity of the body.

This reveals the fact that the gifts were given to each Christian to build up the body of Christ. For this reason, Paul says, "Now to each one the manifestation of the Spirit is given for the common good" (I Cor. 12:7, NIV).

In Romans chapter 12, verses 6-8 list the gifts of the Holy Spirit; immediately before these verses, in verses 4-5, it is indicated that the gifts were given to build up the body of Christ. In Roman 12:4-5 we read, "Just as each of us has one body with many members, and these members do not all have the same function, so in Christ we who are many form one body, and each member belongs to all the others." The Holy Spirit has given each Christian different gifts as a way of apportioning different responsibilities so that Christians will work together to build up one body.[203]

In comparison to I Corinthians 12 or Romans 12, Ephesians chapter 4 more pointedly connects the gifts of the Spirit to the process of building up the body of Christ. The Holy Spirit has designated the believers as apostles, prophets, evangelists, pastors and teachers (Eph. 4:11) "to prepare God's people for works of service, so that the body of Christ may be built up" (Eph 4:12, NIV). The body of Christ must be built up until we can attain "to the whole measure of the fullness of Christ" (Eph 4:13, NIV). Thus, the gifts are given according to necessity in order to build up the body of Christ.

Third, the fact that the gifts are related to love testifies to the necessity of the gifts in building up the body of Christ (I Cor. 12:31; 13:1-13; Rom 12:9-10; Eph 4:15-16).

After listing the gifts of the Holy Spirit in I Corinthians chapter 12, Paul says, "But eagerly desire the greater gifts" (I Cor. 12:31). And then in I Corinthians chapter 13, he speaks of the superiority of love (I Cor. 13:1-3), the characteristics of love (I Cor. 13:4-7), and the eternal aspects of love (I Cor. 13:8-13). This means Paul does not ignore the necessity of the gifts in the Church. Paul knows the proper place of the gifts of the Holy Spirit in the Church. So, Paul

---

203) In I Corinthians 12, Paul explains the two criteria that must be met for a gift to be considered a true gift of the Holy Spirit. First, a true gift of the Holy Spirit must be related to the confession that Jesus of Nazareth is Christ (I Cor. 12:3), and second, a true gift of the Holy Spirit must be beneficial to the building up of the church.

commands us to pursue the "greater gifts." But Paul brings to light about love which, in fact, makes all gifts as useful. So, Paul calls love as "a more excellent way" (I Cor. 12:31).

In I Corinthians 13, Paul compares speaking in tongues to love, prophesying to love, faith to love, and generosity to love, and concludes by saying that love is superior to all the other gifts. Love is not a gift of the Holy Spirit. Rather love is a fruit of the Holy Spirit which helps build up the church and draws out the special qualities of all the other gifts. "Love is a basic thing for it does not just refer to a certain relation, but it governs and sustains all relations, because it indicates a direction of life. Love will enable a person to do many things, such as to believe and to hope (vs. 7) but it will make it impossible for him to hate anything else except sin. Love is the root of all good actions." [204]

Even Peter declared that we must exhibit our virtues through our lifestyles in order to "be partakers of the divine nature." In II Peter 1:5-7 it states, "For this very reason, make every effort to add to your faith goodness; and to goodness, knowledge; and to knowledge, self-control; and to self-control, perseverance; and to perseverance, godliness; and to godliness, brotherly kindness; and to brotherly kindness, love" (NIV). The reason Peter included love at the end of the list of virtues is because love is the foundation of all virtues. In order for all the other virtues to yield much fruit, they must work with love hand-in-hand. As an experimental case, let us remove love from all the virtues to which Peter alluded. The result teaches us an important lesson.

When love is removed from faith, the result is legalism (much

---

204) F. W. Grosheide, *Commentary on the First Epistle to the Corinthians* (*NICNT*) (Grand Rapids: Eerdmans, 1968), p. 313.

like the Pharisees and Sadducees). When love is removed from goodness, the result is empty dignity and honor. When love is removed from knowledge, the result is dead orthodox. When love is removed from self-control, the result is stinginess (much like Scrooge). When love is removed from perseverance, the result is self-abhorrence (bitterness). When love is removed from brotherly kindness, the result is egotism (dispute over the inheritance among brothers).

It must be noted that the study of the gifts of the Holy Spirit has thus far proved that there are supernatural gifts as well as ordinary gifts that should be manifested in the daily lives of all Christians. In addition, we saw that every gift is necessary to build up the church, which is the body of Christ. As we remember that the description of love listed in I Corinthians 13 is enclosed in the context which deals with the full reference to the gifts of the Holy Spirit, we can assert that it is necessary for those who have received the supernatural gifts to humbly exercise their gifts with loving hearts for the growth and benefit of the Church.

6. What is the relationship between gifts and talents?

Some people have musical talents. Others have athletic talents. We call those who are excellent in certain talents, "men of talents." So it is sometimes hard to distinguish talents from the gifts of the Holy Spirit. There are several differences between the gifts of the Holy Spirit and inherent talents. The gifts of the Holy Spirit are apportioned to Christians according to the will of the Holy Spirit. The Scripture clearly explains that all gifts are given to individual believer according to the will of the Spirit. "All these are the work of one and the same Spirit, and he gives them to each one, just as he determines"

(I Cor. 12:11, NIV). However, inherent talents are inherited genetically. God providentially allows certain genes of the parents to be transmitted to their children. The gifts of the Holy Spirit are given to people after they have been born-again, but inherent talents that are immanent from birth and can be developed through practice and study. While the gifts of the Holy Spirit add to the richness of the body of Christ and are used to spread the Gospel, inherent talents add to the richness of people's lives and are used for the benefit of society.

The Holy Spirit helps us to better develop our inherent talents so that they will benefit the church community. He calls those who are naturally gifted with public speech as evangelists, those who are musically talented to minister musically and glorify God in music, and those who are gifted in letters to clearly expound God's word. In such ways, the Holy Spirit guides the believers to use and develop the inherent talents for God's glory.

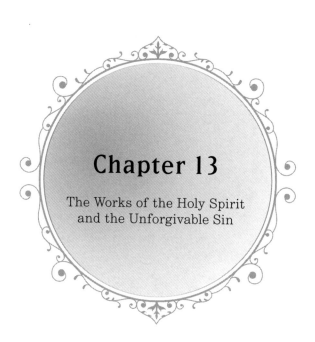

Chapter 13

The Works of the Holy Spirit
and the Unforgivable Sin

The sin of blaspheming the Holy Spirit is used identically as the sin against the Holy Spirit. Therefore, I am going to use these terms interchangeably in this chapter. The sin against the Holy Spirit is drawing much concern from the believers. This concern results from the clear words of Jesus that "every sin and blasphemy will be forgiven men, but the blasphemy against the Spirit will not be forgiven" (Matt. 12:31, NIV). Therefore, it is evident that blasphemy against the Holy Spirit is a serious sin and is serious enough that once we commit it, then we will never be forgiven.

For this reason, we raise a question for ourselves. Did I perhaps commit the sin of blaspheming the Holy Spirit in the past? There is a very serious sin I committed in the past that I have not yet revealed to others. Does that sin perhaps belong to the category of sin against the Spirit? Why did Jesus say that the sin of blaspheming the Holy Spirit is more serious than the sin against Jesus the Son of God? When we deal with the sin against the Holy Spirit, these questions confront us for consideration.

1. How can a man blaspheme against the Holy Spirit, the third person of the Trinity?

God is truly mysterious in His working. Though He is omnipotent, he does not use that almighty power recklessly. Though He has sovereignty over all things, He does not exercise His authority needlessly. In case of saving people from sins, He does not use a method of coercion but persuasion by the Spirit for man to accept Jesus as his Savior. God saves us by His grace only, but He works our salvation as if we are under the false impression that it is we who have a greater part in our salvation. In that way, God is achieving His works without failure.

Such is possible because the Holy Spirit has a personality. The Holy Spirit is not just "an influence," nor a "certain power." He is the third person of the Trinity who has a personality. This is the reason why the Scriptures describe the Spirit, not as an object, but as the One who has a personality. The Scriptures are witnessing to the personal character of the Holy Spirit in various ways.[205)]

First, the Scriptures testify that the Holy Spirit has a disposition or moral nature and intelligence. He knows the things of God. "For who among men knows the thoughts of a man except the man's spirit within him? In the same way no one knows the thoughts of God except the Spirit of God" (I Cor. 2:11, NIV). The mystery of Christ has been revealed by the Spirit to God's holy apostles and prophets (Eph. 3:3-5). The Holy Spirit will teach the disciples all things and will remind them of everything Jesus has achieved in His death and resurrection (John 14:26). Thus, the fact that the Spirit has a moral character and intelligence proves that the Spirit has a personality.

Second, the Scriptures testify that the Holy Spirit has an emotion. The Spirit can be tested (Acts 5:3, 9), can be resisted (Acts 7:51), can be grieved (Eph. 4:30), can be insulted (Heb. 10:29), and can be blasphemed (Matt. 12:31; Mark 3:29). The Holy Spirit intercedes

---

205) George Smeaton (*The Doctrine of the Holy Spirit,* Carlisle: The Banner of Truth Trust, 1974, p. 109) illustrates the personality of the Holy Spirit in six categories.: (1) The personal actions ascribed to Him abundantly prove it (John 14:26; I Cor. 12:11), (2) His distinction from the Father and the Son, and His mission from both, prove it (John 15:26), (3) The co-ordinate rank and power which belong to Him equally with the Father and the Son prove it (Matt. 28:19; 2 Cor. 13:13), (4) His appearance under a visible form at the baptism of Christ and on the day of Pentecost proves it (Matt. 3:16; Acts 2:1-4), (5) The sin against the Holy Spirit implying a Person proves it (Matt. 12:31-32), (6) The way in which He is distinguished from His gifts proves it (I Cor. 12:11). Cf. C. R. Vaughan, *The Gifts of the Holy Spirit* (Carlisle: The Banner of Truth Trust, 1975), p. 406: "*Personal actions are* ascribed to him. He is said to *teach,* to *strive,* to *comfort,* to *lead,* to *intercede,* to *bring to remembrance,* to *create,* to *regenerate,* to *search all things,* yea, even the deep things of God" (italics original).

for the saints in accordance with the will of God (Rom. 8:27), and He will testify about the Son of God (John 15:26). All these verses of the Scriptures clearly testify that the Spirit has an emotional character which gives witness to His personality.

Third, the Scriptures testify that the Holy Spirit has a will or volition. Hebrews 2:4 says that "gifts of the Holy Spirit distributed according to his will" (NIV). The Holy Spirit gives His gifts to the believers just as he determines (I Cor. 12:11). The Spirit convicts the world of guilt in regard to sin, righteousness and judgment (John 16:8) and sends out missionaries for the Gospel proclamation (Acts 13:2-3). The Holy Spirit prohibits certain works according to His will (Acts 16:6-7) and guides the church by His will (Acts 15:28). The Scriptures testify that the Spirit is the One who exercises His will in various ways.

Thus, it is evident that the personal character of the Holy Spirit is manifested in possession of His moral nature, His emotion, and His will. It is also certain that the personal character of the Spirit is clearly revealed in the relationships with the first and second persons of the Trinity. Clear evidence is in place because the Scriptures are often describing the personal character of the Father and the Son and explaining the works of the Spirit in relationship with the works of the Father and the Son. Therefore, if it is proven that the Father and the Son have personal characters, then it is also clear that the Spirit has personal characters.

Then what is the relationship between the fact that the Holy Spirit has personal characters and the sin of blaspheming the Holy Spirit? There is an unavoidable relationship between the two. Man is created in the likeness of God. He is created to have an ability to reason and think logically that sets them apart from the animal world.[206] Men were given mental capacity, such as will power and emotional feelings. When God created man, He created him as God's image bearer. It is because of these aspects of man that he is able to approach God, the Creator. From the same perspective, the Scripture confirms that the Holy Spirit begins to dwell in the believer when he confesses Jesus as the Lord (I Cor. 12:3; Rom. 8:9-11; 10:9-10). Thus, the body of believers is a temple of the Holy Spirit (I Cor. 3:16; 6:19).

Now we can come to a conclusion that since the Holy Spirit possesses personal characters and is not a machine void of emotions, sin against the Holy Spirit is possible for man to commit. In the same line of thought, the Scripture expresses that man can grieve the Spirit (Eph. 4:30), quench the Spirit (I Thess. 5:19), and even blaspheme the Spirit (Matt. 12:31).

2. What is not "the sin against the Holy Spirit"?

Before we consider the sin of blaspheming the Holy Spirit, it is useful to discuss about what is not "the sin against the Spirit." By doing this, we can pinpoint what is "the sin of blaspheming the Spirit."

Firstly, the sins we commit knowingly or the sins against our consciousness are very serious sins, but they are not referring to the sin against the Spirit. For they who committed those sins still have an opportunity of repentance and are able to be forgiven of their sins. Jesus refers to a specific sin when He mentions the sin of blaspheming the Spirit by saying that "I tell you the truth, all the

---

206) Wayne Grudem, *Systematic Theology: An Introduction to Biblical Doctrine* (Grand Rapids: Zondervan, 1994), pp. 446-447.

sins and blasphemies of men will be forgiven them. But whoever blasphemes against the Holy Spirit will never be forgiven; he is guilty of an eternal sin" (Mark 3:28-29, NIV). What Jesus here is affirming is that the sin against the Holy Spirit does not include the sins we commit knowingly and with consciousness.

Secondly, the sins which are very serious according to a worldly criterion do not belong to the sin of blaspheming the Spirit. When a believer commits such a serious sin, we might consider that it is not possible for him to be forgiven from the sin. Yet, in truth, it is possible for the sin to be forgiven when the believer repents. Therefore, such a sin cannot be categorized as the sin against the Spirit which can never be forgiven.

King David committed the sin of adultery and the sin of homicide, but he was forgiven from such sins because he repented thoroughly (II Sam. 12:13; Psalms 51:1-19). The sinful woman who anointed Jesus at his feet with expensive perfume (Luke 7:36-40) and the prodigal son who wasted his father's property in profligate living were also forgiven (Luke 15:11-32) though their sins were regarded as very serious.

It appears that Peter's intentional denials of Jesus three times are serious enough not to be forgiven (Matt. 26:69-75; John 18:15-18). However, he was forgiven from such sins (Luke 22:31-32; John 21:15-17). Even though such sins appear to be heinous in human eyes, such sins do not belong to the sin of blaspheming the Holy Spirit and can be forgiven.

Thirdly, the sins committed mistakenly or unconsciously do not belong to the sin of blaspheming the Holy Spirit. The sin against the Spirit is the willful sin that does not attribute the works of salvation to the Holy Spirit while the works are clearly manifested as the work of the Spirit. Therefore, when a man sins mistakenly or unconsciously, that sin is not considered as the sin of blaspheming the Spirit because there is a possibility of repentance. Any sin that can be repented does not belong to the sin against the Spirit.

Fourthly, even though a man teaches to distort the Bible, he does not commit the sin of blaspheming the Spirit. There is always a possibility for the person who distorts the message of the Bible to repent. For instance, a man was a founder of a heretic group, and he manipulated the message of the Bible to accommodate his purpose. But when he repented of his sin of making heresy and accepted Jesus as his Lord, he can be saved. Distorting the message of the Bible does not deprive one of the possibility of repenting and of being saved. Therefore, distorting the Bible is not the sin of blaspheming the Spirit.

Fifthly, the sin which blasphemes Jesus the son of God or God the Father does not belong to the sin against the Spirit. When a man blasphemes God, he is blaspheming the power and dignity of God. In this case, God Himself can be the direct object of being blasphemed (Rev. 13:6) or the revelation of God can be the object (Titus 2:5). When one blasphemes Jesus, he is insulting Jesus publicly (Mark 15:29; Luke 22:64-65). For example, Jesus was blasphemed when Jesus was hung on the cross; the passers-by, the leaders of the religion in those days, and the robbers insulted Jesus (Matt. 27:38-44). They insulted Jesus on the cross, "You who are going to destroy the temple and build it in three days, save yourself! Come down from the cross, if you are the Son of God!"….."'He saved others,' they said, 'but he can't save himself! He's the King of Israel! Let him come down now from the cross, and we will believe in him'" (Matt. 27:40-42, NIV).

It is a serious sin when one blasphemes Jesus and God, but he can be forgiven of his sins just like the one of the robbers who repented from his sins on the cross (Luke 23:40-43). He repented his sins by saying that "We are punished justly, for we are getting what our deeds deserve. But this man has done nothing wrong." Then he said, "Jesus, remember me when you come into your kingdom." Jesus answered him, "I tell you the truth, today you will be with me in paradise" (Luke 23:41-43, NIV). Thus, the sin against Jesus or God does not belong to the sin of blaspheming the Spirit because he still has an opportunity to repent.[207]

It is pertinent here to raise a few questions. Why is the sin against the Spirit more serious than the sin against Christ or God? The God of Trinity is God the Father, Jesus Christ, and the Holy Spirit. When one blasphemes the Holy Spirit, does his sin not affect the other two persons of the Trinity? These questions can be automatically answered when we come up with what the sin of blaspheming the Spirit is. One comforting idea is that no matter how serious the sins we commit are, God has provided a way to repent and be saved from the sins.

3. What is then the sin of blaspheming the Holy Spirit?

We find a few verses in the Bible that describe the sin of blaspheming the Spirit. Matthew states, "And so I tell you, every sin and blasphemy will be forgiven men, but the blasphemy against the Spirit will not be forgiven. Anyone who speaks a word against the Son of Man will be forgiven, but anyone who speaks against the Holy Spirit will not be forgiven, either in this age or in the age to come" (Matt. 12:31-32, NIV). And the parallel verse in Mark says, "But whoever blasphemes against the Holy Spirit will never be forgiven;

---

207) Park Hyung Yong, *An Exposition of the Four Gospels* (I) (Korean) (Suwon: Hapshin Press, 1994), p. 348.

he is guilty of an eternal sin" (Mark 3:29, NIV). Luke reads on this matter, "And everyone who speaks a word against the Son of Man will be forgiven, but anyone who blasphemes against the Holy Spirit will not be forgiven" (Luke 12:10). From these three verses, we have direct references for the sin of blaspheming the Spirit.

In regard to the sin of blaspheming the Spirit, we need to make sure that Jesus Christ did not alleviate the importance and necessity of repentance. "Every sin will be forgiven" in Matthew 12:31 appear to mean an implication against the emphasis on the serious nature of repentance, but Jesus always teaches the seriousness of repentance (Luke 13:1-5). "The sin against the Spirit" is not included in "every sin" in this context. Jesus used "the sin against the Spirit" in a particular sense, but he used "every sin" in general sense.

Now let us discuss what the sin of blaspheming the Spirit is on the basis of the verses in the Gospels and consider how it is related to our daily lives. When a text is not clear, we should interpret the text in light of the broader context. Such is also the case with the sin of blaspheming the Spirit.

In light of the context, Jesus explains the sin of blaspheming the Spirit with qualifications. Jesus says that "every sin" and "a word against the Son of Man" will be forgiven, but anyone who speaks against the Holy Spirit will not be forgiven, either in this age or in the age to come" (Matt. 12:31-32, NIV). Jesus is contrasting here "every sin" with "the sin of blaspheming the Spirit" and "the sin against the Son of Man" with "the sin of blaspheming the Spirit." Therefore, "every sin" in this context is not used quantitatively which includes all sins in all circumstances. Rather, "every sin" is used qualitatively that refers to "all kinds of sin" or all sins in general. Then Jesus concretely singled out "the sin of blaspheming the Spirit" by comparing it with "all sins in general." He even contrasted "the sin against the Son of

Man" with "the sin of blaspheming the Spirit. He is using "the sin of blaspheming the Spirit" in a qualified sense. What Jesus is teaching in this context is that he is separating actions against Him and His works from the intentional negation of the saving works of the Holy Spirit. Guthrie notes, "Evidently Jesus makes a distinction between general opposition to himself in his teaching ministry and a deliberate distortion of the Holy Spirit's ministry within him." [208]

When we look into the context where "the sin of blaspheming the Spirit" is mentioned, the sin is explained in association with Jesus' work of driving out Satan. Even though Pharisees clearly knew the works of driving out Satan was done by Jesus Christ Himself, they intentionally claimed that "it is only by Beelzebub, the prince of demons, that this fellow drives out demons" (Matt. 12:24, NIV). Jesus, being conscious of the sin of the Pharisees, uttered that "anyone who speaks against the Holy Spirit will not be forgiven, either in this age or in the age to come" (Matt. 12:32, NIV).

The context indicates that the sin Pharisees committed is the sin of blaspheming the Spirit. Since it is clearly manifested that Jesus drives out Satan through the help of the Holy Spirit, the Pharisees, hating Jesus intentionally, ascribe the activity of Jesus to the activity of Satan and regard the good works of Jesus as the evil works of Satan. Their judgment was very much biased because their eyes were blind. So Jesus Christ said, "make a tree good and its fruit will be good, or make a tree bad and its fruit will be bad, for a tree is recognized by its fruit" (Matt. 12:33, NIV).

It is certain from this perspective that the sin of blaspheming the Spirit mentioned in this context is not associated with the nature of the Holy Spirit, but with the manifestation of the grace of the Holy

---

208) D. Guthrie, *New Testament Theology* (Downers Grove: IVP, 1981), p. 521.

Spirit that is applied to the believer. That is, when the works of the Holy Spirit are undoubtedly manifested and we ascribe them to the works of Satan, then it will not be forgiven. Bruner defines the sin against the Spirit by saying that "But intentionally to speak against the Holy Spirit powerfully at work then in Jesus and now in the church's message of Jesus, to question Jesus' motives or 'spirit,' so that others will not place their trust in him -- this is quite another 'spirit,' and it will not be forgiven."[209]

When Jesus says, it will be forgiven when one oppose the Son of God but it will not be forgiven when one blasphemes against the Holy Spirit, he does not mean that the Holy Spirit is superior to Jesus Christ. In the verses under discussion, Jesus wants to point out that if a mind of a person is evil enough to deny the clear works of the Holy Spirit and to ascribe them to Satan, he has nothing to do with the Holy Spirit. For he denies the saving works of the Holy Spirit. If a man is in such a case, he cannot be forgiven of his sins. Therefore, the sin against the Holy Spirit is the sin where one denies the clear manifestation of the works of the Spirit in saving sinners. Such a man cannot repent, so he commits the sin against the Spirit. He falls into eternal damnation.

The sin against the Holy Spirit means to refuse God's forgiveness willfully. It can be defined as the rejection of God's comprehensive offer of amnesty and forgiveness.[210] Loevestam more precisely calls blasphemy against the Spirit the "opposition to God as seen in his eschatological, redemptive activity wherein the gift of forgiveness of

---

209) Frederick Dale Bruner, *The Christbook: A Historical Theological Commentary* (*Matthew 1-12*) (Waco: Word Books, 1987), p. 462: "In context, in all three Gospels, the sin against the Spirit is not some arbitrary curse of deity or some foolish remark about either God or the Spirit per se, *it is trying to ruin Jesus in the eyes of others"*(italics original).

210) Robert A. Guelich, *Mark 1-8:26: Word Biblical Commentary,* Vol. 34A (Waco: Word Books, 1989), p. 180.

sin has its basis and its starting point."[211] So, the sin against the Holy Spirit is not simply the sin of disbelief or the sin of rejecting Jesus Christ. Grudem defines that the sin includes "(1) a clear knowledge of who Christ is and of the power of the Holy Spirit working through him, (2) a willful rejection of the facts about Christ that his opponents knew to be true, and (3) slanderously attributing the work of the Holy Spirit in Christ to the power of Satan. In such a case, the hardness of heart would be so great that any ordinary means of bringing a sinner to repentance would already have been rejected."[212]

It is pertinent here to mention briefly about the relationship between "a sin against the Holy Spirit" and "a sin that leads to death." "A sin that leads to death" in I John 5:16-17 is explaining the sin of blaspheming the Spirit in another way. John compares "a sin that leads to death" with "a sin that does not lead to death" (I John 5: 16-17). When a believer commits a sin that does not lead to death, there is hope of forgiveness left for him. So, we should pray for their repentance. However, when a man who commits "a sin that leads to death," he is alienating himself completely from God. He cannot inherit the redemption which Jesus Christ accomplished in His death and resurrection. He does not belong to the kingdom of God. Calvin is of the opinion that John's use of "a sin that leads to death" is an identical meaning to "the sin against the Holy Spirit."[213] A man who commits "a sin that leads to death," has a reprobate mind and has no hope of forgiveness. Therefore, "a sin that leads to death" is considered the same as "the sin against the Spirit."[214] The references

---

211) E. Loevestam, *Spiritus Blasphemia: Eine Studia zu Mk 3,28f//Mt 12,31f, Lk 12,10* (Lund: Gleerup, 1968), p. 62.

212) Wayne Grudem, *Systematic Theology: An Introduction to Biblical Doctrine* , p. 508.

213) John Calvin, *The Gospel According to St. John Part two 11-21 and the First Epistle of John*, Trans. T. H. L. Parker (Grand Rapids: Eerdmans, 1974), p. 311.

214) The sinners that commit "a sin that leads to death" in these verses do not have a

in Hebrews 6:4-6 (Cf. Heb. 10:26) and in I John 5:16 ("the sin that leads to death") are indirectly a reminder of the sin of blaspheming the Holy Spirit.

A Closing Word

The reason why the sin against the Spirit would not be forgiven is because it removes the possibility of repentance. One can repent only through the help of the Holy Spirit. When a man blasphemes the Holy Spirit, then he does not recognize the saving activity of the Spirit.[215] He who commits the sin against the Spirit does not willfully want to repent. He is indifferent to the works of salvation of the Spirit; he refuses to accept the counsel of the Spirit; and he does not listen to the warnings of the Holy Spirit. In this way he leads himself to destruction.

Then how do we apply the sin against the Spirit to our lives? A faithful believer will never ascribe the clear works of the Holy Spirit to the works of Satan. But we do not know who is a faithful believer. We can only judge that, as a tree should be judged by its fruits, so is

---

fellowship with the Father and the Son (I John 1:3), are excluded from eternal life (I John 5:12), and do not belong to the community of faith (I John 2:19). Cf. Simon J. Kistemaker, *James and I-III John (NTC)* (Grand Rapids: Baker, 1986), p. 363; Stephen S. Smalley, *1, 2, 3 John (WBC)* (Waco: Word Books, 1984), pp. 297-300: "Those who choose such a path are committing an unpardonable sin (cf. Mark 3:28-29=Matt. 12:31-32=Luke 12:10)" (p. 298); However, Grudem is of a different opinion that "this sin (in John 5:16-17) seems to involve the teaching of serious doctrinal error about Christ." ….."Many people who teach serious doctrinal error have still not gone so far as to commit the unpardonable sin and bring on themselves the impossibility of repentance and faith by their own hardness of heart." Cf. Wayne Grudem, *Systematic Theology: An Introduction to Biblical Doctrine* (Grand Rapids: Zondervan, 1994), p. 509.; David Scholer agrees with Grudem on this matter by saying that "nor is it said that one who commits the 'sin unto death' is forever beyond the hope of becoming a member of the believing community." Cf. David M. Scholer, "Sins Within and Sins Without: An Interpretation of I John 5:16-17," *Current Issues in Biblical and Patristic Interpretation,* ed. G. F. Hawthorne (Grand Rapids: Eerdmans, 1975), p. 243.

215) R.C.H. Lenski, *The Interpretation of St. Luke's Gospel* (Minneapolis: Augsburg, 1961), pp. 680-681.

a man by his deeds. We can come to the conclusion whether or not a man commits the sin against the Spirit and who is a faithful believer by observing his deeds.

A believer should be reminded as a warning that he might commit the sin against the Spirit when he moves from a stage of grieving the Spirit (Eph. 4:30) to a stage of resisting the Holy Spirit (Acts 7:51), and from a stage of resisting the Holy Spirit to a stage of quenching the Holy Spirit (I Thess. 5:19). However, when a believer is grieving for any sin whether it belongs to the sin against the Spirit, it is certain that he does not commit it. When a believer has a fear that the sin he committed might be the sin against the Spirit, there is a possibility of repenting the sin, and therefore, he does not commit the sin against the Holy Spirit.[216]

---

216) A. G. Hebert, "Blaspheme, Blasphemy," *A Theological Word Book of the Bible,* (ed) Alan Richardson (New York: Macmillan Publ. Co., 1962), p. 32. "People who are distressed in their souls for fear that they have committed the sin against the Holy Ghost should in most cases be told that their distress is proof that they have not committed that sin."

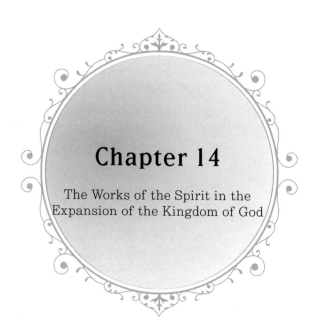

Chapter 14

The Works of the Spirit in the
Expansion of the Kingdom of God

When we study Luke's writings, we need to approach the Gospel of Luke and the Acts as one unit, to see the Gospel of Luke as the first half and Acts as the second half of one book. This is attested in the preface of the Gospel of Luke. Luke says that "Many have undertaken to draw up an account of the things that have been fulfilled among us" (Luke 1:1, NIV), and he has carefully investigated everything from the beginning and wanted to write "an orderly account" of the things that have been fulfilled in the life of Jesus Christ. Luke wants to report what he has investigated to Theophilus. Then, in the preface of Acts, Luke summarizes the content of the Gospel of Luke by saying that "In my former book, Theophilus, I wrote about all that Jesus began to do and to teach until the day he was taken up to heaven, after giving instructions through the Holy Spirit to the apostles he had chosen. After his suffering, he showed himself to these men and gave many convincing proofs that he was alive. He appeared to them over a period of forty days and spoke about the kingdom of God" (Acts 1:1-3, NIV). In light of this content, it is safe to say that Luke intended to write the acts and teachings of Jesus from His Incarnation to His Ascension in the Gospel of Luke. Then, in Acts, he wanted to report to Theophilus what the exalted Jesus is doing through His Church.

As considered above, the Pentecost in Acts 2 occupies a pivotal place in the works of Jesus Christ when we view the Gospel of Luke and Acts as one unit. The Pentecost is the turning point in the combined history of the Gospel of Luke and Acts. In fact, it is not possible to understand them properly unless we have a proper perspective on the Pentecost.

1. The Relationship Between Luke 24 and Acts 1

Let us now consider the overlapping contents of Luke 24 and Acts 1 which manifest a clear relationship between the two chapters. The Synoptic Gospels do not address the events that have happened between the resurrection and the ascension of Jesus Christ with much concern. The Synoptic Gospels do not describe the events of Jesus' life in that time period. It is crystal clear that, in this short period of forty days, Jesus the Messiah was in the exalted state which begins from His resurrection (Compare Phil. 2:6-8 with Phil. 2:9-11). It is somewhat unclear what the exalted state of Jesus Christ is, but it is very clear that this exalted state is a very important one.[217]

In Luke 24:44ff., we are able to see what events have happened between the resurrection of Jesus and His ascension. In Luke 24:44, Jesus teaches His disciples that what happened in His life is the fulfillment of the Old Testament's prophecies. Jesus says, "This is what I told you while I was still with you: Everything must be fulfilled that is written about me in the Law of Moses, the Prophets and the Psalms" (Luke 24:44, NIV). During the forty days

---

217) Korean Kaeyuk translations in John 20:17 give the impression that Mary could not hold Jesus because He has not returned to the Father. Ladd said that "Mary apparently was able to cling to him (John 20:17) as though not to let him get away." (p. 306). He further said that "Jesus is merely reassuring her that he is to be with her and the other disciples for a brief period before he leaves them to return to the Father." (p. 335). See, G. E. Ladd, A *Theology of the New Testament* (Grand Rapids: Eerdmans, 1974), pp. 306, 335. Morris (Leon Morris, *Commentary on the Gospel of John, NICNT.* Grand Rapids: Eerdmans, 1971, p. 841) interprets the verse in the same sense that "It is as though Jesus were saying, 'Stop clinging to Me. There is no need for this, as I am not yet at the point of permanent ascension. You will have opportunity of seeing Me.'" Ridderbos (Herman Ridderbos, *The Gospel of John: A Theological Commentary.* Grand Rapids: Eerdmans, 1997, p. 638) comments that "What is referred to is not touching but 'clutching at' (with the intent or result of) 'holding onto,' 'holding back' (cf. Lk. 7:14)."

Strauss, not being able to accept the supernatural aspect of the resurrection, interprets this verse that "Jesus forbids Mary Magdalene to touch him, because his wounded body was as yet too suffering and sensitive; but eight days later, he himself invites Thomas to touch his wounds." See, David F. Strauss, *The Life of Jesus Critically Examined* (Philadelphia: Fortress, 1972), p. 730.

between His resurrection and His ascension, Jesus Christ manifests His victory over His suffering, and He rests from His redemptive labor. The resurrected Christ explains and declares the meaning of His suffering and the cross. In reality, Jesus Christ, from the post-resurrection perspective, teaches the disciples "a short Old Testament hermeneutics." He explains that His resurrection holds the pivotal place in redemptive history. In particular, Jesus teaches that His earthly ministry which includes His death and resurrection, is a backbone of the teachings of the whole Bible (Luke 24:27, 44).[218] Jesus Christ was the most important character of the entire Old Testament.

The teachings of Jesus in His earthly ministry are essentially identical with the teachings of the Old Testament. The phrase "while I was still with you"[219] in Luke 24:44 refers to the period prior to His death and resurrection. Jesus, in this period of public ministry, taught about the Kingdom of God. The contents of the four Gospels attested to the fact that the first proclamation of Jesus was concerning the Kingdom of God (Matt. 4:17; Mark 1:15) and that He personally said, "I must preach the good news of the Kingdom of God to the other towns also, because that is why I was sent" (Luke 4:43). The Gospels attested to the realization of the Kingdom of God by means of "the physical presence of Jesus Christ," "His proclamation of the Word," and "performing of His miracles" (Cf. Mark 1:15; Luke 4:16-21; Matt. 12:28; 13:16-17). The fact that Jesus cleansed those who were seized with evil spirits and healed the sick is an indication of turning the old distorted order by Adam's sin into a new order (Matt. 12:28). Thus, it is safe to say that Jesus' teachings "while I was still

---

218) "Moses and all the prophets" (Luke 24:27) and "the Law of Moses, the Prophets and the Psalms" (Luke 24:44) in the New Testament generally refer to the entire Old Testament. Cf. I. Howard Marshall, *Commentary on Luke* (*NIGTC*) (Grand Rapids: Eerdmans, 1978), p. 897.

219) Ἔτι ὢν σὺν ὑμῖν. (while I was still with you: NKJV, ESV, NIV, NASB).

with you" are a summary of the Kingdom of God.

Luke records in Acts, too, that Jesus taught His disciples about the Kingdom of God during the period between His resurrection and ascension. The resurrected Christ "appeared to them over a period of forty days and spoke about the kingdom of God" (Acts 1:3, NIV). Thus, Jesus has had much concern about the Kingdom of God before His resurrection, as well as, after. When the disciples asked the resurrected Christ, "Lord, are you at this time going to restore the kingdom to Israel" (Acts 1:6, NIV), Jesus responded by saying, "It is not for you to know the times or dates the Father has set by his own authority. But you will receive power when the Holy Spirit comes on you; and you will be my witnesses in Jerusalem, and in all Judea and Samaria, and to the ends of the earth" (Acts 1:7-8, NIV). Jesus' response meant that the disciples should not be concerned about the future development of Israel but rather be concerned about the gospel proclamation which is the works of the Kingdom of God. It is very clear that Jesus teaches the Kingdom of God during the period between His resurrection and ascension with much concern.

2. The Expansion of the Kingdom of God and the Gospel Proclamation of the New Testament Church

We are informed from Acts that it is the works of the Kingdom of God which Jesus works through His disciples after His ascension. In the Book of Acts, the use of the Kingdom is especially associated with the gospel proclamation. The term "the Kingdom of God" stands out as a characteristic of the proclamation of the apostles (Cf. Acts 8:12; 19:8; 20:25; 28:31). The last verses of the last chapter of Acts prove this point in a succinct manner. "For two whole years Paul stayed there in his own rented house and welcomed all who came to see him. Boldly and without hindrance he preached the Kingdom of God and taught about the Lord Jesus Christ" (Acts 28:30-31, NIV). This is a summary showing how Paul continuously preached the gospel. The core contents of the Apostles' proclamation of the gospel were about the Kingdom of God and Jesus Christ.

With Luke's Gospel and Acts as one unit, Luke explains the events of the Pentecost from the perspective of the Kingdom expansion. The two essential truths of Christianity are listed in Luke 24:46-47. The first important truth is the death and resurrection of Jesus Christ (Luke 24:46). The second essential truth is that "repentance and forgiveness of sins will be preached in his name to all nations, beginning at Jerusalem" (Luke 24:47, NIV). The second essential truth depends on the first essential truth. Without the second essential truth, however, the first essential truth does not have any significance. It is interesting to note that the first essential aspect is recorded in the Luke's Gospel that contains the suffering of Jesus which culminates in His death and resurrection, while the second aspect of the essential truth is explained in Acts. At the time when Jesus was saying these words, the first essential truth was already accomplished by Jesus Himself. Then Jesus was asking the believers to accomplish the second essential truth as stated in Luke 24:48, which says that "you are witnesses of these things." It is "you," the believer who will proclaim the gospel from Jerusalem to the ends of the world (Luke 24:47; Acts 1:8). That is, it is the Church of Christ that should fulfill this purpose.

However, the Pentecost, the outpouring of the Holy Spirit, must occur before the New Testament Church begins to fulfill this work (Acts 1:5). This point is attested by the verses, "I am going to send you what my Father has promised; but stay in the city until you have been clothed with power from on high" (Luke 24:49,), "Do not leave

Jerusalem, but wait for the gift my Father promised, which you have heard me speak about" (Acts 1:4), and "But you will receive power when the Holy Spirit comes on you; and you will be my witnesses in Jerusalem, and in all Judea and Samaria, and to the ends of the earth" (Acts 1:8, NIV). Prior to the universal proclamation of the gospel, the outpouring of the Spirit at Pentecost should occur in order to seal the Church and empower her for the gospel proclamation. It is necessary for the Church to be empowered with the Holy Spirit for the universal expansion of the Gospel.[220] Without the power of the Holy Spirit, the New Testament Church cannot fulfill the task. The task laid before the Apostles was to expand the Kingdom of God by the witness of the Gospel.

From this perspective and when we consider the Gospel of Luke and Acts as one unit, the Pentecost was a must event for the expansion of the Kingdom. The Pentecost was one of the redemptive events which began by the coming of the Messiah-King Jesus Christ, so it should be treated as a phenomenon of the Kingdom of God. The Pentecost began an eschatological order which was accomplished by the advent of the King of the Kingdom of God. Therefore, the records of the life of the early Church in Acts were not selected to show merely the heroic days of the early Church. Neither was it true that the future generations read those heroic records in order to praise the early Church and be encouraged by her. Acts was not written only for us to be challenged by the early Church as we imitate her heroic activities. Rather, it was written to show the role of the New Testament Church in the task of expanding God's Kingdom. Acts

---

220) We do not find the word "kingdom" (βασιλεία) in Matthew 28:18-20, but Matthew clearly proves that the Kingdom of God is expanded by the Gospel proclamation. Matthew 28:18ff explain that Jesus' command for the universal gospel proclamation is based on the authority given by God. In the Synoptic Gospels, the word "authority" (ἐξουσία) is used in association with the concept of the Kingdom.

clearly manifests the eschatological character of the Church from the outset and shows that the gospel proclamation of the Church is a manifestation and an expansion of the Kingdom of God accomplished by the power of the Spirit.

The Pentecost events were epochally unique and once-for-all event which laid a foundation to expand the Kingdom by the Gospel proclamation. Though we experience the same kind of works of the Holy Spirit, they are not a repetition of the Pentecost. For the Pentecost holds a special position in the redemptive history. The Pentecost events laid a foundation to realize the eschatological order, and it is the event that Christ began to expand His Kingdom through His Church. When we consider the Gospel of Luke and Acts as one unit, we understand easily that the Pentecost events hold an important place in the expansion of the Kingdom. As we recognize that the Kingdom is related to the Pentecost events, the relationship between the Holy Spirit and the Kingdom of God is clarified.

3. The Role of the Holy Spirit in the Expansion of the Kingdom of God

We must understand that the Holy Spirit has the most important role in preaching of the Gospel. When Jesus preached at the synagogue in Nazareth, He says, "The Spirit of the Lord is on me, because he has anointed me to preach good news to the poor. He has sent me to proclaim freedom for the prisoners and recovery of sight for the blind, to release the oppressed, to proclaim the year of the Lord's favor" (Luke 4:18-19, NIV). It was not possible even for Jesus to preach without the power of the Holy Spirit. In the same sense, we should understand the fact that when Jesus was baptized, the Spirit came upon Jesus like a dove empowering Him to continue the works of God's Kingdom. Ferguson rightly says, "The Spirit's role in Jesus' ministry is now evident. He serves as the heavenly cartographer and divine strategist who maps out the battle terrain and directs the Warrior-King to the strategic point of conflict. He is Christ's adjutant-general in the holy war which is waged throughout the incarnation."[221] Just as the Holy Spirit helps Jesus to continue the Messianic works, so the Spirit continuously empowers the New Testament Church to continue expanding the Kingdom that Jesus had begun (Matt. 4:17; Mark 1:15; Luke 24:48-49; Acts 1:8).

Then how is the Kingdom expanded? It is expanded by individuals who are saved by faith and become members of the Kingdom. The Church, God's people, is responsible for its expansion, for it is directly related to the salvation of individuals who will live out the principles of the Kingdom in this world, thereby expanding God's rule on earth. "God's sons are to exhibit the family trait of holiness, and this implies putting sin to death through the power of the indwelling Spirit (Rom. 8:13). The Spirit whom believers have received is, not a spirit of bondage, but the 'Spirit of sonship.'"[222] The Holy Spirit is the very agent who, not only helps one to be saved, but empowers one to live out the rules of the Kingdom.

The Scripture clearly says that if we confess Jesus as Lord and believe the death and resurrection of Jesus Christ in our hearts, we are saved. "If you confess with your mouth, 'Jesus is Lord,' and believe in your heart that God raised him from the dead, you will be saved. For it is with your heart that you believe and are justified, and it is with your mouth that you confess and are saved" (Rom. 10:9-10, NIV). We have not seen the historical Jesus and His death and resurrection with our own eyes. Then how can we believe in Jesus

---

221) Sinclair B. Ferguson, *The Holy Spirit* (Downers Grove: IVP, 1996), p. 50.
222) Sinclair B. Ferguson, *The Holy Spirit*, p. 183.

as Lord and in His death and resurrection? Who can bridge the gap between Jesus of history and us? It is the Spirit who bridges the gap and helps us to recognize Jesus as Lord our Savior. The Scripture says, "No one who is speaking by the Spirit of God says, 'Jesus be cursed,' and no one can say, 'Jesus is Lord,' except by the Holy Spirit" (I Cor. 12:3, NIV). It is the Spirit's role to bridge the gap between the historical Jesus and the believers who put their faith in Him and recognize Him as Lord though they do not even see Jesus Christ in person.

When the believer recognizes Jesus as Lord by the help of the Spirit, the Spirit begins to dwell in the believer. The Spirit takes His seat in the heart of the believer. The Scripture testifies that the believer is a temple of the Holy Spirit. "Don't you know that you yourselves are God's temple and that God's Spirit lives in you?" (I Cor. 3:16, NIV). "Do you not know that your body is a temple of the Holy Spirit, who is in you, whom you have received from God? You are not your own; you were bought at a price. Therefore, honor God with your body" (I Cor. 6: 19-20, NIV). It is possible for the believer to become a temple of the Holy Spirit because Jesus Himself is the temple of God. In the temple courts, when Jesus was asked to perform a miracle, He responded to the Jews, "'Destroy this temple, and I will raise it again in three days.' The Jews replied, 'It has taken forty-six years to build this temple, and you are going to raise it in three days?' But the temple he had spoken of was his body." (John 2:19-21). Jesus is the temple because He accomplished all the functions of the Old Testament temple through His life, death, and resurrection. Just as God's people in the Old Testament period had been reconciled with God through the sacrifices for their sins in the temple, the believers can be forgiven of their sins by believing in Jesus Christ who offered Himself as the final sacrifice. It is clear that the believer is a temple because he is united with Jesus Christ who is the temple.

A Closing Word

When the believer believes in Jesus as Lord, he is united with Him in his death and in his resurrection (Rom. 6:5-7). "God, who is rich in mercy, made us alive with Christ even when we were dead in transgressions--it is by grace you have been saved. And God raised us up with Christ and seated us with him in the heavenly realms in Christ Jesus" (Eph. 2:4-6, NIV). The believers are completely united with the life of Jesus Christ in His death, resurrection, and ascension.

Now, the believers or the Church is responsible in expanding the kingdom of God through the preaching of the Good News and the lifestyle of the Kingdom. They should proclaim the Gospel of Jesus and live out the rules of the Kingdom. Believers have to work out their salvation with fear and trembling (Phil. 2:12). The believers' entire lives are involved in expanding the Kingdom of God. What we are to witness here is that the Holy Spirit is present and active from the beginning stage of the establishment of the Kingdom by the works of Jesus to the consummation stage of the Kingdom by the preaching of the Church. It is certain that the power of the Spirit is involved in every stage of the expansion of the Kingdom of God.

Bibliography

Bibliography

Ahn, Young Bok. *A Right Understanding of the Work of the Holy Spirit* (Korean). Seoul: Christian Literature Crusade, 1987.

Andry, E. R. *Journal of Biblical Literature,* 70(1951): x vii.

Arndt, W. F. and Gingrich, F. W. *A Greek-English Lexicon of the New Testament and Other Early Christian Literature.* Chicago: The University of Chicago Press, 1979.

Austin, Bill R. *Austin's Topical History of Christianity.* Wheaton: Tyndale House Publishers, Inc., 1983.

Baltensweiter, H. "ἐγκράτεια," *The New International Dictionary of New Testament Theology,* Vol. 1. Grand Rapids: Zondervan, 1975, pp. 494-497.

Barnes, Albert. *Notes on the New Testament: Ephesians, Philippians and Colossians.* Grand Rapids: Baker, 1980.

Barrett, C. K. *The Acts of the Apostles: I.C.C.* Vol.1. Edinburgh: T&T Clark, 1994.

Basham, Don. *A Handbook on Holy Spirit Baptism.* Springdale: Whitaker, 1969.

Bauckham, Richard J. *Jude, 2 Peter: Word Biblical Commentary,* Vol. 50. Waco: Word Books, 1983.

Beasley-Murray, George R. *John: Word Biblical Commentary.* Vol. 36. Waco: Word Books, 1987.

Behm, J. "ἀρραβών," *Theological Dictionary of the New Testament.* Vol. 1. Grand Rapids, 1972, p. 475.

Bengel, John A. *Bengel's New Testament Commentary,* Vol. 2. Grand Rapids: Kregel Publications, 1981.

Berger, K. "χαρά," *Exegetical Dictionary of the New Testament,* Vol. 3. Grand Rapids: Eerdmans, 1993, pp. 454-455.

Berkhof, L. *Manual of Christian Doctrine.* Grand Rapids: Eerdmans, 1973.

Berkhof, L. *Principles of Biblical Interpretation.* Grand Rapids: Baker Book House, 1952.

Berkouwer, G. C. *Holy Scripture*. Grand Rapids: Eerdmans, 1975.

Bruce, F. F. *The Acts of the Apostles: The Greek Text with Introduction and Commentary*. Grand Rapids: Eerdmans, 1975.

Bruce, F. F. *The Book of the Acts: NICNT*. Grand Rapids: Eerdmans, 1970.

Bruce, F. F. *The Spreading Flame*. Grand Rapids: Eerdmans, 1964.

Bruner, Frederick Dale. *A Theology of the Holy Spirit*. Grand Rapids: Eerdmans, 1976.

Bruner, Frederick Dale. *The Christbook: A Historical Theological Commentary (Matthew 1-12)*. Waco: Word Books, 1987.

Cairns, E. E. *Christianity through the Centuries*. Grand Rapids: Academie Books, 1981.

Calvin, John. *The Epistles of Paul the Apostle to the Galatians, Ephesians, Philippians and Colossians*. translated by T.H.L Parker, Grand Rapids: Eerdmans, 1974.

Calvin, John. *The First Epistle of Paul to the Corinthians*. translated by John W. Fraser. Grand Rapids: Eerdmans, 1973.

Carson, D.A. *Showing the Spirit: A Theological Exposition of I Corinthians 12-14*. Grand Rapids: Baker, 1987.

Carson, D. A. *The Farewell Discourse and Final Prayer of Jesus: An Exposition of John 14-17*. Grand Rapids: Baker, 1980.

Carson, D. A. *The Gospel According to John*. Grand Rapids: Eerdmans, 1991.

Carter, Howard. *The Gifts of the Spirit*. Minneapolis: Northern Gospel Publishing House, 1946.

Cho, David (Cho Yonggi). *The Holy Spirit*. (Korean). Seoul: Seoul Seojeok, 1992.

Chung, Won Tai. *Fervent Calvinism* (Korean). Seoul: Christian Literature Crusade, 1984.

Churchill, Robert K. *Glorious is the Baptism of the Spirit*. Nutley: Presbyterian and Reformed Publishing Co., 1976.

Clowney, Edmund P. *The Church*. Downers Grove: IVP, 1995.

Conn, Charles. *Pillars of Pentecost*. Cleveland, Tenn.: Pathway, 1956.

Dennis and Bennett, Rita. *The Holy Spirit and You*. Plainfield, N.J.: Logos International, 1971.

Dosker, Henry E. "Pentecost," *The International Standard Bible Encyclopaedia* (Grand Rapids: Eerdmans, 1939), Vol. 4. pp. 2318-2319.

Drummond, Henry. *The Greatest Thing in the World*. New York: Grosset and Dunlap, 1981.

Duffild, Guy and Van Cleave, N. M. *Foundations of Pentecostal Theology*, Trans. Yulsoo Lim. Seoul: Sungkwang, 1992.

Dunn, J. D. G. *Baptism in the Holy Spirit*. Naperville: Alec R. Allenson, 1970.

Dunn, J. D. G. *Jesus and the Spirit*. London: SCM Press, 1975.

Dunn, J. D. G. "Feast of Pentecost," *The New International Dictionary of New Testament Theology*, Vol. 2, pp. 783-787.

Ervin, Howard M. *Conversion-Initiation and the Baptism in the Holy Spirit: An Engaging Critique of James D.G. Dunn's Baptism in the Holy Spirit*. Peabody, MA: Hendrickson Publishers, Inc., 1984.

Eusebius, P. *The Ecclesiastical History*. Grand Rapids: Baker, 1977.

Evans, C. F. *Resurrection and the New Testament. Studies in Biblical Theology*, 2nd Series, 12. London: SCM Press, 1970.

Fee, Gordon D. *God's Empowering Presence*. Peabody, M.A.: Hendrickson Publishers, Inc., 1994.

Fee, Gordon D. *The First Epistle to the Corinthians: NICNT*. Grand Rapids: Eerdmans, 1987.

Ferguson, Sinclair B. *The Holy Spirit: Contours of Christian Theology*. Downers Grove: IVP, 1996.

Finney, Charles G. *Lectures on Systematic Theology*. edited by J. H. Fairchild. South Gate, Calif.: Colporter Kemp, 1944.

Finney, Charles G. *Memoirs*. New York: Fleming H. Revell Co., 1903.

Gaffin Jr., R. B. "The Holy Spirit," *The Westminster Theological Journal*, Vol. X L III, No.1. (Fall. 1980), pp. 58-78.

Gaffin Jr., R. B. *Perspectives on Pentecost*. Grand Rapids:Baker, 1979.

Gee, Donald. *Pentecost.* No. 34 (December 1955).

Geldenhuys, Norval. *Commentary on the Gospel of Luke: NICNT.* Grand Rapids: Eerdmans, 1968.

Gordon, A. J. *The Ministry of the Spirit.* Grand Rapids: Baker, 1964.

Green, Michael. *2 Peter and Jude: Tyndale New Testament Commentaries.* Grand Rapids: Eerdmans, 1987.

Green, Michael. *I Believe in the Holy Spirit.* Grand Rapids:Eerdmans, 1977.

Grosheide, F.W. *Commentary on the First Epistle to the Corinthians: NICNT.* Grand Rapids: Eerdmans, 1968.

Grudem, Wayne. *Systematic Theology: An Introduction to Biblical Doctrine.* Grand Rapids: Zondervan, 1994.

Guelich, Robert A. *Mark 1-8:26: Word Biblical Commentary,* Vol. 34a. Waco: Word Books, 1989.

Guthrie, D. *New Testament Theology.* Downers Grove, IVP, 1981.

Hagner, Donald A. "The Old Testament in the New Testament," *Interpreting the Word of God.* edited by S. J. Schultz and M. A. Inch. Chicago: Moody Press, 1976, pp. 78-104.

Harrison, E. F. *Acts: The Expanding Church.* Chicago: Moody Press, 1975.

Hendriksen, William. *The Exposition of the Gospel According to John: NTC.* Grand Rapids: Baker, 1975.

Hendriksen, William. *The Gospel of Luke: NTC.* Grand Rapids: Baker, 1978.

Hendriksen, William. *The Gospel of Matthew: NTC.* Grand Rapids: Baker, 1973.

Hendriksen, William. I – II *Timothy and Titus: NTC.* Grand Rapids: Baker, 1974.

Henry, Carl F. H. "Inspiration," *Baker's Dictionary of Theology.* Grand Rapids: Baker, 1960, pp. 286-289.

Hermas *The Shepherd* (Parable 5.3:1,2; 5.5:1; 5.6:8; 8.11:1; 9.11:9).

Hoekema, Anthony A. *What about Tongue-Speaking.*Grand Rapids: Eerdmans, 1966.

Hoekema, Anthony A. *Holy Spirit Baptism.* Grand Rapids: Eerdmans, 1972.

Hollander, Harm W. "μακροθυμία," *Exegetical Dictionary of the New Testament,* Vol. 2. Grand Rapids: Eerdmans, 1991, pp. 380-81.

Jeremias, J. *Jerusalem in the Time of Jesus.* Philadelphia: Fortress Press, 1978.

Jeremias, J. *New Testament Theology: The Proclamation of Jesus.* New York: Charles Scribner's Sons, 1971.

Kelly, J. N. D. *A Commentary on The Pastoral Epistles.* Grand Rapids: Baker, 1981.

Kendrick, Klaude. *The Promise Fulfilled: A History of the Modern Pentecostal Movement.* Springfield, Mo.: Gospel Publishing House, 1961.

Kistemaker, Simon J. *Exposition of the Acts of the Apostles: New Testament Commentary.* Grand Rapids: Baker, 1990.

Kistemaker, Simon J. *James and* I −III *John: NTC.* Grand Rapids: Baker, 1986.

Kistemaker, Simon J. *Peter and Jude.* Grand Rapids: Baker, 1987.

Ladd, G. E. *A Theology of the New Testament.* Grand Rapids: Eerdmans, 1974.

Lampe, G. W. H. *The Seal of the Spirit.* London: S.P.C.K., 1976.

Lee, Jae Bum. "The Worship in the Pentecostal Church," (Korean). *Bible and Theology,* Vol. 6 (1988), pp. 91-112.

Lee, Jae Bum. *Right Understanding on the Holy Spirit Movements* (Korean). Seoul: Boice, 1985.

Lee, Sang Kun. *The Lee's Commentary on I and II Corinthians* (Korean). Seoul: General Assembly Education Committee Press, 1985.

Lehman, Chester K. *Biblical Theology,* Vol. 2. *New Testament.* Scottdale: Herald Press, 1974.

Lenski, R. C. H. *The Interpretation of St. Luke's Gospel.* Minneapolis: Augsburg Publishing House, 1961.

Lenski, R. C. H. *The Interpretation of the Acts of the Apostles.*

Minneapolis: Augsburg Publishing House, 1961.

Lloyd-Jones, D. M. *Joy Unspeakable.* Trans. Won-Tae Jung. Seoul: Christian Literature Crusade, 1986.

Lloyd-Jones, D. M. *God's Ultimate Purpose.* Carlisle: The Banner of Truth Trust, 1978.

Loevestam, E. *Spiritus Blasphemia: Eine Studia zu Mk 3,28ff//Mt 12,31f, Lk 12,10.* Lund: Gleerup, 1968.

Longenecker, Richard N. *The Acts of the Apostles: The Expositor's Bible Commentary,* Vol. 9. edited by Frank E. Gaebelein. Grand Rapids: Zondervan, 1981.

Louw, J. "Wat wordt in II Peter 1:20 gesteld," *Nederlands Theologische Tijdschrift,* 3 (1965), pp. 202-212.

Lull, David John. *The Spirit in Galatia.* SBL Dissertation Series 49. Ann Arbor: Edwards Brothers, Inc., 1978.

MacArthur Jr., John F. *Charismatic Chaos.* Grand Rapids: Zondervan, 1992.

Macleod, Donald. *The Spirit of Promise.* Ross-shire, Scotland: Christian Focus Publications, 1986.

Marshall, I. H. *Biblical Inspiration.* Grand Rapids: Eerdmans, 1983.

Marshall, I. H. *Commentary on Luke.* Grand Rapids: Eerdmans, 1975.

Marshall, I. H. *Commentary on Luke: NIGTC.* Grand Rapids: Eerdmans, 1978.

Marshall, I. H. *The Acts of The Apostles: NTC.* Grand Rapids: Eerdmans, 1980.

Martin, Ralph P. *New Testament Foundation,* Vol.2. Grand Rapids: Eerdmans, 1978.

Morgan, Campbell. *The Acts of the Apostles.* Old Tappan: Fleming H. Revell Company, 1924.

Morris, Leon. *The Gospel According to John: NICNT.* Grand Rapids: Eerdmans, 1971.

Morris, Leon. *I Believe in Revelation.* Grand Rapids: Eerdmans, 1976.

Morris, Leon. *I Corinthians: Tyndale New Testament Commentaries.*

Grand Rapids: Eerdmans, 1990.

Murphy-O'Connor, Jerome. *Paul: A Critical Life*. Oxford: Oxford University Press, 1997.

Murray, John. *Redemption Accomplished and Applied*. Grand Rapids: Eerdmans, 1955.

Murray, John. *Systematic Theology*, II, trans. Park, Moon Jae. Seoul: Christian Digest, 1991.

Myung, Sung Hoon, *With the Holy Spirit* (Korean). Seoul: Credo, 1993.

Nolland, John. *Luke 1-9:20 : Word Biblical Commentary*, Vol. 35a. Dallas : Word Books, 1989.

Packer, J. I. *Keep in Step with the Spirit*. Old Tappan: Fleming H. Revell Company, 1984.

Packer, J. I. "Biblical Authority, Hermeneutics, Inerrancy," *Jerusalem and Athens*. Philadelphia: The Presbyterian and Reformed Publishing Co., 1971, pp. 141-153.

Park, Hyung Yong. "The Lord is the Spirit," (Korean). *Presbyterian Theological Quarterly*, Vol. 45, No. 1 (Spring, 1978), pp. 28-39.

Park, Hyung Yong. "The Pentecost Event in the History of Salvation," (Korean). *Journal of Reformed Theology*, Vol. 12, No. 1 (May, 1994), pp. 7-51.

Park, Hyung Yong. "Love as the Cardinal Virtue," (Korean). *Journal of Reformed Theology*, Vol. 11, No. 2 (November, 1993), pp. 339-382.

Park, Hyung Yong. "The Baptism with the Holy Spirit in the Life of the Believers," (Korean). *Journal of Reformed Theology*, Vol. 9, No. 1 (July 1991), pp. 24-56.

Park, Hyung Yong.. *A History of Criticism on the Gospels: An Appraisal from Reformed Theological Perspective on the Study of the Historical Jesus* (Korean). Seoul: Sungkwang Publishing, Co., 1985.

Park, Hyung Yong. *An Exposition of the Acts of the Apostles* (Korean). Suwon: Hapshin *Press, 2003/2007.*

Park, Hyung Yong. *An Exposition of the Four Gospels,* Vol. I (Korean). Suwon: Hapshin Press, 1994.

Park, Hyung Yong. *An Exposition of the Four Gospels,* Vol. II (Korean). Suwon: Hapshin Press, 1994.

Park, Hyung Yong. *Biblical Hermeneutics* (Korean). Suwon:Hapshin Press, 2007.

Park, Hyung Yong. *The New Testament Canon* (Korean). Suwon: Hapshin Press, 2002.

Park, Hyung Yong. *An Exposition of the Letter to the Ephesians* (Korean). Suwon: Hapshin Press, 2006.

Peck, John. *What the Bible Teaches about the Holy Spirit.* Wheaton: Tyndale House Publishers, 1979.

Richardson, Alan., ed. *A Theological Word Book of the Bible.* New York: Macmillan Publ. Co., 1962.

Ridderbos, H. *The Coming of the Kingdom.* Philadelphia: The Presbyterian and Reformed Publ. Co., 1962.

Ridderbos, H. *The Gospel of John: A Theological Commentary.* Grand Rapids: Eerdmans, 1997.

Robinson, John A.T. *The Body.* London: SCM, 1952.

Salmond, S. D. F. *The Epistle to the Ephesians: Expositor's Greek Testament,* Vol. 3. Grand Rapids: Eerdmans, 1980.

Sand, A. "ἀρραβών," *Exegetical Dictionary of the New Testament,* Vol. 1. Grand Rapids: Eerdmans, 1990, pp.157-158.

Sanders, J. Oswald. *The Holy Spirit and His Gifts.* Grand Rapids: Zondervan, 1970.

Schep, J. A. *The Nature of the Resurrection Body.* Grand Rapids: Eerdmans, 1964.

Scholer, David M. "Sins Within and Sins Without: An Interpretation of I John 5:16-17," *Current Issues in Biblical and Patristic Interpretation.* ed. G. F. Hawthorne. Grand Rapids: Eerdmans, 1975, pp. 230-246.

Schrenk, Gottlob. "γράφω," *Theological Dictionary of the New Testament.* Grand Rapids: Eerdmans, Vol. I, pp. 742-773.

Schweizer, E. "θεόπνευστος," *Theological Dictionary of the New Testament,* Vol. 6. Grand Rapids: Eerdmans, 1971, pp. 453-454.

Sherrill, John L. *They Speak With Other Tongues.* Old Tappan, N.J.: Spire, 1964.

Smalley, Stephen S. *1, 2, 3, John: WBC.* Waco: Word Books, 1984.

Smeaton, George. *The Doctrine of the Holy Spirit.* Carlisle: The Banner of Truth Trust, 1974.

Smith, J. B. *Greek-English Concordance to the New Testament.* Scottdale, PA: Herald Press, 1947.

Smith, Morton H. *Systematic Theology,* Vol. 2. Greenville: Greenville Seminary Press, 1994.

Spence, R. M. "Private Interpretation," *Expository Times* 8(1896-1897), *pp. 285-286*

Stanley, D. M. *Christ's Resurrection in Pauline Soteriology.* Romae: E Pontificio Instituto Biblico, 1961.

Stanton, Graham N. *Jesus of Nazareth in the New Testament Preaching.* Cambridge: The University Press, 1974.

Stier, R. *The Words of the Apostles.* Eng. Trans. Edinburgh, 1896.

Stonehouse, N. B. "The Authority of the New Testament," *The Infallible Word.* Philadelphia: Presbyterian and Reformed Publ. Co., 1946, pp. 90-140.

Stott, John R.W. *The Spirit, the Church, and the World: The Message of Acts.* Downers Grove: I.V.P., 1990.

Strachan, R. H. *The Second Epistle General of Peter: The Expositor's Greek Testament,* Vol. 5. Grand Rapids: Eerdmans, 1980.

Strauss, David F. *The Life of Jesus Critically Examined.* Philadelphia: Fortress, 1972.

Summers, Ray. *Commentary on Luke.* Waco: Word Books, 1972.

Thiselton, A. C. "Explain," *The New International Dictionary of New Testament Theology,* Vol. 1. Grand Rapids: Zondervan, 1975, pp. 573-584.

Torrey, R. A. *The Baptism with the Holy Spirit.* Minneapolis: Bethany House Publishers, 1972.

Turner, Max. *Power from on High: The Spirit in Israel's Restoration and*

Witness in Luke-Acts. Sheffield: Sheffield Academic Press, 1996.

Vaughan, C. R. *The Gifts of the Holy Spirit*. Carlisle: The Banner of Truth Trust, 1975.

Vos, G. *Biblical Theology*. Grand Rapids: Eerdmans, 1948.

Vos, G. *The Pauline Eschatology*. Grand Rapids: Eerdmans, 1961.

Wand, J. W. C. *A History of the Early Church to A.D. 500*. Methuan and Co. Ltd, 1963.

Warfield, B. B. *The Inspiration and Authority of the Bible*. Philadelphia: The Presbyterian and Reformed Publishing Company, 1948.

Wesley, John. *A Plain Account of Christian Perfection*. London: The Epworth Press, 1952.

Whale, J. S. *The Protestant Tradition: An Essay in Interpretation*. Cambridge: The University Press, 1955.

Williams, Donald T. *The Person and the Work of the Holy Spirit*. Nashville: Broadman and Holman Publishers, 1994.

Williams, Ernest. "Your Questions," *Pentecost Evangel,* 49 (January 15, 1961).

Yoo, Dongsik. *Hananimeui Sungshoi Kyohoisa (A History of the Assembly of God)* (Korean). Seoul: Seoul Seojeok, 1987.

Yoo, Dongsik. *Hankook Shinhakeui Kwangmaek.* (Korean). Seoul: Jeonmangsa, 1983.

Zerwick, Maximilian. *Biblical Greek.* Rome: Biblical Institute Press, 1985.

Zmijewski, J. "χρηστότης," *Exegetical Dictionary of the New Testament,* Vol. 3. Grand Rapids: Eerdmans, 1993, pp. 475-477.

Index of Subjects and Authors

Index of Scriptural References

Genesis
Gen. 1:26 : *172*
Gen. 2:7 : *203*
Gen. 11:1-9 : *23*
Gen. 11:7 : *189*
Gen. 11:7-9 : *189*
Gen. 12:14-20 : *230*
Gen. 20:1-18 : *230*
Gen. 26:6-11 : *230*
Gen. 38:17ff. : *199*
Gen. 40:8 : *144*

Exodus
Ex. 14:21-25 : *105*
Ex. 14:22 : *94*
Ex. 31:3 : *95*

Deuteronomy
Deut. 21:22-23 : *50*

I Samuel
I Sam. 13:8-14 : *117*

II Samuel
II Sam. 12:13 : *245*

II Kings
II Kings 17:25 : *41*
II Kings 17:28 : *41*
II Kings 17:29-31 : *41*
II Kings 17:32 : *41*
II Kings 17:32ff. : *41*
II Kings 17:33 : *41*
II Kings 17:41 : *41*

Psalms
Psalms 2:7 : *171*
Psalms 51:1-19 : *245*
Psalms 51:11 : *95*

Proverbs
Prov. 16:18 : *118*
Prov. 18:12 : *118*

Isaiah
Isaiah 42:1 : *171*
Isaiah 61:1-2 : *49*

Jeremiah
Jer. 1:11 : *145*
Jer. 1:13 : *145*

Luke 1:39-45 : *168*

Luke 1:41 : *166*

Luke 1:67 : *166, 167*

Luke 1:67-69 : *167*

Luke 1:67-75 : *168*

Luke 1:76 : *168*

Luke 2:1-20 : *169*

Luke 2:27 : *166*

Luke 3:4-6 : *28, 29*

Luke 3:15 : *27*

Luke 3:16 : *18, 19, 22, 24, 25, 27, 30, 31, 87, 90, 126, 172*

Luke 3:16-17 : *19, 84*

Luke 3:17 : *20*

Luke 3:20 : *28*

Luke 3:20-22 : *28*

Luke 3:21-22 : *28, 49, 65, 86, 170*

Luke 3:22 : *171*

Luke 4:1 : *49*

Luke 4:1-13 : *220*

Luke 4:16-21 : *172, 259*

Luke 4:18 : *172, 173*

Luke 4:18-19 : *263*

Luke 4:18-21 : *49*

Luke 4:19 : *173*

Luke 4:21 : *137, 172*

Luke 7:11-17 : *204*

Luke 7:14 : *258*

Luke 7:36-40 : *245*

Luke 8:49-56 : *204*

Luke 9:22 : *90*

Luke 10:25-37 : *123*

Luke 11:13 : *107*

Luke 11:16-17 : *106*

Luke 11:20 : *173*

Luke 12:10 : *248, 250, 252*

Luke 12:12 : *186*

Luke 12:49-53 : *20, 27, 90, 172*

Luke 12:50 : *30, 31*

Luke 13:1-5 : *248*

Luke 13:16 : *174*

Luke 15:11-32 : *245*

Luke 16:16 : *173*

Luke 18:18-19 : *123*

Luke 19:41 : *120*

Luke 21:25 : *23*

Luke 22:20 : *82*

Luke 22:31-32 : *245*

Luke 22:54-62 : *186*

Luke 22:64-65 : *246*

Luke 23:40-43 : *246*

Luke 23:41-43 : *247*

Luke 24:27 : *137, 157, 158, 159, 259*

Luke 24:31 : *204*

Luke 24:32 : *137*

Luke 24:39-43 : *204*

Luke 24:42 : *204*

Luke 24:44 : *156, 258, 259*

Luke 24:45 : *137*

Luke 24:46 : *51, 261*

Luke 24:46-47 : *261*

Luke 24:46-48 : *61, 64*

Luke 24:47 : *51, 261*

Luke 24:48 : *51, 261*

Luke 24:48-49 : *264*

Luke 24:49 : *87, 167, 181, 184, 261*

John

John 1:12 : *81, 169, 231*

John 1:12-13 : *214*

John 1:33 : *18, 200*

John 1:40-42 : *181, 183*

John 1:42 : *62, 63, 181, 182, 183*

John 2:19 : *196*

John 2:19-21 : *265*

John 2:21 : *196*

John 2:22 : *137*

John 3:1-8 : *200*

John 3:3 : *102*

John 3:3-7 : *211*

John 3:5 : *102, 212*

John 3:5-8 : *215*

John 3:6 : *149*

John 3:7 : *102*

John 3:8 : *102, 229*

John 3:16 : *115*

John 4:1-26 : *41, 189*

John 4:20 : *41*

John 4:23 : *18*

John 5:16-17 : *252*

John 5:25 : *18*

John 6:37 : *218*

John 6:48 : *215*

John 6:54 : *215*

John 6:65 : *218*

John 6:70 : *64*

John 7:37-39 : *92*

John 7:38-39 : *126*

John 7:39 : *89, 180*

John 8:56 : *18*

John 10:17-18 : *196*

John 10:35 : *137*

John 11:38-44 : *204*

John 11:50 : *180*

John 13:16 : *69*

John 13:32 : *18*

John 14:6 : *215*

John 14:12 : *88*

John 14:16 : *23, 32, 33,*
88, 157, 180, 200

John 14:17 : *200*

John 14:18 : *33, 34, 88*

John 14:20 : *88*

John 14:26 : *23, 33, 50,*
88, 132, 133, 155,
157, 158, 186, 200,
242

John 14:28 : *89*

John 15:1-9 : *21, 22*

John 15:26 : *32, 33, 50,*
156, 157, 180, 200,
242, 243

John 16:7 : *33, 91, 158,*
200

John 16:7-8 : *32, 179, 180*

John 16:7-13 : *91*

John 16:7-14 : *23, 157*

John 16:8 : *200, 243*

John 16:8-11 : *156*

John 16:8-13 : *212*

John 16:13 : *50, 132, 155,*
156, 158, 180, 200

John 16:13-14 : *32*

John 16:13-15 : *200*

John 16:14 : *156*

John 16:14-15 : *50*

John 16:15 : *156*

John 17:13-26 : *119, 187*

John 18:11 : *30*

John 18:15-18 : *245*

John 20:17 : *258*

John 20:19-20 : *204*

John 21:5-14 : *204*

John 21:15-17 : *245*

Acts

Acts 1:1 : *96*

Acts 1:1-2 : *46*

Acts 1:1-3 : *51, 257*

Acts 1:1-11 : *19*

Acts 1:3 : *83, 260*

Acts 1:4 : *87, 262*

Acts 1:4-5 : *167*

Acts 1:5 : *18, 19, 20, 21,*
22, 24, 25, 26, 30, 31,
90, 101, 102, 105,
106, 172, 261

Acts 1:6 : *260*

Acts 1:6-8 : *65*

Acts 1:7-8 : *260*

Acts 1:8 : *39, 40, 51, 53,*
97, 261, 262, 264

Acts 1:11 : *204*

Acts 1:21-22 : *42, 69*

Acts 1:26 : *96*

Acts 2:1 : *94*

Acts 2:1-4 : *20, 21, 22, 31,*
34, 39, 40, 43, 58, 86,
104, 105, 165, 212,
242

Acts 2:3 : *90*

Acts 2:4 : *23, 110, 218*

Acts 2:6 : *189*

Acts 2:7-13 : *23*

Acts 2:11 : *189*

Acts 2:12-13 : *105*

Acts 2:14-21 : *172*

Acts 2:14-47 : *65*

Acts 2:15 : *24, 110*

Acts 2:16 : *24*

Acts 2:16-18 : *82*

Acts 2:17 : *24, 26*

Acts 2:17-18 : *24, 25*

Acts 2:18 : *26*

Acts 2:19 : *26*

Acts 2:19-20 : *24, 25*

Acts 2:20 : *26*

Acts 2:21 : *27*

Acts 2:31-32 : *45*

Acts 2:33 : *126*

Acts 2:36 : *212*

Acts 2:36-38 : *45*

Acts 2:37-38 : *212*

Acts 2:37-47 : *53*

Acts 2:38 : *45, 126, 187, 213*

Acts 2:41 : *82, 181*

Acts 2:42 : *187*

Acts 2:42-47 : *126, 187*

Acts 2:44 : *187*

Acts 2:44-46 : *187*

Acts 2:46 : *187*

Acts 2:47 : *187, 188*

Acts 3:15-19 : *45*

Acts 3:15-21 : *45*

Acts 4:8 : *106, 109, 166, 186*

Acts 4:10 : *45, 174, 197*

Acts 4:12 : *108*

Acts 4:13 : *186*

Acts 4:18 : *186*

Acts 4:19-20 : *186*

Acts 4:31 : *106, 108, 109, 166, 186, 187*

Acts 4:31-37 : *187*

Acts 4:32 : *108, 187*

Acts 4:33 : *45*

Acts 5:3 : *188, 242*

Acts 5:5 : *188*

Acts 5:9 : *242*

Acts 5:11 : *188*

Acts 5:12 : *188*

Acts 5:14 : *188*

Acts 5:30 : *174, 197*

Acts 5:30-1 : *45*

Acts 5:30-31 : *45*

Acts 5:32 : *107*

Acts 6:3 : *107, 108*

Acts 6:5 : *108, 166, 189*

Acts 6:10 : *107, 108, 166*

Acts 7:51 : *242, 253*

Acts 7:52-56 : *45*

Acts 7:55 : *107, 166*

Acts 8:1 : *39, 40*

Acts 8:4-5 : *39*

Acts 8:4-25 : *39, 189*

Acts 8:12 : *19, 20, 39, 40, 44, 83, 189, 260*

Acts 8:13 : *190*

Acts 8:14 : *43*

Acts 8:14-17 : *44, 52, 61*

Acts 8:15 : *40, 44, 190*

Acts 8:16 : *40, 44, 189, 190*

Acts 8:17 : *40, 44, 51, 57*

Acts 8:18 : *44*

Acts 8:19 : *57*

Acts 8:20-21 : *190*

Acts 8:29-39 : *158, 160*

Acts 9:1-30 : *54*

Acts 9:3-18 : *43*

Acts 9:15 : *56*

Acts 10:1-33 : *51*

Acts 10:1-48 : *54*

Acts 10:3 : *190*

Acts 10:4 : *52*

Acts 10:5 : *190*

Acts 10:5-6 : *48*

Acts 10:13 : *48*

Acts 10:15 : *48*

Acts 10:19 : *190*

Acts 10:34-43 : *49*

Acts 10:38 : *49, 190*

Acts 10:39 : *50*

Acts 10:40-42 : *50*

Acts 10:43 : *48, 50, 159*

Acts 10:44 : *49, 191*

Acts 10:44-48 : *39, 47, 49, 61, 210*

Acts 10:45 : *51, 57*

Acts 10:46 : *51*

Acts 10:47 : *51*

Acts 10:48 : *51*

Acts 11:1-18 : *47, 54*

Acts 11:14-15 : *48*

Acts 11:15 : *57*

Acts 11:15-18 : *210*

Acts 11:16 : *18, 19*

Acts 11:16-17 : *19, 106*

Acts 11:17 : *51*

Acts 11:19-26 : *54*

Acts 11:24 : *107, 108, 123*

Acts 12:1-19 : *54*

Acts 12:2 : *64*

Acts 13:2-3 : *243*

Acts 13:6-11 : *108*

Acts 13:9 : *109*

Acts 13:52 : *109*

Acts 15:1 : *47*

Acts 15:8-9 : *47*

Acts 15:11 : *47*

Acts 15:28 : *243*

Acts 16:6-7 : *243*

Acts 19:1 : *54, 55*

Acts 19:1-7 : *53, 61*

Acts 19:2 : *55*

Acts 19:3 : *54, 55*

Acts 19:4 : *55, 191*

Acts 19:5 : *55*

Acts 19:5-6 : *55*

Acts 19:6 : *56, 57, 191*

Acts 19:7 : *54*

Acts 19:8 : *19, 83, 260*

Acts 19:8-10 : *56*

Acts 20:25 : *19, 83, 260*

Acts 20:31 : *56*

Acts 20:35 : *118*

Acts 20:38 : *120*

Acts 21:4-14 : *71*

Acts 27:14 : *147*

Acts 27:15 : *147, 148*

Acts 27:17 : *148*

Acts 28:23 : *19*

Acts 28:30-31 : *261*

Acts 28:31 : *19, 83, 260*

Romans

Rom. 1:1 : *132*

Rom. 1:1-4 : *232*

Rom. 1:2 : *137*

Rom. 1:3 : *168*

Rom. 2:4 : *122*

Rom. 3:10-11 : *210*

Rom. 4:9 : *95*

Rom. 4:25 : *20, 213*

Rom. 5:1 : *121*

Rom. 5:3-5 : *114*

Rom. 5:8 : *115*

Rom. 5:9 : *121*

Rom. 5:12-14 : *170*

Rom. 5:12-21 : *169*

Rom. 5:25 : *90*

Rom. 6:5-7 : *266*

Rom. 6:6 : *127*

Rom. 6:8 : *127*

Rom. 6:23 : *29*

Rom. 7:24 : *203*

Rom. 8:4 : *218*

Rom. 8:5 : *218*

Rom. 8:5-6 : *218*

Rom. 8:9 : *159*

Rom. 8:9-10 : *185*

Rom. 8:9-11 : *104, 216, 244*

Rom. 8:10 : *159, 198*

Rom. 8:10-11 : *203*

Rom. 8:11 : *159, 174, 198, 200, 201, 218, 222*

Rom. 8:13 : *264*

Rom. 8:14-17 : *185*

Rom. 8:15 : *214*

Rom. 8:17 : *127*

Rom. 8:23 : *199, 222*

Rom. 8:26 : *220*

Rom. 8:27 : *220, 243*

Rom. 8:31-39 : *218*

Rom. 9:2 : *120*

Rom. 10:9 : *174, 197*

Rom. 10:9-10 : *46, 64, 81, 92, 185, 189, 210, 244, 264*

Rom. 10:17 : *46, 210*

Rom. 11:17-24 : *21*

Rom. 12:4-5 : *233, 234*

Rom. 12:6-8 : *72, 227, 228, 232, 233*

Rom. 12:7 : *228*

Rom. 12:9-10 : *234*

Rom. 12:15 : *120*

Rom. 14:17 : *114, 120, 173*

Rom. 15:16 : *159*

Rom. 15:20 : *70*

Rom. 16:26 : *137*

I Corinthians

I Cor. 1:1 : *132*

I Cor. 1:2 : *159, 214, 230*

I Cor. 1:7 : *69*

I Cor. 2:10 : *155*

I Cor. 2:10-14 : *185*

I Cor. 2:11 : *242*

I Cor. 2:15 : *155*

I Cor. 3:10-11 : *53*

I Cor. 3:16 : *22, 104, 107, 185, 198, 200, 216, 244, 265*

I Cor. 3:16-17 : *174*

Ephesians

Eph. 1:1 : *132*
Eph. 1:3 : *126*
Eph. 1:3-6 : *210*
Eph. 1:7 : *231*
Eph. 1:7-12 : *210*
Eph. 1:13 : *216, 217, 222*
Eph. 1:13-14. : *210*
Eph. 1:22 : *214*
Eph. 2:1-3 : *209*
Eph. 2:4-6 : *266*
Eph. 2:6 : *218*
Eph. 2:8 : *185*
Eph. 2:8-10 : *209*
Eph. 2:10 : *122*
Eph. 2:11-18 : *51*
Eph. 2:12 : *210*
Eph. 2:14-18 : *121*
Eph. 2:20 : *53, 64, 69, 70, 93, 132*
Eph. 2:21-22 : *216*
Eph. 3:3 : *146*
Eph. 3:3-5 : *242*
Eph. 3:4 : *146*
Eph. 4:2 : *123*
Eph. 4:2-6 : *17*
Eph. 4:3 : *78, 121*
Eph. 4:4 : *184*
Eph. 4:7 : *232*
Eph. 4:10 : *214*
Eph. 4:11 : *66, 72, 227, 228, 232, 234*
Eph. 4:12 : *82, 234*
Eph. 4:13 : *128, 161, 234*
Eph. 4:15-16 : *234*
Eph. 4:30 : *199, 217, 221, 242, 244, 253*
Eph. 4:31 : *221*
Eph. 5:9 : *114*
Eph. 5:18 : *106, 109, 110, 218, 219*
Eph. 5:18-6:9 : *187*
Eph. 5:19 : *111*
Eph. 5:20 : *111*
Eph. 5:21 : *111*
Eph. 5:22-28 : *112*
Eph. 6:1-4 : *112*
Eph. 6:4 : *112*
Eph. 6:5-9 : *113*
Eph. 6:9 : *113*
Eph. 6:17 : *220*
Eph. 6:18 : *220*

Philippians

Phil. 1:4 : *120*
Phil. 1:25 : *120*
Phil. 2:5-11 : *115*
Phil. 2:6-8 : *258*
Phil. 2:7 : *120*
Phil. 2:7-8 : *118*
Phil. 2:9-11 : *258*
Phil. 2:12 : *266*
Phil. 2:18f : *120*
Phil. 2:25 : *69*
Phil. 3:20 : *218*
Phil. 3:21 : *205*
Phil. 4:6-7 : *122*

Colossians

Col. 1:1 : *132*
Col. 1:11 : *123*
Col. 1:11f : *120*
Col. 1:19 : *214*
Col. 2:12 : *127, 197*
Col. 3:1 : *127, 218*
Col. 3:1-2 : *218*
Col. 3:1-4 : *218*
Col. 3:12 : *123*
Col. 4:16 : *67*

I Thessalonians

I Thess. 1:6 : *121*
I Thess. 1:9-10 : *197*
I Thess. 1:10 : *68*
I Thess. 2:13 : *135*
I Thess. 4:3 : *111*
I Thess. 4:13 : *120, 134*
I Thess. 4:14 : *197*
I Thess. 5:14-15 : *123*
I Thess. 5:15 : *111*
I Thess. 5:16 : *111*
I Thess. 5:17 : *111*
I Thess. 5:18 : *111*
I Thess. 5:19 : *199, 221, 244, 253*

II Thessalonians

II Thess. 1:10 : *69*

I Timothy

I Tim. 1:1 : *132*
I Tim. 1:8 : *73*
I Tim. 1:9 : *75*
I Tim. 1:10 : *73*
I Tim. 1:15 : *74, 78*
I Tim. 1:16 : *122, 75*
I Tim. 1:18 : *73*
I Tim. 1:19 :*75*
I Tim. 2:1 : *75*
I Tim. 2:2 : *75*
I Tim. 2:8 : *75*
I Tim. 2:15 : *75*
I Tim. 3:1 : *74*
I Tim. 3:1-13 : *74*
I Tim. 3:2 : *74*
I Tim. 3:3 : *75*
I Tim. 3:3-4 : *74*
I Tim. 4:1 : *200*
I Tim. 4:5 : *73, 75*
I Tim. 4:6 : *73*
I Tim. 4:8 : *75*
I Tim. 4:9 : *74*
I Tim. 4:12 : *75*
I Tim. 4:14 : *73*
I Tim. 5:12 : *75*
I Tim. 6:5 : *75*
I Tim. 6:11 : *75, 114*

II Timothy

II Tim. 1:1 : *132*
II Tim. 1:13 : *75*
II Tim. 2:3 : *75*

II Tim. 2:9 : *75*
II Tim. 2:11 : *74*
II Tim. 2:12 : *127*
II Tim. 2:15 : *74*
II Tim. 2:21 : *214*
II Tim. 3:5 : *75*
II Tim. 3:10 : *114, 123*
II Tim. 3:11 : *75*
II Tim. 3:12 : *75*
II Tim. 3:13-15 : *136*
II Tim. 3:14-17 : *75*
II Tim. 3:15 : *75*
II Tim. 3:16 : *74, 76, 135,*
    136, 137, 143, 149,
    153, 200,
II Tim. 4:2 : *74*

Titus

Tit. 1:1 : *132*
Tit. 1:5 : *73*
Tit. 1:5-9 : *74*
Tit. 1:9 : *74*
Tit. 2:1 : *74*
Tit. 2:1-10 : *75*
Tit. 2:5 : *246*
Tit. 2:12 : *75*
Tit. 3:2 : *75*
Tit. 3:5 : *76*
Tit. 3:5-7 : *76, 212*
Tit. 3:6 : *76*
Tit. 3:8 : *74*

Hebrews

Heb. 1:1-2 : *43, 68*
Heb. 4:12 : *220*
Heb. 6:4-6 : *252*
Heb. 9:26 : *29*
Heb. 9:27 : *29*
Heb. 10:29 : *242*
Heb. 11:39 : *95*
Heb. 11:40 : *95*

James

James 1:19 : *122*
James 5:9 : *116*

I Peter

I Pet. 1:5-7 : *119*
I Pet. 2:24 : *50*
I Pet. 4:8 : *118*
I Pet. 4:10 : *82*

II Peter

II Pet. 1:5-7 : *114, 235*
II Pet. 1:16-21 : *143*
II Pet. 1:19 : *142*
II Pet. 1:19-21 : *153*
II Pet. 1:20 : *141, 142,*
    143, 144, 145, 149
II Pet. 1:20-21 : *135, 143*
II Pet. 1:21 : *141, 143,*
    144, 145, 146, 148,
    149
II Pet. 2:1 : *143*
II Pet. 3:7 : *25*

II Pet. 3:10 : *25*
II Pet. 3:16 : *133, 134, 143*

I John
I John 1:3 : *252*
I John 1:4 : *121*
I John 2:1 : *200*
I John 2:19 : *252*
I John 3:1-2 : *214*
I John 3:2 : *205, 223*
I John 3:19-20 : *122*

I John 4:8 : *116*
I John 4:19 : *115*
I John 5:12 : *252*
I John 5:16 : *252*
I John 5:16-17 : *251, 252*

Revelation
Rev. 6:12 : *25*
Rev. 13:6 : *246*
Rev. 14:13 : *222*
Rev. 21:9-14 : *64*